LIFE
ABUNDANT

"Sallie McFague offers us a brilliant constructive theology. Here she focuses on the problems of contemporary human existence through a comprehensive analysis of consumerism. She marshals the resources of personal experience, scripture, and tradition to develop a theology that speaks redemptively to our plight, concluding with a challenging vision of life as it could be and can be. This provocative work deserves wide reading. It is a 'must' not only for those who follow the work of this fine theologian, but for all who ask how Christian thinking can today impel our actions toward the creation of beneficent communities."

—Marjorie H. Suchocki
Claremont School of Theology

LIFE
ABUNDANT

Rethinking Theology and Economy
for a Planet in Peril

Sallie McFague

Fortress Press
Minneapolis

Cover art by Harnett/Hanzon copyright © 2000 Photodisc, Inc.
Cover and interior design by Beth Wright
Author photo by Harry Redl, courtesy of *The Chronicle of Higher Education*

Pages 161–71 were originally published in Sallie McFague, "An Ecological Christology: Does Christianity Have It?" in D.T. Hessel and R.R. Ruether, eds., *Christianity and Ecology: Seeking the Well-Being of Earth and Humans* (Cambridge, Mass.: Harvard University Center for the Study of World Religions, 2000) 29–45, copyright © 2000 by the President and Fellows of Harvard College, and are reprinted by permission.

A study guide written by David C. Teel is available at:
http://www.fortresspress.com
(In the Quick Search box, type: Life Abundant)

Library of Congress Cataloging-in-Publication Data
McFague, Sallie.
    Life abundant : rethinking theology and economy for a planet in peril /
    Sallie McFague.
        p.   cm.
    Includes bibliographical references and index.
    ISBN 0-8006-3269-9 (alk. paper)
        1. Economics—Religious aspects—Christianity. 2. Human ecology—
    Religious aspects—Christianity. I. Title.
    BR115.E3 M315 2000
    261.8—dc21
                                                            00-057274

Manufactured in the U.S.A.   AF 1-3269

To my students at Vanderbilt Divinity School
and the Graduate Department of Religion
1970–2000

Contents

Part III: The Content of Planetary Theology

 # Acknowledgments

I AM DEEPLY GRATEFUL to my students of thirty years, who helped me write this book. I owe them a large debt. I have worked out my theology—which is summed up here—in classes, conversation, and mutual criticism with them.

I wish also to thank my colleagues who read all or parts of the manuscript: Janet Cawley, Rebecca Chopp, John Cobb, Paul Lakeland, Marjorie Suchocki, and David Teel.

And once again, I am appreciative of the encouraging and insightful guidance of Michael West, as well as help from the other good folks at Fortress Press.

Finally, a word of thanks to the Vancouver School of Theology, where I wrote this book, as well as two others. I am grateful to its faculty, students, and staff for welcoming me so graciously in the past and look forward to a future with them.

 **Preface**

I HAVE WRITTEN EACH OF MY BOOKS in an effort to make up for deficiencies in the last one. *Life Abundant* is no exception. After completing *Super, Natural Christians*, subtitled *How We Should Love Nature*, I realized love was not enough. I realized that we middle-class North American Christians are destroying nature, not because we do not love it, but because of the way we live: our ordinary, taken-for-granted high-consumer lifestyle. I realized that the matter of loving nature was a deep, complex, tricky question involving greed, indifference, and denial.

So I have set about trying to rectify the inadequacies of my last book with yet another (inadequate) book. The thesis of this one is that we North American middle-class Christians need to *live differently* in order to love nature, and to live differently, we need to think differently—especially about ourselves and who we are in the scheme of things. And by "think differently" I do not mean our conscious, "for publication" thoughts about ourselves, but the largely unconscious picture of who we are that is the silent partner in all our behavior and decisions. These world-pictures or worldviews are formed by many factors, one of which is the religious assumptions about human beings that operate implicitly in a culture. The current dominant American worldview, a legacy from the Protestant Reformation, the Enlightenment, and eighteenth-century economic theory, is that we are individuals with the right to happiness, especially the happiness of the consumer-style "abundant life." The market ideology has become our way of life, almost our religion, telling us who we are (consumers) and what is the goal of life (making money). In report after report from the United Nations Development Programme and similar organizations, the grim results of this lifestyle are becoming apparent: a widening gap between the rich and the poor as well as the unraveling of the irreplaceable life systems of the planet. Is *this* loving nature—or our neighbor?

I don't think so. I realized that a basic deficiency in my last book was the neglect of economics (partly because I thought it was too difficult to understand). There is, however, no avoiding it—and what ordinary people need to know is not its technical side, but the *assumptions* and *results* of consumer-oriented economic theory. We do not love nature or care for two-thirds of the world's people if we who are 20 percent of the population use more than 80 percent of the world's energy. There is not enough energy on the planet for all people to live as we do (and increasingly, most want to) or for the planet to remain in working order if all try to live this way. We are on a path that is unjust to others and unsustainable to the planet. But most of us do not know (or acknowledge) this; we keep ourselves in denial because we *like* this way of life, and our economic system and government collude with us. We middle-class North Americans are addicted to the consumer lifestyle, even if it means depriving others and putting the planet in jeopardy.

Life Abundant is not a feel-good read, at least not initially. Reading it will probably be like writing it was. Eventually, I could imagine *another* abundant life, one that I found deeply satisfying. The route to it, however, for folks like me and you (the presumed middle-class North American reader) involves limitation and sacrifice, a radically different view of abundance. It involves reimagining the good life in just and sustainable ways. Why is this satisfying? I invite you to read on and discover, but most simply, for me, because I sleep better at night, thinking of another possible way to live, one in which most of the world's people would have the necessary basics and the planet could remain more or less intact.

So, this book is about imagining another way to live "abundantly" on planet Earth. The route to this other way, to what I call the ecological economic model, is a bit circuitous because I want to show how *I* got there. I believe that all Christians must have a *working theology*, one that can actually function in their personal, professional, and public lives. Gradually, over many years I have developed one, and it is a theology for just and sustainable planetary living. I will share my theological journey as a possible case study for readers who might want to undertake a similar one. I decided to write the book this way in part to demystify theology: there is nothing special about theology—every Christian has one. The question is how good, appropriate, and functional is it?

One way to test your theology—those deeply held, perhaps subconscious beliefs about God and the world that profoundly influence your actions—is to examine it. This is an old Christian practice, epitomized in Augustine's plea, "For Thy mercies' sake, O Lord my God, tell me what Thou art to me."[1] One undertakes a contemplative exercise for the purpose of living with God and for neighbor more appropriately and fully. It is a way of doing theology that begins in experience and ends in a conversion to a new way of being in the world. Developing a working theology is not "doing one's thing" or finding a comfortable view of God; on the contrary, it is undergoing the discipline of the examination of conscience for the purpose of living the Christian life more deeply and fittingly in one's own time. Needless to say, if this exercise does result in a view of abundant living, it will not be the popular contemporary one. Perhaps Dorothy Day summed it up best when she wrote: "I wanted life and I wanted the abundant life. *I wanted it for others too*" (italics added).[2]

This book, then, has a dual aim: to describe a Christian theology of the good life and to show how I have come to this theology. Needless to say, this is only *one* such theology. Whether it is helpful toward attaining a just, sustainable planet and whether it is Christian is for readers to judge. At the very least, I hope it helps you work out your own theology.

Given this dual purpose, the first three chapters are "how I got there." Chapter 1 is a brief religious autobiography and credo, while chapters 2 and 3 try to answer the questions of what theology is and how one might do it (my version, of course). Those readers who have less interest in such topics might read chapter 1 and then skip over to chapters 4 and 5. These chapters are central ones: they lay out two major economic models—the neo-classical contemporary one and the ecological alternative one. These chapters try to answer the question of who we are in the scheme of things: they look at the deep world-pictures of two understandings of where human beings (and especially we middle-class North American ones) fit into the planet. These very different world-pictures suggest different behavior by us and result in different views of the abundant life. The last part of the book (chapters 6-8) spell out the theologies that emerge from these two worldviews. We will look at God and the World (chapter 6), Christ and Salvation (chapter 7), and Life in the Spirit (chapter 8) from the perspective of the neo-classical economic worldview and the ecological economic worldview. The resultant theologies are very different. I will be asking which one is both better for people and the planet as well as a more appropriate interpretation of Christian faith for our time. The Appendix is a brief summary of the book in the form of a manifesto, which can serve as an introduction to the main issues.

In closing, I want to underscore the limitations of the theology I am proposing. It will not restore the planet or stop the greedy. The kind of theology suggested in these pages fills just one small niche: that part of us which acts out of our assumptions, especially about who we are and where we fit. Many other tasks are more important: feeding the hungry, clothing the naked, healing the sick—not to mention voting for the legislators who will pass laws supporting justice and sustainability as well as encouraging the forest, land, water, and climate experts. Other theologians see other tasks for theology to do. The point is not to find *the* solution (for there is no *one*), but to foster all the ways that every human enterprise, including theology, can help us imagine and live a different abundant life, one that will make the earth healthier and people happier.

This is the great work of the twenty-first century. Never before have we had to think of everyone and everything all together. We now know that if we are to survive and our planet flourish we will do so as a whole or not at all. Christians believe we do not have to do this alone: "I came that they may have life and have it abundantly" (John 10:10).

 **Part I**

The Practice of Planetary Theology

1. A Brief Credo

The glory of God is every creature fully alive.
>—in the spirit of Irenaeus, third cent. C.E.

We beg you, God, make us fully alive.
>—Bishop Serapin, fourth cent. C.E.

A Religious Autobiography

FOR MANY YEARS I have taught a course on religious autobiography; it was the first course I taught, and I am still teaching it. Why? Because I am very interested in people who try to live their faith, who have what I would call a "working theology," a set of deeply held beliefs that actually function in their personal and public lives. Augustine, John Woolman, Sojourner Truth, Dietrich Bonhoeffer, Dorothy Day, and Martin Luther King Jr. are a few of these people. Each of them struggled to discern God's action in and through their lives and then to express that reality in everything they did. Their theologies became embodied in themselves; as disciples of Christ they became mini-incarnations of God's love. We call such people "saints," reflections of God, images of God with us in the flesh. They are intimations of what it means to be "fully alive," living life from, toward, and with God. They are examples to the rest of us of what a Christlike life is. They fascinate because in them we see God and the human in intimate connection, human lives showing forth different facets of divine power and love.

While it may seem outrageous to suggest, I believe each of us is called to this vocation, the vocation of sainthood. Each Christian is asked to examine his or her life with the goal of discerning the action of God in it and then to express God's power and love in everything. Each of us is expected to have a working theology, one that makes a difference in how we conduct our personal lives and how we act at professional and public levels. Becoming a mature Christian means internalizing one's beliefs so that they are evident in whatever one says or does. Made in the image of God, humans are called to grow into that image more fully—to become "like

God," which for Christians means becoming like Christ, following Christ. And following Christ means following One who, like us, was flesh and bones, of the earth, earthy. It means that Christian saints focus on God's work of helping to make all of us, every creature on the planet, fully alive. Christian sainthood is, it appears, a very mundane—a worldly, earthly—business.

For all the years I have been teaching the course in religious autobiography, it never occurred to me to write my own. Actually, I wasn't ready. I believe I might be now. I want to see how a few beliefs which I now hold undeniably can function as a working theology for the ecological and justice crises facing our planet in the twenty-first century. A bare bones theology, a few beliefs carefully thought through and actually functioning at personal and public levels, may be more significant than a comprehensive, systematic, but loosely embraced theology. What is one prepared to live? What beliefs are livable; that is, what beliefs will support the flourishing of life?

I want to use my own history as a case study for other Christians who are also trying to integrate their beliefs and their actions at the deepest level, who are trying to be whole, mature Christians functioning effectively in the twenty-first century on planet Earth. The story I will share will be brief, narrow, and focused. It is meant as a pedagogical tool for others and hence will ignore all kinds of personal data (family, schooling, relationships, etc.), which undoubtedly in a full autobiography would be relevant but will be passed over here.

I have had four "conversions," four experiences of such importance that they changed my thinking about God and my behavior. The first, which came in two stages, occurred when I was around seven years old. One day while walking home from school the thought came to me that some day I would not be here; I would not exist. Christmas would come, and I would not be around to celebrate it; even more shocking, my birthday would occur, and I would not be present. It was not an experience of death—and the fear of it; rather, it was an experience of non-being: I simply would not exist. For months, indeed years, I could not get this thought out of my mind; I was fascinated and terrified by it. Eventually, it began to turn into a sense of wonder that I *was* alive—and so were myriad other creatures. Over decades this wonder has stayed with me, growing stronger and deeper until now I believe that one of the most profound religious emotions is wonder at and gratitude for life in all its incredible shapes, colors, and sizes. Along with Annie Dillard I now exclaim, "My God what a world. There is no accounting for one second of it," and along with Alice Walker I notice the color purple in fields when I pass by.[1] That early experience of non-being has eventuated into praise to God for all beings fully alive.

The second stage of my seventh-year conversion occurred one day when the teacher asked the class, "What name will you write more than any other in your life?" Being an eager student, I immediately raised my hand to answer. Fortunately, the teacher did not call on me; had she done so, I would have been red with embarrassment. The correct answer was, of course, one's own name, but I was going to answer, "God." That incident stayed with me as I gradually discerned its meaning. I have decided I was not wrong: "God" is the name beneath, with, and in each of our names. As I have come to realize that we all live and move and have our being in God, the names of each person, species, creature, and element are superimposed over God's name. God *is* reality; God is the source of the reality of each of us. Panentheism seeing the world as *in* God—puts God's "name" first, but each of our names are included and preserved in their distinctiveness within the divine reality. My early experience of God's name as primary, the experience of divine transcendence and preeminence, would stay with me and grow.

It lay dormant, however, during my teenage years growing up in Boston as a member of a conventional Episcopal church. At most, God was the Great Moralizer, the upholder of proper appearances and conduct. My second conversion occurred at college while reading Karl Barth's *Commentary on Romans.* Suddenly the transcendence of God took on a whole new meaning for me. I began to have a glimmer of what the word "God" meant. My boxed-in, comfortable, tribal notion of God was split wide open and like a cold, bracing mountain wind, the awesome presence of the divine brushed my life. That evening I walked home from the library in a daze; I had seen something I would never forget: that God is God and nothing else is. My teacher and mentor, H. Richard Niebuhr, would call it "radical monotheism," and Paul Tillich described it as the Protestant Principle. It is Christianity in its "Protestant" or prophetic mode and a necessary component, I believe, of any theology. For years, however, it would keep me from recognizing and growing into my early sense of wonder at life and its grounding in God (the "Catholic" side that every theology also must have). It created a dualism in my belief and actions that sent me on a long detour, a detour in which the world was not *in* God and God was not *with* the world. The child's love of nature was set aside for the budding theologian's dedication to the transcendent—and distant—God.

Eventually, I found a way back (or one was given to me, as I now see it). The way back was through nature—I became a hiker. I did not find God in nature, but I found a sense of belonging, of being the "proper size" in the forest. Whenever I got on a trail, I immediately had a sense of proportion, of fitting in, of being neither too big nor too small, but "just right" in relation to the trees above me, the bushes and flowers beside me, and the earth under my feet. I felt *in* nature; it surrounded me; I was part of it. It felt like coming home. After many years, this experience on the trail came to symbolize how we (all of us creatures) fit into God's world, each with space and a place. What had been an experience of overwhelming and distant transcendence became one of equally awesome but now immanent and intimate transcendence. God's magnificence, God's preeminence, God's "Godness" was manifest *in and through and with* the earth and all its creatures. I learned this first through nature; eventually, I would see it as what Christians call "incarnation"—God with us here and now for the flourishing of all living beings. Nature can seduce us with its beauty and right order to love and glorify God. This is the way it happened to me.

My third conversion occurred when I was teaching theology at a divinity school. I had several books published and was progressing nicely up the career ladder. There was just one problem: most of my theology was still in my head. It wasn't bad theology; in fact, it was pretty good. It just didn't actually function in my life and I didn't hold to my beliefs with much fervor. I was a theologian but I didn't have a vocation. However, around 1980 I read an essay by another theologian, Gordon Kaufman, in which he claimed that, given the nuclear and ecological crises facing our planet, theology could no longer proceed with business as usual. It must deconstruct and reconstruct its central symbols—God, Christ, human being—from within this new context.[2] What would Christians say about God and the world if they took the planetary ecological situation as our interpretive lens? How different would Christian faith be if the well-being of human beings were not the only criterion? What would Christianity look like from a cosmological rather than just an anthropocentric perspective?

I believed that Kaufman was dead right. I revamped my teaching and research agendas in this direction and settled down to learning something about cosmology, evolutionary biology, and ecological science—about which I knew nothing. It has been a deeply instructive exercise, given me some "ecological literacy," and shown me the tiny niche that my work can fill for the planetary agenda. It also refashioned my sense of who we are in the scheme of things. My sense on the hiking trail that we humans fit into nature, can feel comfortable in our proper place, was confirmed by my readings. We do indeed fit here, but not at the top of the heap as we have supposed. Rather, we fit as one species among millions of others on which we depend for the air we breathe and the food we eat and for whom we are increasingly responsible. What I learned about our place in the scheme of things has become central to my belief that a paradigm shift in our consumer lifestyle will be critical to our well-being as well as our planet's.

This third conversion, while intellectual and theological, was certainly vocational as well. I believed that teaching and writing books that attempt to help people, especially Christians, shift from an anthropocentric to a cosmological paradigm—a way of being in the world that supports the flourishing of all life—is a form of activism. I saw it as a way in which my beliefs, which were increasingly becoming more defined and deeply held, could be embodied. I believed that this kind of work was a form of Christian activism.

But there was still a piece missing. That piece was me. I have always been intrigued by Dietrich Bonhoeffer's comment that he began as a theologian, became a Christian, and finally grew into a "contemporary."[3] I think what he meant was that he started as an academic Christian, became a practicing Christian, and finally became an embodied, "present" one. In other words, God finally became daily and immediate to him; God's presence was the *milieu*, the "world" within which he lived when imprisoned during World War II. Certainly from his letters one gains the sense of a man whose faith became immediate, present, and functional in the daily horrors and infrequent joys of prison life. He had no use for the distant, metaphysical God of his own past nor the God-of-the-gaps invoked by prisoners during air raids. Rather, for him God was the incarnate Christ, present with him in his suffering during interrogations by the Nazi officials, but also present when he could sit in the sun, watch an anthill, or eat a piece of fruit. The embodied, present God accompanied Bonhoeffer in his daily life, whatever that life brought. This God had gradually been fashioning Bonhoeffer in the divine image, into an embodied, present Christian who lived his faith.

My fourth conversion has been something like Bonhoeffer's sense of becoming contemporary with God. Finally, after years of talking *about* God (what theologians are paid to do!), I am becoming acquainted *with* God. This conversion has occurred quite deliberately: I engaged a spiritual director and have undertaken a daily pattern of meditation. I am doing what is called "practicing the presence of God," setting aside time for relating to God. To say that it has been instructive would be a gross understatement; it has been revelatory. Revelation, as I now see it, is God's loving self-disclosure, and that is what I have experienced. I am meeting *God* and God is *love*. How outrageous as well as platitudinous that sounds! I can scarcely believe I am writing it, let alone intending to publish it. Why am I doing so? Simply because it is true; it is what has happened, is happening, to me.

Let me back up and try to flesh this out a little. When I was young I recall hearing the grown-ups whispering in the kitchen on holidays—usually the women preparing dinner. I was convinced that they were talking about things that mattered, what life was all about, how everything fit together. I could not have articulated it that way then, but I recall from a very early age having a sense of the mystery of things and my ignorance about all of it. I wanted to find out; I thought the whispering women were talking about it (I am sure now they were talking about things never discussed openly in the 1940s—cancer, divorce, mental illness, unwanted babies, etc.). Gradually, over the decades separating my six-year-old self from my sixty-plus-year-old self, the mystery has been revealed to me—or so it seems, at least. I quote from an entry in my journal: "I feel as though I finally understand what life is about. It is, quite simply, acknowledging how things are—living in the truth. And the truth is that God is the source and sustainer of everything." Since I have undertaken the daily practice of prayer, I have gradually felt my center, the center of my being, shifting from myself to God. From the burdensome task of trying to ground myself in myself, I have let go and allowed God to become the One in and for whom I live.

I hasten to add two qualifications. First, I am a newcomer to living in this reality—I know little about it except the undeniable belief that it *is* reality, mine and that of everything else. Second, trying to live in God's reality in no way detracts from *my* reality; in fact, it enhances and fulfills it. I feel more "me" than at any other time in my life. I am also more aware of the distinctiveness and concrete particularity of other things: faces are more luminous, the color purple in fields is brighter.

The overwhelming emotion that I have experienced from this revelation of the mystery of things—from meeting God and knowing that God is love—is similar to Ebenezer Scrooge's on Christmas Day. He kicked up his heels, exclaiming, "I didn't miss it after all!" I feel this way. In the sixth decade of my life I have been invited on a new journey, which seems like a great adventure, perhaps the greatest adventure of which human beings are capable.

Some Reflections

Several things have already come clear to me about this journey. It becomes immediately evident that one learns as much about oneself and the world as one does about God. In prayer a reversal occurs: we do not talk about God and the world but begin to see ourselves and the world *in* God. We begin to see human life and the world from the divine perspective, from a broader and more inclusive point of view than we are otherwise capable of holding. We begin to recognize who we are in the scheme of things from the perspective of the Creator and Redeemer of everything that is. We are no longer the center (a definition of sin); we know God is the Center (a definition of salvation).

Another thing that is becoming clear to me is that God is always available; the problem is, we are not. Whereas I used to think God was distant (because transcendent), now I realize that God is "ubiquitous," an old, quaint way of saying that God is everywhere all the time. As I become aware of God's presence in my life, I realize that there is nothing special about this—I am not special to be experiencing God's presence and it is not remarkable for God to be present. God is available all the time to everyone and everything. *We* have to become conscious of God's presence. At one level, it is no different from any important relationship: one has to pay attention to the other, listen, and be open. To say God is always present is simply to acknowledge that God is reality, the breath, the life, the power, the love beneath, above, around, and in everything. This is divine transcendence *immanently* experienced; it is the magnificence and awesomeness of God *with us*.

This brings me to a further insight from "the neophyte's notebook." It is alright to be excessive: one can't love God *too much*. It's a relief to finally find the proper object of insatiable desire. Augustine and Thomas were right: our hearts are restless until they rest in God, and we were made to know and enjoy God forever. One doesn't have to hold back; the *sanctus* is the proper primary prayer; we were made to glorify God—and it feels good to do so. But once again, it is not an either/or—God or the world. The incarnation has taken on a whole new meaning for me: it means God is forever and truly the God with and for the flesh, the earth, the world. Many of the saints who speak about loving God know that it is easier to love God than the neighbor. Hence, the best test as Teresa of Avila shrewdly suggests, is to stick with the neighbor: "And be certain that the more advanced you see you are in love for your neighbor the more advanced you will be in the love of God."[4] The briefest of my credos, then, might be: "We live to give God glory by loving the world and everything in it."

Third, this adventure is showing me how deeply interconnected are the active and contemplative dimensions of the Christian life. I learned this first from teaching the religious autobiography course: all the people we read were social activists. None of them were hermits or New Agers, interested only in their own individual spiritual development. On the contrary, they knew they had to be deeply rooted in God in order to do their justice work in the world. Dorothy Day could never have lasted decades in New York's Bowery ministering to the homeless, the alcoholics, and the destitute without a deep spiritual life. Like Bonhoeffer's God, Day's was immediate, present, and functional—the power that guided and sustained her. We misinterpret God's love when we think it is merely for our comfort or even our spiritual growth. If the saints give us a lesson, it is that God's presence in our lives should turn us into workers for an alternative world.

Finally, these initial reflections have suggested to me that working for an alternative world is a prime directive for Christian living. Do I mean another, supernatural world? Does practicing the presence of God mean leaving this world as so much Christian asceticism and fundamentalism advocate? By no means (as the incarnation insists), but it does mean trying to live *differently* in our one and only world. My reflections coalesce around this point: what I have learned about who God is, who we are, and where we fit into the scheme of things tells me that the one thing needful in a theology for twenty-first century North American middle-class Christians is an alternative view of the abundant life from that of our consumer culture. *Life Abundant* is about this reconstruction. We will take as our context for revisioning theology the well-being of our planet and all its creatures, seeing that project against the deterioration of nature and the injustice to poor people that the religion of our time—consumerism—is bringing about. If one believes that "the glory of God is all creatures fully alive," then our current worldview and its lifestyle are wrong. It is more than that: it is sinful and evil, for it is contrary to God's will for creation.

This sounds like a universal and universalizing project. Actually, it isn't. I will be interpreting this problem and its alternative through a narrow lens: the little bit I know, the few beliefs I hold undeniably. For many years I have been aware that most good (coherent, interesting, plausible) theology grows from a central insight—one possible, deeply held, and thoroughly embodied statement about God and the world. A few examples: for Paul it was being made righteous by God through Christ; for John it was the Word made flesh; for Thomas it was the nature/supernature relationship; for Schleiermacher it was the feeling of absolute dependence; for Barth it was the radical transcendence of God; for the liberation theologians it is the preferential option for the poor. None of these is wrong, but all of them are partial. There is no such thing as a complete theology; there are only piecemeal theologies, the best efforts of human beings to state what they have found to be undeniable through their experience of God and as members of the Christian community. It is as if a tiny bit of God is available to each creature, whatever aspect of God that creature needs and can absorb. Most of us cannot absorb very much of the infinite Divine Being. At most we might come to reflect a smidgen of it in our thinking and actions. No one has ever seen God, so what more can we expect? But a tiny bit is enough; that is, enough if it is deeply held, well understood, and carefully argued—and if it is open to the many other bits from other Christians as we all struggle to discern God's will for our world.

As I come to the end of these reflections on my religious journey, I will try to summarize them at the level closest to my experience. In the next section I will express them more systematically in a credo and in the remainder of the book expand them into a working theology, but here I want to suggest the heart of my theology, the core that informs the whole.

We live and move and have our being in God. God is closer to us (to every iota of creation) than we are to ourselves. God is the breath of our breath, the love with which we love, the power that sustains our work. When we become aware of God, who is the Alpha and Omega, as the source and goal of everything and of all life, love, and power, then we become channels for these realities, both in our own lives and for others. We become available to be "saved" (restored to health and happiness) and to help "save" others. Salvation means living in God's presence, in imitation of divine love for the world. Each of us can love only a tiny fragment of the earth, but that is our task.

I am slowly learning to live and think and act within the divine *milieu*. I sense the world (and myself) becoming ordered by that gracious Presence. I am beginning to see things within that Light and everything seems different. Things are neither chaotic nor ordered in relation to me and my wants. Everything is ordered by God and in relation to God. Reality "makes sense," not according to worldly standards (nor mine), but in terms of the love that created everything and wants it to flourish. Ecologically, theologically, and personally it makes sense: the world is characterized by radical relationality ordered by and to the Power in the universe, who is love. It is the reality in which all are to live together in community to glorify God and to share with each other. Such reality has order and harmony; the disorder and confusion come when we fail to acknowledge this order and try to reorder things around ourselves.

From my growing acquaintance with God has come confirmation of my earliest religious experiences: gratitude for life and glory to God. Pierre Teilhard de Chardin said that from the time he was a child he had two passions: a passion for the world and a passion for God, and his lifelong goal was to bring these two together.[5] I think my journey has been similar: the "Catholic" sacramental appreciation of the world joined with the "Protestant" prophetic witness to divine transcendence. The key to their unity, of course, is the incarnation which, in its profound simplicity, means "God with us," God with the world and the world within God. The incarnation, it seems to me, is not merely or solely about Jesus. It is more radical than that, although for Christians Jesus is the paradigm of both God with us and the world within God. The incarnation reveals God as *always* with us and our being *defined* as within God. The incarnation is the solution to the "two worlds problem": the problem of how to love God and the world. There is only one world, a world that God loves. Since God loves it, we not only *can* but *should*. In fact, loving the world (not God alone), or rather, loving God *through* loving the world, is the Christian way.

The above paragraphs are a summary of my most deeply held beliefs. This theological core has implications for Christian discipleship in twenty-first century North America. The Christian way (according to this view) inevitably leads to an understanding of salvation as deification, becoming like God. Made in God's image, we are to grow into that reality by doing what God does: love the world. Jesus Christ is the incarnation of God because he did that fully—his mind, heart, and will were one with God's love for the world. We see this in his ministry to the outcast, oppressed, and sick as well as in his death on a cross in defiance of the powers of greed, hatred, and domination. But we also are called to this vocation: Christian discipleship is loving the world. As we see in the story of Jesus and the stories of the saints (all Christians who try to do this), it is not easy or pleasant. While appreciating the color purple is one dimension of passion for the world, identifying with its sufferings is another.

Such identification is, I believe, increasingly essential for favored North American Christians who, along with other Westerners, are experiencing the highest level of the "good life" that any human beings ever have. The context in which we experience this consumer abundance, however, is one of a widening gap between the well-off and the poor of the world, as well as an increasing deterioration of the "resources" (the natural world) that fund our abundance. We cannot, in good conscience "love the world"—its snowcapped mountains and panda bears—while at the same time destroying it and allowing our less well-off sisters and brothers to sink into deeper poverty. Hence, I believe Christian discipleship for twenty-first-century North American Christians means "cruciform living," an alternative notion of the abundant life, which will involve a philosophy of "enoughness," limitations on energy use, and sacrifice for the sake of others. For us privileged Christians a "cross-shaped" life will not be primarily what Christ does for us, but what we can do for others. We do not need so much to accept Christ's sacrifice for our sins as we need to repent of a major sin— our silent complicity in the impoverishment of others and the degradation of the planet. In Charles Birch's pithy statement: "The rich must live more simply, so that the poor may simply live."[6] While not all North American Christians are "rich," most of us are avid consumers, and few Christian churches have suggested alternative visions of abundant living. We should be doing so. Christians have the obligation not just to live differently themselves, but to recommend an alternative to the paradigm of unlimited consumption. Can an alternative life be good, be abundant? I believe it can be but only within God's ordering of reality, in which right relations (what is good for the planet) becomes our standard.

Since the world, according to the incarnation, is where God dwells, it is God's "house," and we should abide by God's house rules. The house rules for the whole earth are right relations among all creatures, relations governed in basic ways by economics. What God's house rules are—in terms of ecological and economic imperatives—is one of the major tasks of Christian discernment. I am suggesting that the context within which North American Christians should undertake such discernment is a cruciform one: the recognition that a *different* way of living in the world is called for rather than the dominant consumer model.

Thinking Theologically

Our progression has been from a narrative, first-order experience of God to reflections on that narrative. We now take a further step to thinking theologically, toward a credo. A credo is the thoughtful expression of what one believes most deeply and is prepared to act on. John Cobb makes a helpful distinction between "avowed beliefs" and "real beliefs," between "beliefs that Christians avow because they think they are Christian and the ones that constitute their real convictions."[7] While a Christian hopes that his or her real beliefs will be Christian, one cannot fall back on avowed beliefs in fear of what the real ones may or may not produce. The Christian tradition is wide and deep, with more room for genuinely held and carefully thought through positions than many suppose. And, as the saints often remind us, right action is more essential than right doctrine, or as John Woolman, the eighteenth-century Quaker abolitionist, put it, "Conduct is more convincing than words."[8] Indeed it is.

So, thinking theologically is not an end in itself; it is for the purpose of right action, for discipleship. It is to make our action as close to God's will as we can discern. Theology is therefore essential, even though it is not the central enterprise of the Christian life. The goal of theology, as I see it, is to be *functional,* that is, to actually work in someone's life. It is meant to be an aid to right living, the supposition being that examining one's beliefs (which may be only implicit, perhaps even chaotic or inconsistent) is necessary to acting thoughtfully and persuasively on the issues facing twenty-first-century Christians. Anselm in the twelfth century said it well: faith must seek understanding. Not only do many contemporary Christians know little about their faith, both its tradition and their own personal beliefs, but they (we) also know little about the ecological and justice crises that constitute our planet's situation. "Christian literacy" and "ecological/justice literacy" are knowledges that we need if we are to become thinking Christians. Hence, the movement that we are tracing here from first-person narrative expressions of experiences of God to reflections on the narrative, eventuating in a credo, is not finished with the credo. The next step is to understand one's faith within the context of our planet's situation (which we will undertake in chapters 4 and 5). It is not enough that a Christian theology be meaningful to an individual; it must, if it is to be Christian, speak of God's love for the world and whether that world is flourishing as God wishes it to.

Not only must a credo be relevant to the pressing public issues of one's day, but it must also be "Christian." A credo is not just a matter of personal experience or private revelation. While personal experience confirms and deepens beliefs, these beliefs, if they are to be Christian, cannot be totally idiosyncratic. They must be in the Christian tradition or shown to be consonant with it. For instance, since beginning a practice of daily prayer, I have become convinced that God is love—total, radical love that wants nothing except the flourishing of creation. I have known that God is love all my life; it is the most common "platitude" of Christianity. One hears it constantly in Christian prayers and hymns; it seems sometimes trite, overdone, and sentimental; in fact, it often seems false, if not repulsive, in light of the horrors of history, especially those perpetrated by Christians (anti-Semitism, the Inquisition, missionary genocide, American slavery, etc.). But when I began to experience God's love in my own life, when God came to me as totally gracious, giving and forgiving, the platitude became a luminous, precious reality. Nothing seemed more profound, more welcome, richer with unplumbed depths than the simple statement, "God is love." I did not create that insight, nor was it revealed to me alone. It is the central belief of the religious tradition to which I belong; all that has happened is that it has become a reality in my life. Hence, a credo by a Christian is not a statement of original or novel beliefs; on the contrary, it is the personal embrace, the personal representation, of beliefs central to the Christian tradition. I have been formed by that tradition throughout my entire life as a Christian and as a theologian. My credo is simply my attempt to embody, take into myself, the central tenets of Christian faith. Whether the way I represent the beliefs that I embrace is Christian is for the community to judge.

The following brief credo is my initial contribution to a functional theology. It is part of the work of becoming clear concerning which beliefs from the tradition are most central for us today, how we should express them for maximum effectiveness, and whether we hold them with sufficient conviction to make a difference in our personal and public lives. This is an inductive way of doing theology, moving from experience outward toward a more or less comprehensive interpretation of God and the world. Presumptuous as that may sound, it is actually very modest, for it not only admits that theology is nothing but one Christian's experience of God and the tradition, but it shows the all-too-human moves by which theologies develop. Theology, that most pretentious, abstract, and obscure enterprise, is merely attempts by human beings to speak of God from their own experience in light of Christian faith. This book tries to show how that attempt grows from a bare skeleton of a few deeply held beliefs to a fleshed-out theology for twenty-first-century Americans faced with unprecedented global crises. My hope is that other Christians, and not just theologians, will reflect upon their own beliefs so that they can function effectively in the situation facing us. We cannot "love the world" if we do not know it *or* if we do not know what Christian love for the world means.

A Credo
God and the World

I believe that we live and move and have our being in God, that we are not our own but belong to God. I also believe that we are not *on* our own; we live in God's world. We come from God and return to God and in the meantime, we are to live in the presence of God. God is, then, reality: God is the source, the sustainer, and the goal of everything that is. This in no way undercuts the reality of the world; on the contrary, the world is real and significant because God is incarnate—God is enfleshed, God is worldly. I believe a Christian cannot speak of God without speaking of God incarnate, for we do not know a distant, disembodied God but an intimate, embodied one. Because of the incarnation, we can speak of the world as God's body and hence when we say that God is reality we mean that reality is both with us and beyond us, both immanent and transcendent, both physical and spiritual.

Because of the incarnation, I believe that God is love: God loves the world. I believe God loves the world with various kinds of love—the love of a creator, a friend, a mother and father, an artist, a lover, a scientist. God loves the world with disinterested aesthetic appreciation (in Genesis, God says seven times of creation, "It is good") and with exorbitant passion for justice on behalf of all creatures who are oppressed, outcast, or deteriorating. Love is not God; rather, God is love—God defines love. As the Incarnate One, the embodied God, God's love is particular, constant, and universal: it is oriented toward each creature in its particular needs and desires; it is never absent; and it extends to everything that is. God is radical relationality, in intimate relationship with everything as the source, sustainer, and goal of every scrap, every quark, of creation. God wishes everything well, is interested in every creature, and wants nothing other than the flourishing of all. To each and every element in creation God says, "Where you are, I am and I wish nothing other than your health and joy."

I believe God is personal but not a person. To say that God is love means that God is personal, but I also find metaphors such as spirit, life, light, water, and truth, which are impersonal or less personal, significant ways to express belief in God as love, as the source of creation's flourishing. Several of these metaphors are able to include aspects of creation other than human beings and are especially helpful to theologies from a cosmological context. But to human beings, at least, God cannot be less than personal; to other dimensions of creation God is undoubtedly whatever is necessary to relate to them intimately and effectively. I believe God is personal because I have experienced God this way in prayer; I am conscious of being with a Presence, a Thou, not an It.

I believe, then, in God—though what this means I cannot fully say. I know that "God" is beyond all our imaginings, all our thoughts, all our statements. The little I can say can be summed up as follows. To me God is reality and the source of our reality. While God and the world—God's reality and ours—are not identical, they are ontologically related. That is, the world's reality derives from God, but just as important, the world is God's beloved which is joined to God: the world is God's body. I believe we can therefore love God by loving the world. We need not leave the world to be with God (nor even look upward when we pray). God is with us here and now; God always has been and always will be—the incarnation is the eternal truth about God and the world. The transcendent, glorious, awesome God, the maker of stars and galaxies, the Being of all beings, is with each and every one of us as our most intimate Friend. And for each and every one of us God wishes nothing but our flourishing.

As outrageous as this sounds (especially in light of our planet's present deteriorating state and the misery facing many of its human inhabitants), what else could *God* be? If God is not love and life and hope and goodness and peace, then something else is. "God" must be the power of life and the love that wills its fulfillment. This is the God I have learned about from my tradition (both the Hebrew and Christian parts of it), that the incarnation attests to, and that my own experience confirms.

Jesus as the Christ

I believe in Jesus as the Christ. For shorthand purposes, one can say Jesus Christ, but a space, a gap, should always be silently present between Jesus and Christ. For the earliest Christians and for all subsequent ones, Jesus of Nazareth became the Christ as they (we) confess that he is the revelation of God. In his face, Christians see the hidden face of God; in his ministry, death, and resurrection, they perceive the way God would have them live. Jesus' life is a parable of God for Christians and a model for our own lives. He is the mediator, the channel, between God and the world which allows us to say who God is and how human beings should live in the world. But certainly for me (and it seems for many other Christians as well), this belief in Jesus *as* the Christ, as the face of God, is a risk-filled one. Christ is not Jesus' last name; it is a title that Christians confer on him with considerable daring and hope.

He was, after all, only a man, only a human being. He was not a walking God. This is the Jesus side and one that Christians have insisted upon vehemently. I believe deeply in this side: the historical, prophetic, "Protestant" side of Jesus as the Christ. Here we learn the *content* of God's way with us and the way we should respond. The destabilizing parables of Jesus that overturn conventional hierarchies, his ministry to the sick, his practice of eating with outcasts, his end on a cross (the expected punishment for someone who sides with the oppressed)—all of this tells us what it means to confess that *God* is with us. If Jesus was totally open to God, a perfect channel for God, then we can see in his life and death God's way with the world, God's intention toward and activity within the world. We can also see who we are in the scheme of things—God's beloved, and especially beloved are the poor, the dispossessed, the outcast. Since the God whom Jesus reveals is the Creator of everything that is, the "beloved" must include *all* dispossessed, outcast creatures and not only human ones.

But Jesus, according to Christians, was more than a human being: he was the revelation of God, the Christ. He was the incarnation of God, not just a prophet. And here the "Catholic" side emerges, which is just as important as the "Protestant" side. When I confess that Jesus is the Christ, I am saying that he is paradigmatic of what we see everywhere and always: God with us, God with and for *all* of us, all creatures, all worldly processes and events. Jesus as the Christ means God is our *milieu*, that all of us (and not just Jesus) live and move and have our being in God. God is incarnate *in the world*. Jesus is the clue to this, the place where Christians look to see what it means, but divine incarnation is not limited to Jesus. Each creature is a microcosm of divine incarnation; each of us is made in the image of God; and the destiny of all creation is to grow more fully into that reality. If incarnation were limited to Jesus of Nazareth, it would not only be a surd (and hence, absurd), but paltry in comparison to God's embodiment in *all* of creation. This in no way lessens the importance of Jesus Christ to Christians, for he is, to us, the revelation of God, the one who allows us to see what divine incarnation means and how we, too, can live within God's reality.

So, in sum, I believe in Jesus, the strange, enigmatic prophet who lived two thousand years ago, as the Christ of God. In his life and death I learn who God is, and I learn that the God revealed here is incarnate also everywhere else. Jesus as the Christ means God's way with, in, and for the world. Finally, in Jesus' resurrection I can hope that the love of God for the dispossessed and oppressed will not die but live again for us and in us.

The Spirit of God

I believe in God's Spirit as the source of all life and love. Life in the Spirit is the only place where human beings can live fulfilled lives. This is the case because God *is* reality and in God we live and move and have our being. God is not an "extra" added on to life, but life itself—and as we learn from Jesus as the Christ—God's intention is that all life should flourish. Life takes place in love and for love.

Hence, Christian anthropology occurs *within* theology: the doctrine of who human beings are and what we should do is understood within the doctrine of who God is and what God has done and is doing. In no way, however, does this undercut the worldliness, the particularity, the diversity, the uniqueness of each and every creature. In fact, just the opposite is true because of the incarnation of God in the world. An incarnate theology overcomes two-world thinking: there is only *one* world. The question for Christian anthropology is how human beings should live *in this world*.

We learn how we should *not* live ("sin") by becoming aware of how we *should* live ("salvation"). When we accept that we were created by love and for love, that all things come from overflowing divine abundance and are intended to flourish through interdependence with God and others, then we begin to sense what salvation is. We have a new sense of who we are (God's beloved) and where we fit into the scheme of things (in the beloved community along with all God's other creatures). We no longer need focus on the self and its insecurities; we have found our home and can feel some detachment from the pressure to find our place. We *have* a place and a vocation: our place is planet Earth, and our vocation is working with God toward the flourishing of all life in our home.

We now see, as well, what sin is. If salvation is living appropriately on our planet, living as the one creature who can consciously help bring about God's beloved community, then sin is living in a way opposed to that goal. Sin is centering life in the self, trying to establish the self in itself for itself. Sin is living a lie: it is living contrary to God's ordering of things. God's order is one in which the self is *de*centered as focused on itself ("selfishness") and *re*centered as grounded in God and focused on one's neighbors ("deification"). Living a lie is living a selfish life; living the truth is living a deified life. The first assumes that life is found in the self; the second, that life is found in God.

Since sinful living is false, it will result in disorder and chaos, in a distortion and perversion of what matters. The abundant life will be seen as consisting of material things—money, fame, power, consumer goods—all of which are sought in order to bolster the fragile ego, the insecure self. The seven deadly sins are indeed deadly because they contribute to disorder and perversion. Caught in the nets of pride, envy, lust, greed, and so on, we cannot imagine a different rendering of the good life, of what matters. But if that stranglehold is broken and we realize we are God's beloved, a wholly different way of seeing the world and our place in it emerges.

We now understand the abundant life as living from and toward God: "To know you is eternal life, to serve you is perfect freedom."[9]

The good life is life lived in God's ordering of reality: it is life as disciples of Jesus Christ, which is to say, life in the process of becoming like God (deification). We are won over to this service not out of a sense of duty, but out of gratitude, of wonder, for being accepted as God's beloved. What we have struggled for all our lives—to establish the self as worthy—has simply been given to each and every one of us unconditionally.

We want to give back. Hence, life in the Spirit is becoming like God, conforming our wills to God's will, doing God's work in the world. The empty self can now become full of God; detachment from the distorted goods (money, power, fame) allows for attachment to genuine goods (God, other people, the natural world).

I would underscore two points on deification, one that the saints of all ages emphasize and the other that has particular relevance for our time. The first is the basic criterion of deification: if one wants to know whether one is becoming like God, look to the neighbor. "If one loves the neighbor, they can truly say, 'I am a child of God'" (Augustine). Deification, it appears, is not mystical ascent to another world. Rather, at least according to the saints, it is just the opposite, attending to the others here on planet Earth. In fact, to *really* love others appropriately, one must *know* them well. The old adage, "God is in the details," takes on new meaning: deification involves finding out what makes others flourish. (This might mean becoming an expert on logging methods in old-growth forests or global economics and its import for the poor.) Deification is also *empathy* for others, learning how to stand in their place and feel what living a lie or living the truth would be like from their perspective. Deification, then, if it is principally loving the neighbor, is the worldly, secular, mundane process of *knowing* the beloved others and *feeling* with them in their pain and joy. And most of all, it is working for the flourishing of others, which brings us to the second point.

Contemporary North American Christians should understand deification in terms of cruciform living. The abundant life for us must be conducted with a very sharp eye to the way consumerism (the contemporary reincarnation of the deadly sin of greed) is both devastating the natural world and creating great inequities between the poor and the wealthy. We cannot love our neighbors—neither the human ones nor the earth ones—unless we drastically cut back on our consumption. Dostoevsky said: "Love in practice is a harsh and dreadful thing compared to love in dreams." The harsh and dreadful thing we well-off North Americans must do is set our discipleship within a thoroughgoing critique of our culture's current lifestyle and offer some alternative visions of the good life.

*   *   *

My credo, then, can be summed up as follows: I believe in God, the Creator and Sustainer of all life; in Jesus Christ, in whom we see God at work for the flourishing of life; and in the Spirit, who works in us so we might live from, toward, and with God. This trinitarian God is "God with us," as our Source, our Way, and our Goal. This God is radically transcendent and radically immanent: the one who is more awesome than all the galaxies in the universe and nearer to us than our own breath. This God is the One who invites all of us into community to live and flourish together as God's beloved.

As I finish this attempt at a brief credo, I am aware that it ends where it began, with my two deepest passions—in Teilhard de Chardin's words, a passion for the earth and a passion for God. It is profoundly satisfying that I have not had to jettison my two loves in order to be a Christian. In fact, the opposite has been the case; Christianity has educated, deepened, and broadened these passions. From inchoate longings they have become complex, nuanced beliefs with profound implications not only for how I should live my own life but for how we twenty-first-century North Americans might alter our greedy lifestyle. The two dimensions of this love—for the earth and for God—together suggest that a cruciform mode of life is called for. Christian discipleship in our time, if it is to express love for God and for the earth, must be one of self-limitation, sacrifice, and sharing so that the neighbors, all God's creatures, might flourish. Christians are called, I believe, not only to embody an alternative vision of the abundant life, but also to help move our social, political, and financial institutions in this direction. An alternative to individualistic consumerism as the goal of life is surely needed; Christianity, along with the other world religions, can offer an alternative vision. Religions are in the business of recommending counter-cultural visions of the good life; now, more than ever, we need such visions if God and the earth are to be loved.

The love of God and the love of the earth are summed up in Irenaeus's statement with which we began these reflections: "The glory of God is every creature fully alive." We love God, give God glory, by loving the earth, helping all creatures flourish. Short of a radical change in our personal and planetary economics, creatures will not flourish and hence glory cannot be given to God. A cruciform lifestyle is not an option for us; it is the one thing needful for contemporary Christian discipleship.

2. Theology Matters

> . . . Love has its price. God wants to make us alive, and the wider we open our hearts to others or the more audibly we cry out against the injustice which rules over us, the more difficult our life in the rich society of injustice becomes. Even a small love of a few trees, of seals, or of schoolchildren who cry at night in torment . . . is costly. Many cannot afford even a small love for creatures and prefer not to have seen anything.
>
> —Dorothee Soelle[1]

Is Theology Possible for North American Christians?

THE PURPOSE OF THEOLOGY is to glorify God by reflecting on how we might live better on the earth. Theology is about thinking, but it is not primarily an intellectual activity. It is a practical one—so that we might live better, more appropriately, in the world. For Christians, this right living occurs when we bring our wills into line with God's, when we live within the divine ordering of reality. Theology, then, is an aspect of discerning God's will and, hence, cannot be done apart from ethics and spirituality: thinking, doing, and praying belong together. The Christian thinks about God and the world for the purpose of acting rightly in the world, and the primary, the most immediate, context for our thought and praxis is prayer. The liberation theologian, Gustavo Gutiérrez, says it well: "Our spirituality is our method."[2] We cannot think about God or act rightly in the world apart from being grounded in God.

Since theology, ethics, and spirituality are a unit, every Christian is called to be a theologian. There are not categories of Christians—doers, worshipers, and thinkers—since we cannot carry out any of these functions without the others. To be sure, thinking about one's faith is for the purpose of action and is done within the context of prayer, but these conditions do not make theology less necessary. In fact, they make it essential. Theology matters! We can neither praise God nor love the world if we have not thought through who God is and how we should love the world. Reflection is a critical part of Christian discipleship and one, unfortunately, that increasingly seems distant and perhaps unobtainable to many North American Christians.[3] This book is intended to help these Christians develop a working theology—a theology that can actually function in our contemporary world. While the theology elaborated here is only one possibility, it can serve as an example for other Christians who desire to integrate their thinking, action, and spirituality into a coherent theology.

But is theology possible for North American Christians? From both postmodern and liberation perspectives, the theology of North American Christians is suspect. Postmodernism objects to the universalism of theology as well as to its focus on human subjects. Yet, Johann Metz claims theologians are necessarily universalists for they speak of God, world, and human being: "God is either a universal theme, a theme of all humankind, or no theme at all."[4] He also mentions that the human being has disappeared from most fields of study: in the sciences, it is reduced to its DNA, and in the humanities, it is a product of its context. Is theology, then, merely a hold-over from modernity, its last home being post-Enlightenment culture with its "drive to clarity, turn to the subject, the concern with method, [and] the belief in sameness"?[5] Postmodernity, the culture of the late twentieth century, has other priorities: the denial of all fixed certainties and universal assertions, the delight in pluralism and difference.[6] It also insists that subjects do not make statements; rather, interpretations emerge from various contexts with subjects as the channels of these interpretations. Thus, two major characteristics of traditional theology—universalism and subjectivity—are rejected by the contemporary paradigm of thinking and knowing. Universal assertions about God and the world can no longer be made by human beings, who themselves are not coherent subjects but social constructions created by cultural forces. "God," "world," and "human being," the most common terms in theology, are all highly suspect. In fact, theology is often seen by postmodernism as a prime example of illegitimate, presumptuous, and illusory discourse. It is not only empty but dangerous, for its universalism rejects diversity, and its focus on subjects clouds the ways in which cultures form us.

Postmodernism is a healthy and necessary critique of theology's past—as well as much of its present. Theology has often been presumptuous, incredible, and imperialistic. One has only to consider the ways in which it has contributed to colonization, anti-Semitism, genocide, ethnic wars, homophobia, fundamentalism, and so on, to agree. Whenever and wherever theology has joined hands with nationalism, commercialism, militarism, racism, and sexism, as well as all forms of mind control, it merits—and benefits from—the critique of postmodernism.

That critique is joined by various liberation theologies that have also found traditional theology at fault. Interestingly—and undoubtedly not by coincidence—these theologies focus on the same two issues: universal assertions and the nature of the subject. The reasons for objecting, however, are different. Liberation theologies see universal statements as masks for theology's dominant voice: the white, Western male voice. The universal statements of this voice are exposed as partial, biased, and often oppressive to others. Liberation theologians will themselves talk about God, world, and human being, but now from the perspective of the many unheard voices from the underside of history. These theologians object as well to the subject, to the representative human being as white, Western, and male. For them, the representative human being of the twenty-first century will be poor and probably a woman from the third world.

Again, this critique is valid and necessary. The liberation theologians have removed theology from Western, male-dominated, academic institutions where the subject was the alienated modern individual and replanted it in the soil of everyone's yard, but especially in the plots of the poor and the dispossessed. As Gutiérrez eloquently says, "even the poor have the right to think." In fact, we all do—and must. Liberation theology has democratized theology as the right and responsibility of every Christian.

When we consider, then, whether theology is possible today for North American Christians, we are faced with two main questions. If not universal statements, then what kind of statements can our theology make about God, world, and human being? If we accept the critique of the subject of modern theology—the white, Western, male (or female) individual—then what understanding of the human subject is possible for us today? These are such important issues that a brief answer to them seems necessary as we begin, although we will return to them several times in the course of the book. I will make comments on these issues from the position of my own theology—again, as a case study to help other North American Christians answer them from their own perspectives.

Taken together, these two questions ask how mere human beings who are deeply conditioned by their historical and cultural situations can make statements about the Power in, over, and for the universe, statements that are intended to be the truth about this Power and relevant to all people. The answer, of course, is that we cannot. Fundamentalism is the refusal to acknowledge our limitations: it is the attempt to avoid the risky business that theology intrinsically is by claiming that "revelation," usually in the form of an inerrant Scripture, is the literal Word of God. The critiques of theology by postmodernism and the liberation theologies are too accurate and too helpful to be dismissed by a turn to authoritarianism. Rather, the appropriate response is to acknowledge their validity and re-examine the nature of theological statements and the subject making them.

My shorthand suggestion, which I will try to unpack, is that theological statements are open-ended faith statements made by unstable, incomplete subjects in the process of formation, and within many different contexts.[7] In other words, there is considerable uncertainty, partiality, and openness in both the statements and in their source. At the same time, there is a strong sense of conviction and a kind of universalism in many of the best theological statements. When Martin Luther pinned his Ninety-five Theses on the church door and later exclaimed, "Here I stand; I can do no other," his certainty about his assertions and his sense of their importance did not come from himself, but from their object, God. In other words, theologians make universal statements—that is, statements about God, world, and human beings—realizing that the statements are hypothetical, partial, risky, and limited. Theological statements are universal in scope but not in quality of judgment. Another way to express this proper stance of the theologian is to insist on "radical monotheism": the *only* absolute, the only certainty, the only universal, is God.[8] Postmodernism and the liberation theologies are not the first to remind theology of this; in fact, it has been the awareness of every great theologian.[9] All have been conscious that certainty is neither in oneself nor in one's words, but in God alone. It is, however, the sense of certainty about and trust in the one, absolute, universal God—perhaps the most defining characteristic of the Jewish and Christian traditions—that accounts for the rightful sense of conviction in theological statements. For example, from Paul and John, the first two Christian theologians, to current liberation theologians, statements have been made about God's comprehensive, absolute, and permanent love. It makes no sense, at least in this tradition, to speak of God as "maybe" loving the world, or loving "parts" of it, or loving it "now and then." The point of uncertainty is what *we* say about God's love, how *we* understand it, how *we* apply it.[10] Theological statements, then, are risky, partial, uncertain assertions made by relative, historically bound creatures about universal matters—God, world, and human beings.

Are such statements "true"? Obviously not, if judged by a crude correspondence view—that our statements "correspond" to God's reality. We have no way of judging that. All that we can say is that from our own experience and within the parameters of our tradition, we have been persuaded to stand on this or that carefully thought-through interpretation of God's relation to the world. The theologian will say: "I believe it. I believe it is Christian. I believe it is good for the world."

To flesh out this understanding of theology a little, let me describe a few of its characteristics. It begins with "a relative absolute," a central conviction that is neither a foundation nor the "essence" of Christianity, but a deeply held, abiding insight into God's relation to us.[11] As I indicated earlier, my relative absolute is that we live to give God glory by loving the world and everything in it. This is not an absolute, because I know it is simply my interpretation of the relation between God and the world, but it is a relative absolute because it informs everything else I say about God and the world (all the doctrines of Christian faith), and I hold it with a deep and growing commitment. It has been developing in me throughout my entire life, and I could no more deny it than deny myself. The value of a relative absolute is that it gives unity and coherence to a theology, but in a fluid, open, changing way.

Having acknowledged the relative, all-too-human starting point of theology in one's own central conviction, the theologian then realizes that all theological statements are metaphorical.[12] Our language about God is not descriptive; no one has ever seen God; no one can make empirical statements about who God is or what God is doing. This is so obvious that it scarcely merits mentioning, but, curiously, we human beings have a strong propensity to be most definite about what we know least. Theological language is *necessarily* metaphorical, and this means relying on the relations, objects, and events in our familiar world as metaphors for what we do not know how to articulate. Poets use metaphors to express experiences of love and loss, death and grief, friendship and betrayal, joy and sorrow—our most important but hard-to-define experiences. Likewise, all theistic religions use metaphors to speak of God: God as father, mother, lover, friend, lord, king, sun, rock, thunder. Elizabeth Sewell, a poet and literary critic, says that there are five major sources for poetic and religious imagery: breath, water, sex, food, and blood.[13] They are central because they involve the beginning, continuation, and end of life. The Christian tradition is full of these most ordinary—and central—realities of life as the basis for metaphors of God's relation to the world. Metaphorical language as theology's language is simply the acknowledgment that everything we say about God is partial, risky, and uncertain—and very human.

Another important characteristic of any theology is the context in which it occurs. In my theology, that context is not me and my salvation nor even the salvation of human beings, but the planet's well-being. There are three classic contexts in which Christian theologians have done theology: the individual, the human community, and the planet, or the psychological, the political, and the cosmological.[14] A theology that begins with the statement that we live to give God glory by loving the world has two foci: a theocentric and a cosmocentric one, with the work-a-day emphasis being on the second. This is a "universal" context, to be sure, but as is becoming increasingly evident, the well-being of all particular oppressed groups of human beings (as well as the deteriorating parts of nature) are united in complex networks of interdependence. It is difficult to see how individuals or even the human community can prosper apart from a sustainable planet where basic needs are supported by equitable sharing. Thus, I believe that the planetary agenda, the well-being of the whole, is the context within which theology should operate. This does not mean, however, that theology becomes universal or that there is only one kind of human subject. Within the planetary agenda there are an infinite number of tasks that need to be done, each of them particular and concrete, and calling for the knowledge, training, passions, and sensibilities of many different kinds of people. There is no one universal solution to the planet's ills; there are only millions of people working at millions of different tasks to make things better—from theologians attempting to do cosmological theology to ones functioning as facilitators in Latin American base communities; from soil erosion and climate control experts to teachers of environmental studies and better agriculture methods; from health workers distributing birth control information to parents taking their children for walks in the park. The project, the well-being of our planet, may be universal, but its success depends on the passions, knowledge, work, and care of every human being on the earth.

The view of the self or subject that emerges within this context for theology is not the individual who is "saved" for life in another world, but a thoroughly embodied, relational subject who understands herself or himself as interdependent with everyone and everything else. The subject that both postmodernism and the liberation theologies rightly object to is the separate, individualistic, selfish, pretentious self who refuses to acknowledge its radical relativity. The "ecological self" is totally different: it realizes it is one among six billion other members of its own species as well as dependent on millions of other species for its food and next breath. This realization alone is rich in implications for how one sees oneself in the scheme of things and hence how one acts toward others. Such a person understands the absurdity of "going it alone" and the injustice of trying to do so.

Thus the *context* of theology is a critical issue: a cosmological context says that theology should be done from the perspective of the well-being of the entire planet and all its creatures in which I am a subject in a community of subjects, both human and earth subjects, all of whom have value.[15] There are "universal" notes in this theology as well as a focus on the "subject," but the universality is simply the dimensions of our planet (the "universe" for which we are responsible), and the subjects are all the creatures who inhabit it.

Finally, a word about the goal of this theology and its mode of operation. The goal is a functional one—to help the world prosper—

and its mode of operation is one of advocacy and collegiality. The goal is not refinements on the doctrine of God or Christology for their own sake, although these doctrines, as we shall see, are very important, for they help us love the world rightly.[16] We do theology, we think as well and carefully as we can about God and the world, *in order to* live better in the world. Theology is a mundane, not a religious activity. Theology, then, is a functional activity—its goal is practical and pragmatic. As an advocate of the planet, it is not impartial or "objective." It cares about our planet's well-being and takes sides on issues that affect its health. Advocate theologians are public intellectuals, engaged in political, social, and cultural debates on policies and movements dealing with planetary concerns. Theology is not one of the liberal arts, as Latin American theologian Juan Segundo cogently says; it should be a risky business or it has no business staying in operation.[17] In its advocacy, it is also intrinsically collegial; that is, since its goal is the planet's well-being, it is eager to join with others within the Christian community as well as adherents of other religions, and right-minded folks in economics, public policy, education, law, and the arts to work together for the common good.

Does theology matter? It is certainly not all that matters, and it may not matter as much as theologians think it does. But since people's deepest attitudes and loyalties are influenced by implicit pictures of the relation of God and the world, often formed in childhood and operating as an unconscious ingredient in our attitudes toward nature and other people, then becoming conscious of these root-metaphors would seem to be a critical piece in acting appropriately on our planet. And that is what theology does— make us conscious of our deepest picture-beliefs and hence able to change them if need be. For many people today the basic picture of God and the world is of a distant God relating to the world as its creator as well as now and then in times of crisis, especially natural disasters and personal losses. This picture has clear theological implications: it is not a picture of a deeply caring God who loves the world and wants us to love it also. Rather, it suggests a "hands-off" attitude toward nature as well as toward our human neighbors. It suggests a somewhat indifferent (if not arbitrary) divine attitude to the world and an intermittent relation to it. Theology matters— but we only learn how much when we analyze our deeply held

God/world-pictures in depth. We then can become clear regarding the basic conviction underlying our beliefs—what I have called a relative absolute. We can also decide whether that conviction is worthy of our total loyalty ("Here I stand"), the first step toward a working theology.

Ecological Theology: A North American Liberation Theology

So, if theology is possible for North American Christians, what might one look like? Again, I shall use my own theology as a case study to answer the question. I will suggest an "ecological theology"—one that rests on the relative absolute of giving glory to God by loving the world; that understands its context to be the well-being of the planet and its subjects all creatures; that views its universal statements to be risky and partial, made by culturally formed beings. I do not mean a theology just for nature, but one for the entire cosmos with all its creatures, human and otherwise. An ecological theology of this sort could be a liberation theology for twenty-first-century North American Christians.

Let me explain. The myriad ways in which we North Americans oppress poor people and the natural world by being the world's major economic power and its chief exporter of consumerism suggests a form of liberation theology peculiarly suited to us. The decaying state of nature as well as the growing gap between the rich and the poor point to the need for an ecological theology of liberation, one that can free us from insatiable consumerism and, as a result, liberate others, including the natural world, for a better, healthier life. Theology by relatively comfortable North American Christians ought not to focus on personal salvation, in this world or the next, but on lifestyle limitations, on developing a philosophy of "enoughness," and realizing that the cruciform way of Christ means making sacrifices so that others might live. Many North American Christians have felt left on the sidelines as various groups of oppressed people—women, people of color, the poor, people with disabilities, gays and lesbians—have produced their theologies of liberation. Mainline churches, both Protestant and Catholic, with memberships of mainly white, middle-class people, have often wondered where they fit into the new theological paradigm. They fit, I believe, in the uncomfortable center. That center is the increasingly powerful network of controls by a rampant consumer sensibility and economy that is ravaging the natural world and creating impossible expectations for consumer goods by people around the world. One much needed theological task is the critique of this view of the good life and the envisionment of alternatives, alternatives that North American Christians should both articulate and live.

Let us look at this rather unattractive suggestion more carefully. It is unattractive because it is not like other liberation theologies. Other liberation theologies arise from the cries of the oppressed; but we are not oppressed. This theology will not liberate North Americans from chains of oppression (except, of course, the chains of consumerism!); rather, it implies that *we* are the oppressors and must, *if we are Christians,* liberate others from our domination. That is, a liberation theology for us North American Christians should be based on a cruciform lifestyle, expressing and embodying a way of life that will be liberating *to others.*[18] Henri Nouwen puts it this way: "Faith in God does not consist in asserting God's existence, but rather in acting on [God's] behalf."[19] Or more simply, in the words of a Latin American theologian, "To know Jesus is to follow Jesus."[20] Wiggle as we will, most of us North American comfortable mainline Christians know there is probably something wrong with a Christian faith that does not involve a countercultural stance. Liberation theologies have returned theology to its roots in radical discipleship by reminding us that theology is *for the end* of living with and for others, especially the poor. This is scarcely a novel insight; it is at the heart of the life stories of all the saints. John Woolman or Dorothy Day could have written the following statement by liberation theologian Gustavo Gutiérrez: "When one is concerned with one's own stomach, it is materialism, but when one is concerned with other people's stomachs it is spirituality."[21] This brief statement might be taken as a slogan for an ecological liberation theology for North American Christians.

While an ecological liberation theology would, I believe, be a return to the roots of both the Hebrew and Christian traditions, it appears to be novel due to centuries of focus on human well-being alone, and especially inner human well-being. Since the Protestant Reformation and the rise of science in the seventeenth century, there has been a retreat from the idea of the entire creation as the focus of divine concern into the recesses of the human spirit.[22] But the cosmological setting is the oldest one in both the Hebrew and Christian traditions.[23] Likewise, counterculturalism, the recognition that Christian discipleship involves "living differently" and specifically, living in a cruciform fashion, in solidarity with and sacrifice for others, is central in Christianity, not only in the New Testament but also in the literature and lives of the early Christians. Moreover, it is a significant aspect of most protest and reform movements in the church over the centuries—from the medieval mystics and the founding of monasteries to contemporary Latin American base communities. Hence, an ecological liberation theology, a theology that is cosmocentric, countercultural, and cruciform is, I believe, a profoundly *Christian* theology. It is in no way new or novel.

But it will be very difficult. It will certainly involve different lifestyles for us North American Christians—up-close-and-personal issues like how much we drive our cars, use air conditioning, and eat meat. The most immediate, daily inconveniences and small sacrifices are often the hardest to undertake. They will certainly be necessary, but they are not enough. The issues are global, systemic, economic, and political; hence, the solutions must be as well. An ecological liberation theology will involve at least two such tasks. One is envisioning an alternative good life, and the other is working to make systemic changes, especially economic ones, so that this alternative vision can have a public impact. The alternative notion of the abundant life would be radically different from the current "good life" from which most of us benefit.

Since the decline of communism and socialism, there has been little criticism of the reigning capitalist-consumer paradigm and even fewer alternative visions of how all of us might live together on the planet. This absence suggests a special role for the religions of the world. Religions are in the business of envisioning countercultural alternatives on how to live rightly; in fact, that may be one of few things on which they all agree.[24] They offer different views of it, but generally these views do not propose materialism, consumption, and greed as virtues. On the contrary, altruism, sharing, compassion, self-limitation, detachment, and sacrifice are frequent motifs in most religions. Christianity is but one of these religions whose twenty-first-century task may well be to declare once again with clarity and detail what an alternative good life would be. It is, perhaps, a piece of the planetary agenda that North American mainline Christians have a particular responsibility to undertake. Since we are at the top of the consumer "food chain," we are in an advantageous position to use it as a lens to see what this model is doing to our planet. It could be, I am suggesting, our "liberation theology." It might even help to "liberate the oppressors": as we begin to assess the consequences of our economic model, we might also begin to liberate ourselves from its shackles. The eighteenth-century Quaker John Woolman gave up his prosperous grocery business because, as he put it, he was feeling "encumbered" by it. Apparently, many of us feel encumbered as well: consumer glut is not making us happy and free.[25]

What, then, is the economic paradigm at the heart of the Christian alternative good life? The simplest way to express it is to imagine the whole earth as God's household, God's *oikos.* As in all households, economics matter if everyone is to have a chance to eat. And in this household everyone does eat, as the Lord's Supper—the symbol of the eucharistic banquet where all are welcome—clearly signifies. The roots of ecology, economics, and ecumenicism are all in *oikos:* with the right management of the household—respect for the integrity of nature and equitable sharing of resources—all can be included at the dinner table.[26] This suggests some characteristics of the Christian good life: sustainability; self-limitation both in terms of population and lifestyle, so that others may eat; and inclusion of all, especially the weak and vulnerable. The value of alternative visions is twofold: to critique what is and to reach for something better. They are not utopias; we do not expect them to materialize now—or perhaps ever. But they cut into our complacency, our selfishness, and our despair and make us realize that we are capable of—and want—something better.

I believe this theology matters. I think it could be part of the planetary agenda facing us. It could help to heal our deteriorating natural world by cutting back on our use of its gifts; it might help narrow the gap between rich and poor people. It is certainly not the only kind of theology that matters, nor is theology the only thing that matters. But if theology is to matter, I believe it must speak to the critical public and planetary issues facing us in the twenty-first century. As it does so—as it addresses the cosmological and political issues—it will also include the individual, for we are healthiest, sanest, and happiest when we are doing God's will for the world (or so I believe).

3. The Matter of Theology

Be careful how you interpret the world. It *is* like that.

—Erich Heller[1]

IF WE HAVE MADE A CONVINCING CASE that theology is both possible and important for contemporary North Americans, some other basic questions emerge: What *is* theology? How does one do it? Where does one start? What is its content? What are its criteria? In other words, what is the "matter" of theology, what makes it up, of what is it composed?

The word "theology" means simply "words about God," and in an important sense that says it all. Theology *is* about God; if it isn't, it's not theology. I will suggest that North American theology should be about economics and politics, consumerism and its alternatives, global warming and diversity, but *as they* contribute or diminish to giving glory to God by loving the world. A cosmocentric theology—or any other—must be theocentric: theology is about *God* and the world. Theologians are not politicians or economists, they are not experts on climate change or consumerism; rather, their job is to bring the perspective of the Christian faith to bear on the current and pressing issues of our day.[2] The world does not need theologians to be economists or scientists; it needs them to be theologians. The distinctive voice of theology is the voice that speaks of *God* in relation to the pains and pleasures, the crises and opportunities, the dilemmas and despairs of twenty-first century life on planet Earth.

But "speaking of God" is what we have just described, with the critiques of postmodernism and the liberation theologies, as very difficult. From the North American perspective, it can easily become absolutistic and imperialistic as well as biased toward a particular (and well-off) human being. It often speaks about God and about creation from behind its own self-serving mask. How does one proceed in light of this dilemma? As through a minefield, I believe. Philosopher and literary critic Erich Heller's chilling suggestion reminds us: "Be careful how you interpret the world. It *is* like that."[3] One could add "God" along with world. God and world become what we interpret them to be; thus, extreme caution is necessary in theology. It *is* risky business.

If the first thing to say about theology is that it is about God, the second thing to say is that it is interpretation. Or, closer to Heller's point: theology is *interpreting* who God is and what God does. Theology is talk about God from various points of view and experiences. A working definition of Christian theology, as I understand it, goes like this: Theology is reflection on experiences of God's liberating love from various contexts and within the Christian community.[4] Our experiences of God's love take place within complex and overlapping interpretive contexts (worldviews; familial, cultural, and ecclesiastical circles; economic and political frameworks; gender, racial, sexual differences; physical and mental capabilities, and so on). There is no such thing as raw experience; there is no innocent eye; nothing is seen nakedly; "the eye comes always ancient to its work."[5] In our definition, then, *reflection* or interpretation is the primary focus of a theologian's critical attention. While theology is "about *God*," it is the "about," the various contexts of interpretation that constitute the minefield of theology.

As we turn to the matter of theology, three main areas emerge from our definition: reflection, experience, and Christian community, or interpretation (contexts); God's liberating love (content); and Scripture, tradition, and other sources (criteria).

Contexts

We begin with "reflection . . . from various contexts," so that it will be clear from the outset that North American theology, like all others, is relative and partial. We stand *in this place* as all Christians of all ages have stood in their own places. A straight-forward question with a multitude of different answers makes the point: the question "What is Christianity?" attracts a wide variety of replies. A Jehovah's Witness, a Quaker, a Southern Baptist, an Asian Methodist, a Latin American Roman Catholic liberationist, and an African-American womanist would all answer the question in very different ways. Each stands in a particular place and sees with historically and culturally formed lenses. Some answers might overlap with shared convictions; others would be contradictory at various points.

Even if we turn to the Bible, the founding Scripture acknowledged by all Christians, we find a similar diversity. Instead of homogenizing the story of Jesus into one consistent version, the early Christians accepted four narratives, the Gospels, giving a license for pluralism. These four stories are different from one another and also different from the interpretations of Christianity that followed, both in the tradition and in our own time. It is sometimes assumed that the Bible is "beyond" context, that it is the Word of God, while all subsequent talk of God is just words. It is also sometimes assumed that one kind of theology, traditional (i.e., white, male, Western) theology is context neutral. Neither is the case. The Bible is the attempt by the founding Christian believers to express their experiences of God's liberating love as they saw it in Jesus of Nazareth. They did this in the only way they could, with the images and concepts from their own historical, cultural setting. The New Testament is a product of first-century Mediterranean culture with its worldview that included a three-story universe, Gnosticism, demonology, the inferiority of women, and the acceptance of slavery, among other things. Likewise all other significant interpretations of Christianity, from the fourth-century creeds through the great theologies of Augustine, Thomas, Luther, Calvin, and the liberation theologies of today are the products of various contexts: worldviews, sociological and cultural frameworks, ecclesiastical patterns, and personal experience. Ingredient in all these theologies are assumptions about power and privilege, relations between men and women, and relations between human beings and other life-forms. These assumptions are social constructions from different periods of history. It is not, then, just the contemporary liberation theologies that are contextual: *all* theology is. That this is not widely accepted is evident when the word "theology," with no qualifying adjective, is reserved for traditional theology, while all other theologies must have a preceding adjective—feminist, African-American, Hispanic, ecological, etc. Either all theology should have a qualifying adjective or none should.

So, we stand in this place; we speak from this context—or, more accurately, from these contexts. We will look briefly at two interpretive contexts—worldviews and sociological frameworks (race, gender, class, sexual orientation, etc.). Needless to say, there are many others, but these are illustrative of the central role that interpretation plays in theology.

Worldviews

Worldviews are pictures of reality held at a very deep level. They are the basic assumptions of a culture we learn early in life and usually do not question, in part because we are often not aware of them.[6] Worldviews are anchored by models or root-metaphors, such as machine or organism. The assumption is that the world, reality, is like a machine or like a body. If like a machine, then the parts can be replaced and are only externally related; moreover, reality is not alive, and therefore we have no responsibility toward it—we can use and discard it when worn out. However, if the world is more like an organism, a body, then the parts cannot easily be replaced, though some of them can be renewed through growth. Since the parts are internally related and alive, we are not only responsible for the world's well-being but can sympathize with those parts that may be suffering or in pain. We are seldom conscious of world models; they are simply "the way things are" in a culture. Yet, as is evident in the machine/organism examples, they are value laden and deeply influence our behavior toward other people and toward nature. Worldviews, then, are not innocent; they are similar in many ways to ideologies, and hence we are wise to approach them with a hermeneutic of suspicion.

While they appear to be "natural," they are in fact socially constructed. That is, they are the product of myriad cultural, historical, religious, economic, and other influences that converge slowly, often over many generations. No one person or group consciously creates them; they are, nonetheless, humanly produced. For instance, patriarchalism is a worldview in most cultures. It is based in the experience of relating to fathers (its metaphoric source), but that is only the tip of the iceberg. Issues of gender, power and prestige, money and control, submission and dominance, gods and goddesses, among other things, enter into the complex phenomenon of patriarchalism. Patriarchalism has functioned as the model for governance in families, businesses, universities, nations, and the church. It is ubiquitous and for the most part, at least until recently, unobserved. The recognition that deep interpretive contexts are constructed, has made it possible to envision change. And this is precisely what has happened with patriarchalism: it is increasingly seen as an unhelpful, indeed, oppressive and dangerous, model for interpreting relations between people as well as our relations with nature. Its "associated commonplaces" of hierarchicalism, imperialism, absolutism, and dualism have been brought to the light of day and denounced.

Which world model is the dominant interpretive framework in contemporary North American culture? How does it function as a major context for theological interpretation? Should another world model provide the context for North American theology? The worldview at the base of our culture is one of mechanistic progress. The earth is imagined to be like a machine, with replaceable parts and manipulable by humans—a mechanism we can make better and better for our use and pleasure. The wonders of technology mean that we can manage the planet for our well-being; there is no problem we cannot solve, given human ingenuity and sufficient research dollars. At the heart of this worldview is the picture of an upward line, graphing the abundant life in terms of consumer goods for more and more of the world's people. To be sure, this picture is becoming ragged at the edges as rumbles of climate change, AIDS, poverty and population surges, deforestation, desertification, overfishing, and so on increase, but for most North Americans denial is still possible. The worldview of mechanistic progress goes back several centuries in Western culture and is very difficult to displace. Its source is in seventeenth-century science, the industrial revolution, and the vast improvement in the quality of human life for many during this century. It's hard to deny that "things have gotten better." What is hidden, however, are the doubts nibbling at the edges of this picture: Who is benefiting? How long can this upward line continue? What are the consequences for the planet?

Resting on assumptions that do not allow us to ask these questions, our worldview functions as a cover for denial. Since worldviews are based in metaphors and models, they not only allow us to see some things (the world as a machine), but screen out others (the world as an organism). If the world is seen as a machine that, with human management, will keep on improving, then we will speak of it in terms that emphasize features open to human manipulation and benefit. And our planet has many such features. But the machine model eliminates the possibility of seeing our planet as alive, as finite, as fragile. It also blinds us to seeing ourselves as integral parts of the planet; indeed, as radically dependent parts.

Worldviews and the models in which they are based are our eyes and ears with which we interpret our world and our place in it. Since we *cannot see* apart from these most basic contexts (there is no raw experience or innocent eye), then it matters profoundly *which* worldview is operating in our culture. Until we become conscious of the one (or ones) dominant in our society, we will have no chance of combating their ill effects or changing to another one. Realizing that our current worldview (like all worldviews) is a social construction, as well as only a few centuries old, should make it possible for us to name it as a human creation and to denounce it as a faulty one.

In its place we can begin to live within another one that is closer to the reality of our planet and healthier for all its inhabitants. This worldview is of a sustainable organism. Rather than picturing the world as a machine we manage for human betterment, we should see it as a body, a highly complex one with millions of different parts, living as a community. It is a body able in principle to renew and sustain itself indefinitely. We humans are a part of this organic community—the conscious part—dependent on everything else in the body but also responsible for learning how to make it flourish and committing ourselves to do so. It is immediately evident how different the mechanistic progress and the sustainable organism world models are. Because basic models contain many, far-reaching associations and incipient concepts, they are rich mines for developing new understandings and behaviors. They suggest different views of who human beings are in the scheme of things, how we should behave toward other people and other life-forms, what the good life would be and how to attain it. In the first model, individualistic attainment of material goods, by whatever means and without limit, becomes the desired goal, whereas in the second model, community sharing of all resources within the constraints of sustainability and for the end of universal flourishing is seen as the necessary goal. In the first model, fantasy encourages limitless, individualistic goals; in the second, realism demands constrained, shared ones.

If the world as a sustainable organism or body were to begin to seep into our consciousness, to make sense to us and be our truth about the world, we would take an important first step toward overcoming North American denial concerning our planet. It is, I believe, especially important that North Americans denounce the world model of mechanistic progress and adopt the sustainable organism one. We North Americans are the chief beneficiaries of the progress model, amassing money and great piles of consumer goods, which, for the most part we use for our own individual need and comfort. We epitomize the winners in this model and hence are especially responsible for its downside. Its negative results are currently evident in every ecosystem on our planet (forests, oceans, atmosphere, land), which, treated mechanistically with little regard for its fragility, interdependency, or limits, is now in serious decay. The negative results of this model can also be seen in the two-thirds of the world's people who are the losers, the poor people who have not amassed consumer goods and have often even lost the subsistence living they once had. In other words, North Americans (as well as similar people in other parts of the world) have benefited from this model by robbing other people and nature itself. Most of us have not done this consciously; nonetheless, as we now become aware of the drastic consequences of this model, we should reject it and begin to live otherwise.

Christians should do so especially. Regardless of what our culture condones, we should condemn the mechanistic progress model as sinful. It cannot add to the glory of God by loving the world. It does not help every creature to flourish; on the contrary, it contributes to the misery and destruction of other human beings and nature. While the sustainable organism model is certainly not the only one that Christians might adopt as their basic world-picture, it is a viable possibility that provides a context for earthly flourishing.[7]

Sociological Contexts
The African-American womanist theologian Jacquelyn Grant claims that the question Jesus asks Peter—"Who do you say that I am?"—is addressed to all of us.[8] No longer is there one human problem with one answer: the problem identified by traditional theology as sin against God and its answer the sacrificial death of Jesus. We experience life in many different ways and from different perspectives: there is no universal human being or any one problem we all face. Our answer to Jesus' question—what would liberation or salvation be?—depends in large part on our situation. A

teenage Asian prostitute, a Hispanic-American migrant worker, and a white, middle-class Swiss architect will have very different answers. This does not mean that anything goes, that Christian salvation is whatever people at various times and places need, but it does mean we should recognize that our understandings of God's love are context-dependent. In the last few decades postmodernism and the liberation theologies have made us all very aware of this: the different voices of race, class, gender, sexual orientation, physical capabilities, and so on have unmasked universal, absolute statements as power maneuvers.

We will not repeat the now well-known arguments of this unmasking. What we will do is apply the categories that have been used to dethrone ethnocentric universalism in relations among human beings to the supposed absolutism of human beings over nature. Moreover, we will insist that there is no one human stance in relation to nature, but rather a variety of complex relations that different human beings have with nature. In other words, as we consider how we human beings can give glory to God by loving the world, we need to consider our context as one species among millions of others, as well as the ways we differ within our species in our relations with nature.

The first issue calls into question the rigid dualism between human beings and nature. This ancient hierarchical dualism is similar to other such divisions—culture/nature, spirit/flesh, mind/body, male/female—and denies what is obviously a continuum. Like other categories that were imagined to be absolute, human beings and nature are profoundly linked, not only in ancestry but also in our dependency on the earth's ecosystems. The category "human being" is a construction with fuzzy edges; it is a category that makes no sense apart from the history of life on our planet and the interlocking networks of support that keep all of us in existence. We are, indeed, one species among millions of others. This realization provides us with a major context, a place to stand, as we interpret who we are. It immediately makes us aware of our need of the other species and the ecosystems on which we all depend; it also should call up gratitude in us for the gifts of life and its continuance that the earth provides. Moreover, it should mean that we feel empathy for other creatures, both human and otherwise, with whom we are so intimately connected. For instance, we ought to be able to sympathize with the loss that bears experience when their habitat is destroyed as we empathize with our human neighbors when their house is burned down. As one species among millions of others, we are on a continuity with them, in terms of both need and feeling. We all depend on the health of our planet; we all need food and cover; we all want to raise our young; we can all feel physical pain. Thus, human being is a category that makes sense *only* in relation to other creatures. We are *human* beings to be sure, but the adjective modifies the more important noun, *beings*. Once we see ourselves this way, we will have adopted a very important context for doing theology. When, for instance, we answer the question of who Christ is for us, what salvation is, we will do so with the well-being of all of our earthly neighbors and the planet itself in mind.

At one level, then, we human beings are one: we all belong to one species; we all need nature's bounty to feed, clothe, and warm us; all humans are different from other species (and similar to them) in unique and specific ways. *We* form a species and hence, in many ways, will relate to other species and to ecosystems in similar ways. At another level, however, this is not the case. There is no such creature as "human being." We are a lesbian, Hispanic, poor human being; or a white, male, middle-class, heterosexual, HIV-positive, American one; or an African, elderly, royal human being. Each of these people will have a different relationship with nature. The recognition of human differences and its implication for every relationship, including relationship with nature, is one of the contributions of postmodernist and liberationist thought. Whereas there used to be a "hegemonic human being," there is no longer, although, as we shall see, he dies slowly.[9] This hegemonic human being, the human being who comes to mind when the words are spoken or written, is white, male, Western, heterosexual, youthful, educated, able-bodied, middle-class, and successful. He is the figure in Leonardo da Vinci's drawing of a human being with arms and legs outstretched to the four corners of the cosmos; he is the "man" of the American Declaration of Independence who is given life, liberty, and the pursuit of happiness; he is also the human being who is the object of consumer advertising.

To the extent that one fits the characteristics of the hegemonic human being, one feels at home in conventional Western culture.

But most people, even white middle-class males, do not have all the hegemonic traits. Where one does *not* fit opens a window of opportunity, a window from which to see Western culture in a different perspective. This window has been called a "wild space."[10] Imagine conventional Western culture as a circle with your world superimposed over it. If you are the poor Hispanic lesbian, your world will not fit into the conventional Western one. It will overlap somewhat (you may be educated and able-bodied), but there will be a large crescent that will be outside. This is your wild space; it is the space that will allow—and encourage—you to think differently, to imagine alternative ways of living. It will not only give you problems, but possibilities. You will also have wild space if you are the elderly African, though it will be a different wild space with problems and possibilities the Hispanic woman will not have. Even the American has a wild space—his HIV status—the one place where he does not fit the stereotypical human being.

The people to whom this book is addressed—middle-class North American Christians—fit the pattern of the hegemonic human being reasonably well. Most of us will, however, have some wild space—if we are women, or homosexual, or nonwhite, or disabled, or elderly. Other less evident rifts with the standard successful model can also give us some wild space: the death of a child, experience with substance abuse, a history of clinical depression—whatever helps us to question that model.

We *need* this space. It is, I believe, what helps us to see how those parts of us that fit the standard image of human being are lulled into accepting a definition of the good life that is destroying nature and sending many people into poverty. It is the human being without faults, cracks, differences, problems, pain, or struggles, the hegemonic (plastic) human being, who is the object of our consumer-oriented economy and culture. This human being drives a Mercedes, vacations on the Riviera, has a four-bathroom house with swimming pool, wears designer clothes, and retires at fifty-five. It is the wild space in each of us, whatever does not fit the stereotypical human being, that questions that definition of the good life. The poor Hispanic lesbian, the elderly African, and the HIV-positive man offer possibilities of redefinition. If they are true to their wild space (and not already captive to the consumer image), they might suggest that what would make them really happy is not the Mercedes or the designer clothes, but appreciation of differences; respect for cultural and ethnic traditions; sufficient food, clothing, education, and medical care; close familial and community relationships; and perhaps a walk in the park. Sigmund Freud claimed that the two things that really matter in life are love and work. While he may not have covered all the bases, his definition of the good life is far closer to the wild spaces in us than that of our consumer culture, which defines human satisfaction solely in terms of consumer acquisition. Once we free ourselves, even a little bit, from identification with consumerism and allow our wild space to criticize it, we realize how thin it is.

It is also dangerous and unjust. It is dangerous to our planet and unjust to other, less fortunate people. It sees human beings as individuals whose goals are personal profit and pleasure. The hegemonic human being—the one with arms and legs spread out over the planet—is not integrally related to other human beings or to nature. He/she is superimposed *over* it. No image of humanity could be more fitting as the consumer model. This human being has every right to use whatever amount of the earth's resources he/she can afford, regardless of the consequences to nature or other people. If our image of human being is the individualistic consumption one, we will condone ravaging nature and depriving other people of basic necessities. Or, more likely, we simply will not *see* these consequences; the hegemonic image does not allow us to. But our wild space *will*. Our "failures" to fit the hegemonic image are our opportunities to criticize and revise it. The image we need is not of *one* human being superimposed over the earth, but of millions of different human beings living in and with it.

We need to change the *one* human being into a myriad and move them into the earth. These millions form a community among themselves and with all other life-forms as well as the various ecosystems of the earth. This is a very different model. We can now begin to see that our "failures" to fit the hegemonic image are simply human differences—gender, racial, sexual orientation, class, physical capability differences. There *is* no hegemonic human being: to be sure, some fit the hegemonic model, but the lucky (or reflective) ones become uncomfortable with the model—what could be called "the wild space of privilege."

As we dethrone this image of humanity and its dangerous, unjust relationship with nature and poor people, we allow the many different relationships of actual people with nature to emerge. For a large number of people, that relationship is one of increasing loss. Through either the direct or indirect results of our high energy consumption, many people especially in the third world are experiencing growing poverty. Their subsistence way of life is deteriorating; the gap between the rich and the poor is increasing; and weather crises related to climate change (forest fires, droughts, floods, etc.) are becoming more frequent. A desperately poor African woman gathering the last bits of wood in her village to heat her family's dinner, an Indonesian farmer whose land has been devastated by fire, and an Indian family who sold their daughter into prostitution to support themselves create a very different scenario of human existence on our planet than does the hegemonic consumer model. While these people do not fit the hegemonic ideal, they are closer to expressing what human life will be in the twenty-first century. In fact, the representative human being of our time is probably a poor third world woman of color. Her life, not that of the Western model, is far closer to the typical experience of most people on our planet. This woman and other people like her are the ones we can begin to see and empathize with through our own wild spaces. They come into view when we open ourselves to realizing that our conventional, daily Western consumer lifestyle is having very negative effects on others who, like us, also depend on the earth's finite gifts.

In sum, our sociological contexts make a difference to how we interpret everything, including giving glory to God by loving the world. We well-off North Americans need to look very carefully at these interpretive contexts. Do we unconsciously operate within the hegemonic human being context, trying to fit ourselves into it as best we can and assuming others should as well? Are we silently accepting what this model of human life, the individualistic model of profit and pleasure, is doing to nature and to other less fortunate people? Or do we use our own differences from this model as windows of opportunity to define human life on our planet in alternative ways?

When we attempt to say who we are in the scheme of things, we do so within frameworks—worldviews and images of ourselves—that are very deep and equally difficult even to recognize, let alone change. One of the great discoveries of our time is that we have become *conscious* of them. Unlike countless generations before us, we no longer have to live in them like fishes in the ocean. We realize now they are human constructions; we realize also that each of us, in our wild space, has the opportunity to see human life as it is—infinitely rich and various. We also realize that we can and should live with a construction of human life that is closer to reality than the reigning model: a model of earth as a community of different beings, human and otherwise, all dependent on and needing to share what a sustainable planet can give us.

Content

> . . . I understand the Christian faith, which I confess . . . as a preference for life over against death. Being is better than nonbeing, kissing is better than nonkissing, eating is not only preferable to going hungry but ontologically superior. This ontological surplus of Being in the face of Nothingness is what the Christian religion also tries to articulate.
>
> No accident brought us onto this small blue planet; life itself calls to us to participate in life in a thankfulness which does not cease even in darkness to perceive life as a gift, as grace.
>
> —Dorothee Soelle[11]

> For me theology springs from a *divine passion:* that is, the open wound of God in one's own life and in the tormented men, women, and children of this world. . . . But for me theology also springs from God's *love for life,* the love for life which we experience in the presence of the life-giving Spirit, and which enables us to move beyond our resignation, and begin to love life here and now. These are also Christ's two experiences of God, and because of that they are the foundation of Christian theology too: God's delight and God's pain.
>
> —Miroslav Volf[12]

Through their own experiences, as the deepest conviction from which and toward which they live, these theologians confess God's love for life in spite of all forces to the contrary. This is, for them, the content of theology, its very heart.[13] It came to them as a revelation, a central and encompassing insight; it came through their own experience; it illuminated not just their experience but the entire world and in such a way that a response rose up in them. Three points emerge here. First, experience is the place where Christian faith is manifested; it is the channel, but not the substance. Second, the content of Christian faith comes into our experience as a revelation, a central and commanding insight into God's love. Third, this insight is not limited to the individual's well-being—it is an insight concerning the relationship of God and the world, one of such significance that one's orientation and behavior must change.

Experience as Channel

Let us recall the definition of theology: Theology is reflection on experiences of God's liberating love from various contexts and within the Christian community. The object of reflection here is not experience but God's liberating love. Experience is the channel, the carrier, the means, but not the focus. Neither Soelle nor Volf analyze their experience; rather, they zero in on the central insight—"a preference for life against death," "God's delight and God's pain." These theologians are theocentric and cosmocentric: their central insights are about God's relation to the world, not about "God and me." Theologians who speak of their own experience do so most appropriately when they use it illustratively. Paul spoke of his own inability to do the good that he knew as a way of expressing his conviction that we are justified by grace alone. Augustine's *Confessions* are a marvelous example of experience as channel: he uses his coming to awareness of dependence on God as the way to express the central insight of his theology—everything that exists is radically dependent on God. Experience is the channel, not the content, of Christian theology.

Why emphasize this point? The reason we do so is to dissociate theology for North American Christians from contemporary, therapeutic, New Age thinking that is focused on the inner experience of individuals searching for a meaningful spiritual life. I believe the theology we North Americans need is *one for the world,* one in which God and the world are the focus, not your or my personal problems. *We* fit into this theology as workers called to be God's partners in maximizing delight in the world and minimizing its pain. But the focus is not on our experience.

Nonetheless, experience of God's love is crucial. We do not become Christians without it. I would not be a Christian without my "conversions," those experiences of God's love that have given me a set of deep beliefs that I can articulate and act on. Recognizing both the importance of experience as well as its limitations is crucial. Its limitations include all the criticisms of essentialism and universalism by postmodernism as well as of imperialistic masking by liberationists. Everything said in the previous section, "Contexts," is relevant here: "experience" is a highly contested category, open to charges of deception, absolutism, and fantasy. Is there even a coherent subject who can experience? Is there one human experience or many?[14] Is not experience too amorphous a category to work with?

Experience is open to all of the above charges and questions, but nonetheless it is unavoidable. It is tempting to try to avoid it, however, because it appears to be such an ephemeral basis for making statements about God and the world. Many have sought firmer foundations, from proofs for the existence of God to inerrant Scriptures and direct revelations. But these end-runs around faith (the necessary counterpart to the experiential base) seldom hold firm. Religious belief is trust in the God revealed *through* experience. The believer does not have faith in the experience, but in whom is revealed through it.

But the medium of revelation is experience. This does not mean "religious" experience. It means ordinary experience: the revelation of God's liberating love comes to us in the ordinary round of our lives as we comfort an elderly neighbor who has lost his wife, think about the value of the work we are doing, campaign for a politician who backs public transit, worry about a child's drug use. Through these experiences, we glimpse, now and then, God's liberating love at work.[15] This love comes in and through the fabric of our lives; it does not come above, or apart from, or as indifferent to our lives. If it is revelation of God's love *to us*, then it has to be imbedded, embodied, ingredient *in* our lives, our experience. If it were not, it could not make sense of that experience, it would not be illuminating. Moreover, because revelation—insights into God's love—occurs in our ordinary experience, it is ongoing. Revelation did not stop with the Bible; the experiences of the first Christians of God's love manifest in Jesus of Nazareth are a critical norm for subsequent Christians, but revelation is not a deposit of biblical truths. The Bible is a witness to revelations of God's love coming to the early Christians; these revelations continue as we become aware of God's love in new and different circumstances.

Revelation as Illumination and Encounter

If experience is the channel, revelation is the content of Christian faith. Revelation is that key insight, usually expressed in a sentence or two, that illumines everything else. For the liberation theologians, it is a mere phrase: "God's preferential option for the poor." Revelation for me is the realization that we are created to give God glory by loving the earth. The opening quotations from Soelle and Volf are their revelations. These statements contain Christian faith for them in a nutshell. Revelation is not a set of dogmas—statements about God, Christ, human being, and the church—that Christians must accept, nor is revelation secret truth revealed to privileged believers. *Revelation is an insight about God and the world that changes your life.* Unless it has the power not only to illuminate but to transform, it probably is not revelation. Unless it encounters you with both attraction and demand, with undeniable authority on your thoughts, will, and action it probably is not revelation to you. If revelation were only illumination, it might be an interesting, perhaps even very important, idea about God and the world, but nothing that would or could change one's behavior. But it is not like that. Revelation is the sort of insight that one has to do something about, and that action, like the revelation itself, takes place in ordinary experience. As Soelle and Volf say, Christian revelation to them is about kissing and eating, delight and pain, life and death. Christian revelation is about the *incarnate* God, the worldly God, the earthly God. Whatever illuminations this God gives to us are about living in the real, everyday world. Hence, they not only come to us through our ordinary experiences, but they are about these experiences—about giving glory to God by loving the neighbor. This means comforting the elderly and the grieving, considering the relationship between work and vocation, campaigning for legislators who will make the world a better place, helping young people avoid drugs. As we North Americans enlarge our picture of who the neighbor is—to include the third world woman of color, other creatures, and even oceans and forests—we will begin to experience God's liberating love, and help it to increase, in these places as well. The power of God's love as it touches our deteriorating earth in pain (and lost delight) will touch us also. We will know that God's concern for creation is indeed revelatory: it *is* the way God feels about the world and the way we must also.

Revelation as Solidarity

Genuine revelation is not only an insistent pressure toward change and action; it is also expansive. It may start small—with me and my tribe—but tends to move outward. Since the Redeemer is the Creator, the logic of revelation is toward including all of creation. Augustine's sense of his own radical dependence on God became a belief in the dependence of everything on God; John Woolman saw that the network of greed and overconsumption that supported slavery had the same domino effect in the natural world—mistreating post horses from human selfishness; Dietrich Bonhoeffer's realization that Christ was with him in the sufferings of prison life—as well as in its small joys—became grounds for asserting that God is with all of us in our ordinary, secular lives; Martin Luther King's initial insights focused on freedom for African Americans but moved outward to include other poor and oppressed people. Genuine revelation is seldom individualistic and tribal; it may well start there, but it does not usually end there. Ex-slave Sojourner Truth began her lifetime of activism for the abolition of slavery and for women's rights with a personal, immediate revelation that God was her Friend, close and available to her. This realization gave her the stamina and power to spend her whole life walking from town to town preaching God's desire that *all* people be free. It appears to be the case that the strength of the illumination and encounter of revelation—its impact on one's personal life—become the basis for expanding it to be revelation for all. Revelation thus understood is a matter of solidarity: it is a key insight that calls one to action on behalf of all God's creatures.

A beautiful expression of such revelation is the reflections of the Lakota Sioux Black Elk, while recalling his vision quest as a boy of nine. As an adult he understands it as the universal solidarity of all peoples and all creatures in the hoop of life:

> Then I was standing on the highest mountain of them all, and round about beneath me was the whole hoop of the world. And while I stood there I saw more than I can tell and I understood more than I saw; for I was seeing in a sacred manner the shapes of all things in the spirit, and the shape of all shapes as they must live together like one being. And I saw that the sacred hoop of my people was one of many hoops that made one circle, wide as daylight and as starlight, and in the center grew one mighty flowering tree to shelter all the children of one mother and one father. And I saw that it was holy.[16]

Revelation, when genuine, has a tendency to expand, to be the key insight not just for me and my life, but for all life, human and creaturely. It becomes the expression of "the way things are." Thus, for me, the realization that my own life makes sense when I love both God and the earth, expands to universal dimensions: the glory of God is all creatures fully alive. If genuine revelation has this expansive character that knits everything together, we could say that it is profoundly ecological. That is, revelation is about the living network we call creation: it is about the ways all its parts work together for health—or conversely, for decay and death. Each of our revelations usually focuses on some angle of that network's well-being: its need to be free, to be protected, to be fed, to be included, etc. Each of us who is the channel of a genuine revelation sees some aspect of this living network, this ecological whole, from the perspective of God's love: we see forests needing protection; people under totalitarian regimes needing the right to free speech; African Americans needing justice and inclusion; eroded land and overfished oceans needing time to recover; homeless people needing food and shelter; women needing legislation against sexual and physical abuse. All of these issues are interlocking; the health of our planet is an ecological matter—either all of us will flourish or none of us will. Increasingly, we know this to be the case. As we see the telltale signs of deterioration in the intricate fabric of our planet's ecosystems—weird weather events, the decline of biodiversity, the scarcity of fresh water, global warming, the desertification of land—we see similar patterns of deterioration among its human population—our reckless use of natural resources, the increasing gap between the rich and the poor, ethnic warfare, the AIDS epidemic, the looming threat of starvation. Few of us believe that things will be better for our children and grandchildren; most of us, in our more honest moments, know they will be worse.

What can we do? Each of us can work from our revelatory insight—that particular angle on the earth's flourishing that has illumination, insistence, and built-in activism for us. It becomes for us our "relative absolute." It is the place that contains our passion and our persistence; it is the place that has made sense of our own lives and that we believe is healthy for the planet as well. It will be the niche where we make our contribution. It may involve work with the homeless, gay and lesbian rights, forest rehabilitation, the development of solar-powered and electric cars, grizzly bear protection, or shelters for abused women. I have found that the particular angle revelation focuses on for me is North American overconsumption of energy with the dual result of global warming and increasing injustice to poor people. The insight that came into my own life—that I was created to give God glory through loving the earth—has become contextualized for me in terms of the way I live and people like me live. We are contributing to the deterioration of the earth's systems and to the increasing poverty of people less fortunate than ourselves.

Criteria

We are seeking a functional theology, one that makes sense of both our personal and public lives, one that can actually work for twenty-first-century North American Christians. We are using a definition of theology as reflection on experiences of God's liberating love from various contexts and within the Christian community. We have looked at reflection or interpretation (Contexts) as well as experiences of God's love (Content), and turn now to community—Scripture and tradition (Criteria). In the first two sections of "the matter of theology," we have considered its central content, revelation (God's liberating love), as well as the various contexts in which revelation is experienced. We now have to ask the difficult question of criteria. What makes a revelation of God's love *Christian*? How is it possible to identify a position as Christian and avoid both fundamentalism and radical relativism? How does one argue responsibly and persuasively when answering the question, "What is Christianity?"

My shorthand answer, which I will unpack over the next few pages, goes as follows: There is no one answer, but all answers share some identifiable characteristics that come from Scripture, the tradition, and contemporary resources. This answer contains some basic assumptions. First, fundamentalism is not an option since all theology is contextual and metaphorical. No human interpretation, including the ones in the Bible, is absolute. Second, radical relativism—anything goes—is not an option either, since there are some basic understandings from Scripture and the tradition about God and the world that characterize Christian interpretations.

Third, these understandings are deconstructed and reconstructed in different times and places with the help of knowledges such as economics, sociology, cosmology, anthropology, philosophy, ecological science, etc. Under Criteria, then, we will be concerned with how our passionately held revelatory insights, derived from different contexts and fueling our activism, measure up as "Christian."

Scripture: Revelation or Witness to Revelation?

For some Christians the Bible is what Hans Küng calls "the paper pope," the ultimate and inerrant authority.[17] If Scripture is, as we have suggested, reflection on experiences of God's liberating love by the earliest Christians, then it cannot itself be revelation. Like all other experiences of God's love, those in the Bible are from relative, partial contexts by people limited by their own times. They are, then, similar to other such expressions across the centuries by theologians, poets, hymn writers, liturgists, mystics, and ordinary people. The reflections in the Bible, however, are special. These reports are the earliest we have to the time of the central figure of Christianity, Jesus of Nazareth. They hold a special place in Christianity as the earliest recorded reflections on the ministry of Jesus and the formation of the community that grew up around him.

This means we give particular consideration to the New Testament; it is a principal source, norm, criterion for subsequent Christian expressions of God's liberating love. But we do so, I believe, by considering it as a "classic" and as a "constitution." In analogy with these literary genres, we can give the New Testament a very high—and appropriate—status.

A classic is a piece of literature that continues to speak to people across generations. It has a *functional* authority that wins adherents on its own merits. It does not help the status of a classic to force people to revere or read it; in fact, any book that needs such propping up probably does not deserve classic standing. The fact that the Bible has, over the centuries, inspired such diverse movements as monastic poverty, the Protestant Reformation, rebellion by American slaves, the Latin American base communities, and contemporary Christian feminism is proof of its status as an enduring classic. The content of its revelatory insights, even though they often emerge from misogynist, patriarchal, racist, and imperial contexts, is capable of being recontextualized into new understandings in different times. This text has the ability to change lives for the better, to free people from various kinds of oppression, to give hope where there appeared to be no hope.

This classic text is also the "constitution" of Christianity. It is the document without which one cannot understand Christianity. Just as one cannot understand democracy in the United States apart from its constitution, so an analogous relationship exists between Christianity and the New Testament. This is not to say that Scripture tells us everything we need to know about Christianity, just as the constitution of the United States is only one document among many that we need to be acquainted with if we are to have a full understanding of the nation's form of democracy. The New Testament as constitution means that it is a necessary document, but not the only one. As its founding literature, it is essential but not absolute.

As a religion with a classic, constitutional founding text, Christianity is prone to becoming a book religion, a religion that worships a book. It must not be. If we remember that the church produced the book, and not vice versa, that ordinary people like us recorded their experiences of God's liberating love from their various personal and social contexts, we are less likely to deify the Bible.

To see the Bible as a classic or a constitution is to regard it as a model. We recall that a model is an interpretive grid, a pair of lenses, that allows us to say something about which we do not know how to speak. The Bible, and especially the New Testament for Christians, is such a model. It is our primary interpretive framework, our best pair of glasses, for saying something about God's relationship to the world. As a model, it is not descriptive; as primary model, it is an indispensable medium of Christian expression.

What, then, is its importance? The Bible and the tradition built upon it have proven revolutionary to many generations of people in different times and places. Its importance, in the broadest sense, is *functional*. It changes lives; it has shown itself to be revelatory—to illuminate and transform. It has helped to destabilize oppressive societal structures and introduce more liberating ones (which is not to deny that it has also contributed substantially not only to oppressive, but to destructive, human and environmental structures). It is not important because it tells us "the truth about God and the world"—that we do not know and can never know for certain. People whose lives have been transformed *believe* the New Testament points to such truth, but this text is not primarily a book of true statements about either God or the world. Rather, it is a collection of reflections on experiences of salvation, of God's liberating love, that change people's lives.[18] Transformatory experiences carry their own form of truth and credibility. In other words, while the experience of saving revelation is always subjective (it happens *to* people), what is experienced, the divine grace bringing about the transformation, is claimed not to be. What I experience (God's saving love) is not taken to be simply a figment of my imagination or a totally human construction. It is, I believe, psychologically impossible to believe in a God of one's own making. I believe *what* I believe is, in some sense, "the way things are." I cannot prove that claim—faith is not knowledge—but I can give reasons for holding it. And this moves us into our two final thoughts on Criteria—some characteristics of Christian faith and resources from our culture to help us in reconstructing Christian doctrine. Both of these will help fill out what we mean when we say a theology is Christian.

Characteristics of the Christian Paradigm

In addition to the Bible as classic and constitution, as the text that has proven revelatory over the centuries, transforming lives and revolutionizing societal structures toward liberating the oppressed, Christians also have the "tradition." This tradition includes all the texts, in many genres, orthodox and otherwise, that make up the loosely defined phenomenon known as "Christianity." It is, in Thomas Kuhn's term, a paradigm, a set of assumptions and practices that distinguishes it from other world religions and gives it a distinctive nature. I am not speaking of "the essence of Christianity," some foundational kernel or core that all must adhere to—in fact, just the opposite. I am asking whether there are some historical continuities, some features that have arisen over the centuries and within different contexts, that distinguish this religion. This is an empirical, not a foundational question. Why, for instance, do we call the Nicene Creed, Calvin's *Institutes,* James Cone's *God of the Oppressed,* and Dorothee Soelle's theology all Christian? What identifies this paradigm from others?

Answering the question is a risky business, but it is necessary if we are to avoid both ideological absolutism (there is only one version, one interpretation, of Christianity) and radical relativism (anything goes). I am suggesting that what we call Christianity is composed of many theologies, many interpretations of God's liberating love, which are loosely connected by some common threads. These characteristics have been embodied in different root-metaphors and expressed within many different contexts. They are not universals, but simply some more-or-less identifiable historical continuities that keep appearing in Christian theologies. As we attempt to construct a working theology for twenty-first-century North American Christians, we need to keep in mind both the limitations and the latitude these characteristics allow. We can, of course, debate this list; I am presenting mine to stimulate your reflective consideration and counter-suggestion.

1. GOD: Christianity is a theistic religion. Many religions are not. Historically, its theism has ranged from a transcendent, distant deism (God above and apart from the world) to an immanent, involved panentheism (God in, with, and through the world). It has not accepted pantheism—the identification of God and the world. The most common image of God has been of a Creator who is also Redeemer as well as continuing Spirit. Christianity inherited ethical monotheism from Judaism, keeping the prophetic ethical concern, but modifying monotheism, in light of Jesus Christ, into a trinitarian theism. The Christian God, while imaged in both personal and impersonal metaphors (both father and friend as well as eternal and everlasting) veers toward the anthropomorphic side: God is love, One who understands suffering, judges oppressors, rejoices in creation. Nonetheless, the range is broad: views of God as diverse as those of Irenaeus, Jacob Boehme, Thomas Aquinas, John Calvin, the Quakers, Karl Barth, and Elizabeth Johnson are all included within the Christian paradigm.

2. WORLD: The world is created by God and depends for its existence and continuation on God, but there is considerable variety in terms of the closeness of this relationship. Artistic models of creation (as in Genesis 2 where God sculpts creatures from the earth), verbal models (as in Genesis 1 where God speaks and various elements of creation appear), and emanational models (in which the world emerges from God's being) are all in the tradition. Each model suggests a different understanding of God's distance

from and intimacy with the world. In all cases, however, the world is understood to be real (the world and life in it is not an illusion that one should or can escape from) and good (the world is the object of divine pleasure and satisfaction). The importance of this feature of the Christian paradigm needs to be underscored: it means that earthly, worldly life is where the action is. Our home is the garden, our planet, which we are to cultivate and in which we should flourish. A basic Christian assumption is that worldly life is good.

3. HUMAN BEING: Just as God in the Christian tradition is understood in agential, relational terms, as living and loving, so human beings are as well. The tradition is predominantly activist rather than contemplative or, perhaps more accurately, contemplation is for the purpose of more effective action on God's behalf. Human beings are to make a difference; we are here for a purpose; we are to help make things better for others. We have only one lifetime in which to achieve this; thus, what we do in our brief time on earth matters. We are also, and primarily, relational beings, defined by our radical dependence on God and our interdependence with other people (only recently has this quality been extended to other life-forms and the earth itself). Classic Christian understandings of human life do not promote individualism, nor do they deny the importance of the individual; rather, they promote relationality as basic to human existence and solidarity with the oppressed as its goal.

4. CHRIST: In a sense Jesus Christ is not a fourth topic in the Christian paradigm but the one that qualifies the other three— God, world, and human being. As Christians, we look at each of these through the lens or model of Christ. We look Godward through Christ and say that God loves us; we look at the world through Christ and say it is where God is incarnate and where God wants us to flourish; we look at ourselves through Christ and learn what sin and salvation, living a lie and living the truth, mean. Jesus Christ is the *sine qua non* of the Christian paradigm; we go by his name. One cannot call oneself a Christian unless one's interpretation of God, world, and human being include Christ. Again, the range is enormous—from seeing Jesus as a paradigmatic teacher and guide for life to claiming that he is the incarnation of the second person of the trinity and, more recently, to seeing Christ as

Christa and as an African American. Nonetheless, in spite of the variety, a portrait (which is very different from a photograph) has emerged over the centuries of a man so deeply at one with God that his life on behalf of outcasts of society became for many people God's own love for the oppressed. His distinguishing characteristic is this dual-dimensional love: for God and for others, or, as I would put it, giving glory to God by loving the world.

So, what do these characteristics of the Christian paradigm come to? Not much, in one sense, given how broad they are, but in another sense, perhaps they are helpful in suggesting some guidelines for our working theologies (not everything goes) and some limitations (Christianity is not everything). In other words, Christianity is an identifiable religion (it is not Hinduism or Buddhism), but it is not the one and only religion (Hinduism and Buddhism are also religions). It is one way of modeling God, world, and human being (through the Christic lens); other religions model the sacred (not necessarily theism), world, and human being differently, but in ways that have for many centuries and for many people been revelatory and transformative.

But even continuity with the Christian tradition, fitting into that paradigm, is not the only criterion—in addition to Scriptural reliance—of a good, an appropriate, Christian theology. It is a necessary but not a sufficient condition; it is the needful baseline but not the most interesting or important thing to say about a theology. What is most critical is the *new* way that these continuities of God, world, human being, and Christ are understood in each contemporary era. As one wise interpreter puts it, ". . . we understand in a different way, if we understand at all."[19] We cannot understand the Christian faith in first-century Mediterranean terms; that is not our world. We must understand it as twenty-first century North Americans.[20] This condition leads us into our last criterion for a working theology—the reconstruction of Christian doctrines in and for our time.

Deconstructing and Reconstructing Christian Understandings of God and the World

A working theology for us cannot be one from the past. We cannot merely translate biblical theologies (whether that of Jesus, Paul, or John) or any subsequent ones into contemporary terms.

The metaphors, models, and concepts of these theologies were developed in a different context for a different world. Whether this world be that of first-century Mediterranean culture, the medieval three-story universe, or eighteenth-century deism, it is not *ours*. The theologies of these eras fitted their world: salvation as ransom from the devil, God as King with his loyal serfs, a clockmaker God who started up the world. These models of divine action made sense within their respective worldviews and were, for the people of that time, powerful expressions of God's love. However, they make little sense in our world and are not, for us, compelling expressions of God's love.

A working theology, a theology that matters, must reconstruct its basic understanding of God and the world from and toward *our world*. It must take the contemporary analysis of our planet's plight as its context and its well-being as its goal. A theocentric, cosmocentric theology for twenty-first century North American Christians should begin with planetary literacy, knowledge about the world in which we live our ordinary, daily lives. In addition, then, to reliance on Scripture and the tradition, a theology must be *informed* about the world. The world to which God relates is not, I believe, primarily the inner world (each individual's situation and needs) nor the religious world (the world understood only as creation), but the ordinary world of plants and animals, oceans and skies, people and cities, institutions and governments as well as the knowledges that study and express them—biology, anthropology, sociology, political science, economics, the arts, and so on.

Christians need to reconstruct their theology in terms of the world in which we actually live for three reasons. First, if we do not do so, Christian faith will appear to be a scandal to the intellect. It will be presented to us clothed in miracles and demons, hell and heaven, a descending and ascending savior—in worldviews from another time posing as the substance of faith. Christianity may well be a scandal to the will, as genuine discipleship usually proves it to be, but it need not be a scandal to the intellect. When Christian faith is deconstructed and reconstructed within and for the present world, it does not scandalize the intellect. Second, unless we reconstruct doctrine in the context of our own worldview, Christian faith will be irrelevant. While some will be scandalized intellectually ("I cannot believe that"), others will simply find

Christianity irrelevant ("It doesn't make any difference"). It will seem trivial, unnecessary, extraneous. Unless theology connects to the vital issues of one's day—the economic, political, ecological issues—it *is* irrelevant. Third, unless our own world, *as it is,* forms the context of theology, we can deny that we must attend to its well-being. This last point is the most important one for a North American twenty-first century working theology: unless we know the state of our world and see it as what God loves and we should love, we can continue in a state of denial about its condition. We can pretend that the world's deteriorating state and the increasing gap between the rich and the poor is not God's concern and need not be ours.

For these several reasons, but especially to overcome our denial, we must learn about the state of planet earth. This is not easy in a consumer-driven culture, because the forces behind maximum economic growth and stock market profits do not want consumers to know how their behavior is affecting soil erosion, global warming, the loss of biodiversity and animal habitats, environmental pollution, desertification, poverty in the third world, and so on. They do not want North Americans to change their lifestyle or petition their governments out of concern for what is happening to the planet or to less privileged people. They want us to stay in denial and, for the most part, we comply. It is easy and certainly more pleasant to do so.

As we come to the close of our comments on the criteria for theology, we need to remember that such a reconstruction—an ecological theology for twenty-first-century North American Christians—is nothing more than that. It is relative and limited. It comes through the experience of one North American feminist, experience that has led me to the "relative absolute," which I describe as giving glory to God by loving the earth. I now try to understand how this basic insight can become a theology for people like myself in our present world. It is, needless to say, *one* theology, not *the* theology or even *theology*.

To sum up the matter of theology—its Contexts, Content, and Criteria—here is a list of the most important points I have made.

1. Theology has no absolute foundation, experiences, essence, book, basis, or authority. Theology is not God's Word; it is our words. This is what Paul Tillich meant with his notion of the

Protestant Principle: a protest against all attempts to be God, to let anything be absolute except God, to pretend that our words correspond to God's being, that we know the truth. Theology is a risky business; it is composed of metaphors and models; it is a limited, partial, passing enterprise. All theologies should be and will be replaced.

2. Theology is, then, contextual—always and inevitably. These contexts are of many different kinds and levels, from worldviews and personal experience to gender, race, class, sexual orientation, physical capabilities, age, etc. Theology, then, is always theolog*ies*, many different understandings of God's relation to the world from varying contexts.

3. Nonetheless, given a common text, Scripture, which functions as both a classic and a constitution for Christianity, as well as a tradition with a number of historical continuities with regard to how God, world, Christ, and human life are understood, we can speak of a Christian paradigm. To be a Christian theologian, not anything goes. There are guidelines.

4. It is not enough, however, to merely translate scriptural or traditional understandings of God and the world into contemporary terms, making merely "cosmetic" changes to doctrines. They must be reworked, reconstructed, in light of the novel situation of one's own time. The world as we know it and live in it must be the context within which Christian doctrine is reconceived.

5. The goal of such theology is not theology *as such;* that is, it is not refinements on the doctrines of God or Christology. The goal is the well-being of the planet and justice to its people, especially the oppressed. The goal is understanding what salvation—the liberation of the oppressed—means in our time, and, as disciples, following in that way.

We have a choice. We do not need to live within interpretations of Christian faith created in other times from other contexts for other needs. We can live in theological constructions for and from our own times. This is what theology has always been when it has made sense to people and when it has helped them love the world. If we reconstruct Christian faith for our planet's well-being, we will simply be following in the steps of all good, appropriate theology. But as a closing reminder, we need to construct these interpretations very carefully. They enter not only our minds, but our hearts, our imaginations, our wills, and even our dreams. They become our glasses to the world and affect what we love, how we spend our time and money, what we are willing to work for, how we vote, what we protest, and what we give ourselves to. Remember: Be careful how you interpret God and the world. It *is* like that.

 **Part II**

**The Context of
Planetary Theology**

 **Introduction**

THEOLOGY TAKES PLACE *within* a context, a worldview, of who we are and where we fit. Theology is not about "God and the world," but about God and a particular world, some concrete interpretation *of* the world. These worldviews are usually implicit, a set of deeply held and largely invisible assumptions about the world and especially about *us,* where we human beings fit. They give us a sense of proportion, a sense of our "place," so that we will know how to act in relation to others. Our consumer culture seems to have lost this sense of proportion. Perhaps we need to take a lesson from Goldilocks, who had a sense of what was too much, what was not enough, and what was "just right." Most of us, especially we middle-class North Americans, are all Miss Piggy: "more is more" and there can never be too much of it.[1] What has happened to a society's sense of proportion when "too much" is still not enough? What are the prospects for a people when they lose their sense of limits?

Goldilocks aside, this is a serious question—perhaps the most serious question facing us at the beginning of the twenty-first century. The religions of the world are constantly, in different ways, reminding us of our limits: there is no religion that elevates the proud, the vain, and the greedy. The point is that we human beings need to reflect soberly and often on our position in the world in relation to other human beings and to nature. Giving a thoughtful, open-eyed, honest answer to this question of our place and limits is one of the most difficult and most necessary tasks facing us. It may also prove painful, especially to us better-off human beings, but at least we know, as people in most of human history have not, that "who we are" is an *interpretation,* not a *description.* Therefore, it can be changed. If we discover that our current view of ourselves is destructive—that it is not, in spite of appearances, the good life—we can work toward changing it.

The next two chapters are about two worldviews, two interpretations of human beings and where we fit in the world. These worldviews, like all others, are at base economic; that is, they have

71

to do with how to live together in the household called Earth.
Since "economics is the study of how scarce resources are allocated
among competing uses,"[2] a worldview of planetary living is *necessarily* economic. It is no accident that the Greek word for "house"
(oikos) is also the root of "economics," "ecology," and "ecumenicity." For the universal household called Earth to survive and flourish, certain "house rules" must be obeyed. These house rules are
ecological, economic ones, having to do with the just division of
basic resources among all the members of the family of life.

A caveat is necessary here. We are not doing economics as
trained practitioners do it, engaging in technical discussions of
economic policy. It might have been more accurate to speak of
"political economy" or even "social ethics" than of economics.
Economics, however, is the term commonly used for the phenomenon we are discussing: a consumer-oriented context for the allocation of scarce resources versus a justice and sustainability context.
Moreover, allowing the economic guild alone to use "economics"
suggests that it is a neutral, objective science. On the contrary, we
are claiming that economic policies assume and imply worldviews:
who we are and how we should act in the world.

The two worldviews we will consider are dramatically different,
each carrying directions for human action—or, particular house
rules. The first model sees the planet as a corporation or syndicate,
as a collection of individual human beings drawn together to benefit its members by optimal use of natural resources. The second
model sees the planet more like an organism or a community that
survives and prospers through the interrelationship and interdependence of its many parts, both human and nonhuman. The first
model rests on assumptions from the eighteenth century in its view
of human beings (as individuals with rights and responsibilities)
and the world (as a syndicate or collection of individual parts,
externally related to one another). The second model rests on
assumptions from postmodern science in its view of human beings
(as the conscious and radically dependent part of the planet) and
the world (as a community or organism, internally related in all its
parts). *Both* are models, interpretations, of the world; neither is a
description. This point must be underscored because, as we shall
see, the first model seems "natural," indeed "inevitable" and "true"
to most middle-class Westerners, while the second model seems

novel, perhaps even utopian or fanciful. In fact, *both* come from assumptions of different historical periods; both are world-pictures built on these assumptions, and each vies for our agreement and loyalty.

These chapters will suggest that the syndicate or corporation model is injurious to nature and to poor people, while the other one, the community or organism model, would be healthier for the planet and all its inhabitants. In other words, we need to assess the economy of both models, their notions of allocation of scarce resources to family members, to determine which view of the good life is better.

To appreciate, however, how deeply the first model is rooted in Western society—and increasingly, in most others—we need to realize that *all of us* are players in it, whether we want to be or not. For example, while North Americans express deep concern for the environment when polled, we do not vote this way: most of us talk "green" and act "brown." This is so in part because the *structures* of our society, its institutions and laws, are derived from the first model, the model that focuses on individual human beings bettering themselves—at nature's and other people's expense, if necessary. Hence, we do not need to *deliberately* harm nature; we *will* do so simply by being favored players in Western culture. There are not "green saviors" and "evil exploiters" so much as *structures* that determine how we all, willy-nilly, will act: "Chrysler and General Motors and you and I are caught together in modern society, acting out our roles in a cultural act we did not write."[3] But try to live differently—"simply"—without a car, television, or mall shopping, and one immediately encounters culture shock. It is very difficult to live simply and does not seem to make much difference anyway.

Moreover, we are also as North Americans privileged players in the global economic game. Just as we do not deliberately harm nature, so most of us do not set out to make other people poor. But those of us who are citizens of the United States benefit from our accident of birth: in the growing global divide between the rich and the poor, most of us end up on the plus side. The United States is politically and economically dominant in this game and via its investments, loans, military aid, and cultural exports, controls the board for our benefit. Americans are impressively charitable when natural disasters hit anywhere, but the largest number of deaths worldwide are not from disasters. They come simply by being too poor to survive within the present global economic structures. These deaths occur in "ordinary times."[4] Environmental ethicist Larry Rasmussen surmises that future generations will be stunned as they look back at our era, at "the collective arrogance and pathology of ordinary Western ways."[5] But it is hard for us to recognize this because our ways seem so "natural"; we middle-class Americans see ourselves simply living as "everyone lives."

This is the way beguiling major models—worldviews—operate: they cover the world with their interpretive grid and we *cannot* see the world otherwise. And not being able to see the world differently, we cannot *act* differently either. While there is not a direct correlation between seeing and acting, seeing differently at least raises the *possibility* of acting differently. Thus, one very important piece of the planetary agenda is envisioning alternatives to the dominant economic worldview. It is difficult to appreciate the dire circumstances of our deteriorating planet as well as the one-fifth of its impoverished human population *unless* we change our conventional glasses for new lenses.[6] Environmental degradation and death from poverty are not conspicuous disasters like war; rather, they are usually silent and to many of us invisible. And yet we North Americans increasingly suspect things are not right, that our view of the world and the behavior it promotes may be eating away at the planet and creating poverty. The Millennial Edition of *State of the World* puts it this way: "So far, the world order emerging is one almost no one wants," with its shrinking forests; accumulating greenhouse gases; polluted air and dying species; dwindling fresh water, fisheries, and farmland; and increasing numbers of poor people.[7] But like it or not, we do not seem able to do much about it. Caught as we are in a system so wide and deep that we usually don't see it as *a* system, but as *the* system, we despair, even in our moments of awareness, of being able to act differently within it, let alone change it. Paralysis is widespread, a paralysis especially easy for well-off North Americans to endure; in fact, waking up and taking action seems painful by comparison. No people who have ever lived have had it as good as we do—why change anything? Why indeed? There are several ways to answer this question and the rest of Part II is one attempt to do so.

4. The Contemporary Economic Model and Worldview

In so far as Americans have a *collective identity* it is as *Homo oeconomicus*—the mass person, the consumer who lives amid unprecedented material splendor and the producer who bends the earth to virtually unrestrained human purpose.

—Max Oelschlaeger[1]

Neo-classical Economics and Its Worldview

To MOST ORDINARY PEOPLE, economics is a mystifying, difficult topic that they consider beyond their comprehension and best left to the experts. This is true of much of its daily transactions and details, concerned as it is with vast sums of money and complex mathematical calculations. But, at base, economics is simple: it is about dividing up whatever is scarce among competing uses and users. It is, for instance, about divvying up a candy bar among three children; or about deciding how to spend an hour's free time (reading a book, watching television, or doing the laundry); or about whether to log an old-growth forest, preserve it for wilderness, or use it for recreation.[2] Economics is not, then, just about money; it is present wherever and whenever *scarcity* exists. We do not have to worry about economics with things like love and friendship, since they grow rather than diminish with use. Therefore, in making economic decisions, money is not the only value to be considered. Many other values are present in decisions concerning scarce resources: from the health of a community to its recreation opportunities, from the beauty of other life-forms to our concern for their well-being, from a desire to see our own children fed and clothed to a sense of responsibility for the welfare of future generations. The "bottom line" is not our only value when faced with making decisions about competing uses for scarce commodities. It is important to underscore that economics is not *primarily* about money; more fundamentally, it is about decisions concerning scarcity from the perspective of a number of values, *one* of which is money.[3]

75

If this is the case, then there are different levels of economics. One is the complex, mathematical level that most folks find too difficult to follow and is part of every field of study: physics, literary theory, and sociology each has its specialized language and methods of analysis. But another level is the value decisions embedded in a particular economic system. On what basis are scarce resources allocated? What are an economic system's implicit values concerning human life and its goals?

The theorists of neo-classical economics, however, do not believe that economics contains values; they believe it is "objective," similar to a science such as physics (of course, one could ask whether science is value-free, but that is another topic). The point is that contemporary economics has fashioned itself on the sciences as Milton Friedman's distinction between "normative" and "positive" economics makes clear.

> Normative economics is speculative and personal, a matter of values and preferences that are beyond science. Economics as a science, as a tool for understanding and prediction, must be based solely on positive economics which "is in principle independent of any particular ethical position or normative judgments."[4]

The critical point is economics' claim of neutrality from all normative or ethical values or preferences.

Is this possible? Let us look at a few definitions and descriptions of neo-classical economics. By neo-classical economics we mean market capitalism as conceived by Adam Smith in the eighteenth century and, more particularly, the version of it practiced by the major economies of our time. The key feature of market capitalism is the allocation of scarce resources by means of decentralized markets: "system-wide resource allocation occurs as a consequence of many individual market transactions each of which is guided by self-interest."[5] Or, the same point in different words: market capitalism is "a giant machine operated by numerous investors, whose motives are neither vicious nor benign, who merely seek to maximize their returns."[6] At the base of neo-classical economics is an anthropology: human beings are individuals motivated by self-interest. The value by which scarce resources are allocated, then, is the fulfillment of the self-interest of human beings. The assumption is that everyone will act to maximize their own interest and by doing so all will eventually benefit—the so-called "invisible hand" of classical economic theory. This is Adam Smith's "market mechanism" of supply and demand, which operates spontaneously (according to him) to bring about the optimal price and quantity of goods. As Smith colorfully expressed it in 1776: "It is not from the benevolences of the butcher, the brewer, and the baker that we expect our dinner, but from their regard for their own self-interest."[7] The key concept in neo-classical economics is the argument that freely acting, acquisitive individuals will eventually, though not intentionally, work out the best solution for production and consumption in a society.[8]

In other words, neo-classical economics is not value-free; its central value is the gratification of individuals competing for scarce commodities. This gratification is understood entirely in monetary terms and the assumption is that all individuals in such an economy—like parts of a smoothly running machine—will profit from the system. Neo-classical economics has *one* value: the monetary fulfillment of individuals provided they compete successfully for the resources. But what of other values? Two key ones, if we have the economics of the entire planet in mind (and economics is increasingly global), are the just distribution of profits from the earth's resources and the ability of the planet to sustain our use of its resources. However, these matters—distributive justice to the world's inhabitants and the optimal scale of the human economy within the planet's economy—are considered "externalities" by neo-classical economics.[9] They are not considered intrinsic to economic theory; the government should attend to distributive justice through taxes and individuals through philanthropy, while the various sciences will hopefully find substitutes for non-renewable resources. In other words, the issues of who benefits from an economic system and whether the planet can bear the system's burden are not part of neo-classical economics.

In sum, the worldview or basic assumption of neo-classical economics is surprisingly simple and straightforward: the crucial assumption is that human beings are self-interested individuals who, acting on this basis, will create a syndicate or machine, even a global one, capable of benefiting all eventually. Hence, as long as the economy grows, all individuals in a society will sooner or later participate in prosperity. These assumptions about human nature and its goal are scarcely value neutral. They indicate a preference for a certain view of who we are and what the goal of human effort should be: the view of human nature is individualism and our goal is growth.

This anthropology rests on the Enlightenment's central insight: the importance of the individual. To us contemporary middle-class North American people, this may sound like a platitude. But to a culture where most ordinary people lived under the rule of king and church, as well as in the patriarchal family and were limited by inherited employment, it was the announcement of unheard-of freedom. Immanuel Kant's motto "Dare to think for yourself!" declared liberty to those bound in mind, spirit, and body by the chains of tradition and institutional control. A similar anthropology had lain behind the Protestant Reformation: the right of individuals to approach God directly, free of the mediation of clergy and church. Much that we cherish in American democracy today is from this dual heritage of eighteenth-century culture and the Reformation church: the right of every individual to choose what he or she wants and finds fulfilling. Those who have lived under totalitarian regimes know how precious the "platitude" of the importance of the individual is: it is non-negotiable.

It is, then, no surprise that modern economic theory, appearing for the first time in the eighteenth century, should assume a version of this anthropology.[10] Moreover, Adam Smith and subsequent economic theorists embraced not only the Enlightenment and Reformation view of the individual, but also the Protestant view of human sinfulness. These folks were not sentimentalists, counting as Smith put it, on the "benevolences" of others for their dinner but, more realistically, on the selfishness of others, their insatiable acquisitiveness, which could, by means of the invisible hand, be harnessed for the common good.

Behind this anthropology lies an accompanying view of the world as a machine with many parts. The scientific revolution of the seventeenth century had overthrown the medieval view of the world as an organism with interrelated members. In its place, as one of the century's prime symbols (the watch) suggests, they substituted a machine, which a transcendent God set in motion and which we can understand by taking apart and studying in detail. The world, then, like a machine, was an object (not a subject), dead (not alive), with all its parts connected only in external ways (as are the separate parts of a watch).[11] Atomistic thinking, imagining the tiniest parts of reality as separate units colliding with each other in random ways but manipulable by human design, began to seep into the cultural consciousness. Newtonian physics contributed its own view of the individual entity, along with the Enlightenment and Reformation Protestantism, to a cultural *milieu* below consciousness but operationally effective in all aspects of eighteenth-century life, including economics. Religion, philosophy, and science joined to create classical economics' view of the nature of human beings and of the world: what better way to conceive of their relationship than as a collection of individuals, all operating separately from self-interest, coming together like the parts of a smoothly operating machine? Just as the Deist God oversaw a world of many individual components operating together for the benefit of the whole, so also eighteenth-century economics imagined a similar economic structure. Like God, man was designer and controller of the world—in each case, for the betterment of all. The vision was elegant, simple, and inviting.

Its goal was similarly simple and inviting: growth. While "growth" may initially appear to be a description—as the economy grows, all benefit—it is in fact a value. That is, as there are other possible goals one might imagine for an economy—such as sustainability—the choice of growth is obviously a preference. As with the value of individualism, the value of growth must not be underestimated. We middle-class North Americans have benefited enormously from it. Our standard of living has skyrocketed during this century, and every one of us enjoys (and takes for granted) its many comforts and conveniences, not just inside plumbing but for many a personal bathroom, not just public transportation but one's own automobile, not just enough food to eat but, for many of us, too much food. We are the world's privileged people, and we owe it to *growth*. While the human population has grown four times the level it was one hundred years ago, the world economy is seventeen times larger than it was in 1900.[12] Growth was the bonanza of Western culture during the twentieth century; it is the means whereby we individuals with appetites for more and more scarce goods have been satisfied.

Again, just as we need to appreciate the importance of individuality and can do so best through the eyes of those under totalitarianism, so also we need to see growth from the perspective of a struggling country that does not have inside plumbing, little transportation other than by bicycle or foot, and a very minimal diet. The comfortable, consumer lifestyle that we enjoy is, understandably, the goal of most other people in the world; it is an inviting vision of the good life and should not be dismissed lightly. The only people likely to do so are those who enjoy its full benefits.

As with neo-classical economics' value of gratifying the individual, however, the value of growth is problematic. Most basically, it is a questionable goal because it is *impossible*. For all the earth's people to enjoy a Western middle-class lifestyle, four more planets the size of the earth would be necessary as the resource base![13] In addition, the value of growth leaves out many other values. This can be clearly seen in the indicator of growth, the GDP (Gross Domestic Product), which is the sum of all financial exchanges that occur within a country. This figure must rise and keep rising for a contemporary economy to be considered "healthy"; in fact, the faster and higher it climbs, the healthier an economy is judged to be. Most people feel good when they hear the country's GDP is growing; what many do not know is that *everything* involving exchange of money counts in this measurement including, for instance, the clean-up and litigation that followed the 1989 Exxon Valdez oil spill in Alaska.[14] Every time someone is treated for cancer or burglarized, every time you turn on an air conditioner rather than open a window or drive your car rather than walk, the GDP goes up. The GDP counts "harmful" activities the same as "beneficial" ones, the clear-cutting of an old-growth forest as well as crime and social decay—whatever brings money into the pockets of some individuals counts. What it does not count, however, is activities that do not involve money: unpaid housework, child or elderly care in the home, or volunteer work. In other words, if we think of our welfare, of the good life, only in terms of the GDP, we are leaving out many things we might consider valuable (such as bringing up children) and counting many things we might consider injurious to ourselves and our planet (such as oil spills). Finally, the GDP does not factor in the depletion of natural resources or the deterioration of air, water, and soil at the front end—that is, as an intrinsic part of an economy. The entire realm of "nature" is considered an "externality" that must be considered only when a company is fined for pollution or must install expensive environmental safeguards. The GDP does not count the "planet's economy," the large household in which we all live; in fact, this household falls outside the loop in neo-classical economics. While contemporary economics does recognize land along with capital and labor as a resource base for production, it does not see the planetary household as the essential context within which capital and labor must operate.

In sum, then, in the neo-classical economic worldview, two values predominate—the individual and growth, or perhaps it is more accurate to see just one value: the satisfaction of the desires of individuals through the means of constant growth. Within this worldview human beings are pictured as separate from one another and isolated from the earth; that is, they are only externally related to both, entering into contracts with other human beings for mutual financial benefit, and vying for the possession of scarce natural resources, which, whether "animal, vegetable, or mineral," are seen as objects for our use. Moreover, this worldview recognizes no limits, neither for individuals nor the planet's resources. Miss Piggy's "more is more" drowns out Goldilocks's quiet murmur, "This is enough."

The neo-classical anthropology and worldview would not be such a serious matter if it were but one of several attractive, vibrant ideologies competing for our loyalty. But it is not: it is the *only* one.

> In so far as Americans have a *collective identity* it is as *Homo oeconomicus*—the mass person, the consumer who lives amid unprecedented material splendor and the producer who bends the earth to virtually unrestrained human purpose.[15]

This identity is not necessarily or in most instances *conscious;* but for that very reason, it is all the more powerful. Becoming conscious of it is the first step; we can then at least decide whether we want to embrace this identity.

The Contemporary Economic Worldview and the Consumer Society

Who Are We? We Are Consumers

As we have seen, religion, political science, and economics came together to create an image of human life, and our place in the world focused on personal acquisition. We must remember, however, that this worldview not only came from noble roots, but was not consciously created (it is not a secret weapon conjured by "big business"). Rather, economics inherited it from religion and political theory. Religion contributed the notion of the sacredness of the individual and the sinfulness of all before God; political science contributed "the rights of man," summarized in the motto "life, liberty, and the pursuit of happiness"; economics combined the religious and political views to create a new creature: *Homo oeconomicus*—one who has the freedom to pursue his or her own personal economic interests. Eighteenth-century men and women, however, experienced restraints that their twenty-first-century counterparts do not. The twenty-first-century economic individual exists *outside* community; the eighteenth-century economic individual lived *within* communities, most notably religious and political communities. As Robert Bellah and others have told us, the strong sense of community generated by our early biblical and civic republican traditions no longer functions.[16] But it was not always so. Economic theory and its view of the acquisitive individual arose first in the context of powerful communal bonds—the biblical covenant uniting all people under God and the civic constitution joining Americans into a republic with shared goals and responsibilities. The individual's rights were balanced with responsibilities for larger goods—the kingdom of God and the republic of men [*sic*].

It is this sense of the individual in community that we have lost. Our assumptions about human life, its rights and responsibilities, no longer begin with a strong sense of solidarity toward others. Of course, contemporary people live in communities, many of them—families, cities, and countries as well as religious and social communities—but the image we have of human life is not fundamentally relational: that is, our primary sense of ourselves is not that "we live and move and have our being" in community. Rather, it is what Bellah identifies as "utilitarian individualism" from the eighteenth century and its present-day modification: "expressive individualism."[17] The common American culture is no longer religious or political. It is neither the covenant nor the republic that is primary, but the right of the individual to financial and personal fulfillment. Popular American religion, whether evangelical or New Age, is focused on the satisfaction of individuals, either through personal rebirth in Jesus or by the inner fulfillment gained from a variety of practices and sources. Neither of these powerful contemporary movements are prophetic calls to solidarity with the poor or oppressed; rather, they fall under "expressive individualism." Likewise, the common interpretation of the goal of America's founding documents is more supportive of "utilitarian individualism" than of civic society. Our motto of "life, liberty, and the pursuit of happiness" is often interpreted in personal, individualistic—sometimes even libertarian—ways, as for instance, in the right to carry a gun or the right to do as one pleases. It is the individual's *rights*, not their responsibilities for the welfare of others, that are primary for many Americans when they express pride in their country.

It is necessary, then, to spread the blame for our present worldview to religion and civic society. Contemporary *Homo oeconomicus* is not just the product of economics; as we have seen, its content comes directly from Reformation Christianity and eighteenth-century political theory. Moreover, the present narrowly individualistic understanding of human life is due in part to the retreat of religious and political communal perspectives. The view of human life shared by religion, politics, and economics—the sinful, but free individual—has lost what religion and politics once provided for it: a powerful sense of community with responsibility for others. As religion and politics have become less public and more private, as they have retreated by failing to provide alternative discourses or worldviews, the image of free individuals bound together by covenant and country has degenerated into a cult of individualism. The fault lies not so much with the hegemony of the contemporary economic worldview as it does with the failure of other forms of discourse to counter it. The last powerful counter-discourse, communism (and socialism), has died an unfortunate death. It is unfortunate because whether or not one agreed with this discourse, it provided a strong critique of capitalism's individualism.[18] It helped to reign in the inevitable excesses that any view of human nature and the world will develop *if it is the only one.*

The supremacy of the neo-classical economic worldview has led some to describe it as a religion—"consumerism"—the civic religion that we all share, regardless of other faith commitments we might have.[19] As one commentator puts it, "After the collapse of communism the market has quickly become a true world religion, the 'most successful religion of all time, winning more converts more quickly than any previous belief system or value system in human history.'"[20] Is this claim of religious authority justified? If religion, most basically, is that which makes us understand the world and our place in it, then market capitalism and its worldview as epitomized in consumerism, is not only *a* religion but surely one of the most successful. It *is* so successful in part because it has few alternative views of the good life with which to contend. As a result, it can become "invisible," the most desired condition for any ideology. That is, the contemporary economic worldview, resulting in our consumer culture, is generally not considered to be *one* way to live, but the *only* way.

"Out of all the alternative styles that history has tried, all the life objectives imagined in utopias or portrayed by philosophers, it is the high-consumption, North American style of life that has become standard for the billion who have attained it and the ideal for the 5 billion that aspire to it."[21] For an increasing proportion of the world's people, consumerism is the accepted and unquestioned way—the good way—to live.

The goal of this invisible religion is personal happiness. "The consumer society promotes the belief that ownership of things and activities that require spending money—and the spending of money itself—are the primary means of happiness. A subtext in such a society is the assumption that happiness is the single real goal of life."[22] The seductiveness of this goal is made all the greater by its invisibility. Since there are few counter-discourses offered to us, we need not become critical of the one we have. As in a totalitarian regime where only one ideology is permitted and therefore it is difficult even to imagine another form of government, so also as we live inside consumerism with no alternative good life available to us, it becomes natural, inevitable, conventional. How else *could* we live, one might ask? And we show our devotion to consumerism by working long hours to attain its rewards, by going into deep debt to remain members in good standing, and by spending many hours a week shopping (ninety-three percent of teenagers claim shopping is their favorite pastime).[23] The "cathedrals" of this religion are everywhere: there are four billion square feet of shopping space in the United States—sixteen square feet for every adult and child.[24]

Consumerism, however, is not just about customers and stores; it is not just a leisure-time activity that some individuals enjoy. It is a *systemic* phenomenon, deeply embedded in every political and economic structure in the world. In present-day culture the world is defined largely *as* a "trade market"; this is the most common metaphor for it. This trade market has five major players: producers, advertisers, the media, national governments, and transnational corporations.[25] Note that consumers do not appear in the list as active players; rather, they are the desired goal of these other forces, especially advertising and the media. Approximately 150 billion dollars a year is spent on advertising in the United States, more than on all of higher education.[26] The goal of advertising is to create customers for the commodities that producers generate, that governments support through tax subsidies and regulations, and that transnational corporations disperse across the planet with the help of free-trade agreements.

The Consumer Society: The Good Life?

The complexity, breadth and depth, power and influence, of this worldwide phenomenon is breathtaking and beyond imagination; its goal, however, is simple: to create customers for products. We need not, then, understand all the details in order to assess its goal—is the consumer life the good life? Does the buying and owning of many possessions bring happiness, and is happiness the proper goal of life? The ordinary citizen and the theologian need not become experts in neo-classical economic theory to judge the basic assumptions—anthropology, worldview, and goal—of a "religion" such as present-day economics. Our answer to this question has two parts: First, does the consumer society make those of us who have it happy, as claimed, and, second, is it the good life for all people and for the planet? The first question asks whether the goal of consumerism—happiness—is achieved by the one billion people who live this life. The second question inquires whether this ideology is achievable by the five billion who want it, as well as whether it is good for the rest of life on planet Earth.

The first question is tricky: Does the consumer life make its most faithful adherents happy? "The percentage of Americans calling themselves happy peaked in 1957—even though consumption has more than doubled in the meantime."[27] This statistic gives us pause. It appears that the relationship between consumption and happiness is by no means simple; in fact, a number of studies have concluded that money has little effect on happiness except for poor people.[28] Lottery winners are no happier than others: human beings are highly adaptable and can become used to almost anything, including substantial increases in income.[29] Having money wears off after a few months, as does buying a new car or a fancy dress. Material goods appear to make little difference in psychological or physical well-being, *after* basic needs are met. But there is a further twist: some people can *feel poor* with an annual income of $100,000. Consumption, for many, is a *relative* matter: we consume to keep up with others.[30] And since, for many people, this does not mean merely keeping up with the Joneses next door but with the lifestyle of the very wealthy as seen on television, the more people make, the more unhappy they can become.[31]

Curiously, then, it appears that having more money (after a certain level) does not make for greater happiness; in fact, it often leads to greater dissatisfaction as the bar is raised concerning what is "enough." If consumption is relative, enough is never enough: there will always be some people out there with more money than you have. What does seem to make people more content is *overall* reduction—that is, reduction for everyone, such as took place with rationing during World War II. If the consumption of an entire society is reduced, the bar of "enoughness" is lowered for all.[32] People in countries less well off than the United States do not feel deprived unless they compare themselves, as they increasingly do, to the consumption levels of Western countries.[33] It appears that consumption has a complex psychological component, resting on issues of self-respect and superiority (Who gets to wear the Nikes? Does this car "make a statement" about me?).

But for the very poor, consumption not only makes for happiness, but their increased consumption is essential. The bottom one billion of the world's population needs to consume more, much more.[34] These are the people who do not have enough to eat, often not adequate shelter, medical care, or education. As the top one billion should consume less, the bottom billion needs to consume more. The ideal level of consumption would be somewhere with the three billion people in the middle: they have adequate food, clothing, and shelter as well as access to some medical care and education.[35] This suggests a *reduction* in our lifestyle: would this make us unhappy? It is too early to attempt an answer to this question, but it is an interesting one that we will keep in mind.

The answer to our first question, however, the one on whether consumerism makes us happy, is very mixed. We all need to consume—*consumption* is not a bad word—since we are animals dependent on our planet's resources for everything we use to survive and flourish. A full stomach and a warm house are minimal consumption necessities, and they *do* make us happy. So does buying a special book, owning one's first car, or purchasing a long-awaited vacation package. But what pleasure does the one thousandth book, the Mercedes sportscar, or the tenth trip abroad provide? Perhaps some, but probably with diminishing returns. Can we say, as the religion of consumerism suggests, that human beings find their happiness in buying and owning goods or even that happiness is the goal of life?

We will let this question simmer as we look at the second issue: Is consumerism the good life for all people and for the planet?

The Consumer Society: The Good Life for All?

"The western economic model—the fossil-fuel based, automobile-centered, throwaway economy—that has dramatically raised living standards for part of humanity during this century—is in trouble."[36] We all know the dismal facts—the disappearing rainforests, the looming scarcity of water and arable soil, the increase in world poverty, the threat of global warming, the decline in biodiversity. The litany of planetary woes and human misery is endless and, finally, numbing. We can't take another grim statistic; we turn aside in despair, feeling there is little we can do. Reciting a list of problems is not, however, the best way for us to approach the issue. Rather, we need to see our *own involvement* in these problems: it is the question we have been pursuing from the beginning—who are *we* in the scheme of things and how do we *fit into* the earth? Even more specifically, we need to ask who we *middle-class North Americans* are and how *we* fit into the planet. The reason for posing the issue this way is that we cannot answer the question whether the consumer society is the good life for all unless we take a hard look at the state of the planet after one billion of its inhabitants have lived this way for the past one hundred years. The carrying capacity of the planet in regard to human beings is calculated by multiplying the number of people times their level of consumption.[37] If all consume less, then the planet can support more; if some consume more, then others must consume less. "A child born in the industrial world adds more to consumption and pollution over his or her lifetime than do 30 to 50 children born in developing countries."[38] We cannot *all* consume more; the planet cannot support six billion (or more) people living a Western lifestyle. As things now stand we middle-class North Americans are consuming *much* more, while others are consuming less: 20 percent of people in high-income countries account for 86 percent of private consumption, while the poorest 20 percent of the world's population consume only 1.3 percent of the pie.[39] In Africa, the average household consumes 20 percent less than it did twenty-five years ago; two-thirds of the world's population lives on less than two dollars a day.[40]

The problem, then, is not just consumption, but who is consuming and what are they consuming? We Western middle-class people are consuming much too much, and a good deal of our consumption is of luxuries while others do not even have the basics. Therefore, one critical issue is *who* benefits from the consumer good life? *Can* all have the good life? Only if the definition of what is "enough" changes radically for us high consumers; in other words, if all people are to have some form of the consumer good life, it must be different from the present one in which some individuals benefit enormously and others suffer deeply. It must be consumption for human *development* rather than consumption for individual aggrandizement. Consumption should be seen as a means to human development, "enlarging people's capabilities to live long and to live well"—*all* people, not just the fortunate one-fifth of the world's population.[41] This already suggests a different form of the good life, one that focuses on basic needs and is inclusive of all. We are far from this at the present time. Currently, Americans spend $8 billion annually on cosmetics and Europeans $11 billion on ice cream, a total more than it would cost to provide basic education ($6 billion) or water and sanitation ($9 billion) to the more than two billion people worldwide who do not have schools or toilets.[42]

The answer to the question, "Can *all* have the consumer good life?" depends, then, in part on who we middle-class North Americans think we are in the scheme of things: Are we entitled to all we can get or are we under *obligation* to share? Is sharing just a matter of charity (a choice by the wealthy to share their surplus), or is it an implication of *who we are?* The neo-classical economic anthropology does not help us here: as insatiable individuals we have no *obligation* to share the world's resources, though we may be moved by compassion to do so. As we will see, the ecological economic model does contain such an obligation.

We have seen, then, that the simple question, "Can all have the good life?" is deceptive; we have to ask who would be included in the "all" and what sort of good life is entailed. The neo-classical economic anthropology includes only those who can make it on their own, and it entails whatever luxuries these people can afford.[43] Issues of justice, fairness, and obligation, however, hover beneath the surface as well as other possible definitions of the good life.

The Consumer Society: The Good Life for Planet Earth?

When we turn to the second part of the question, "Is the consumer life also good for the planet?" another simple-sounding question will need a complex answer. In answering this question, it matters how we imagine the planet. If, as in the neo-classical economic view the world is a machine or syndicate, then presumably, when some parts give out, they can be replaced with substitutes. If, for instance, our main ecological problem is non-renewable resources (oil, coal, minerals, etc.), then human ingenuity might well fill in the gaps when they occur. Since the earth is considered an "externality" by neo-classical economics, then "good for the planet" can only mean good for human beings to use. The main issue is whether or not there will be enough materials to satisfy human needs and desires.

The state of the planet at the beginning of the new millennium, however, is far different than simply the loss of non-renewable resources. In fact, that problem is of less importance than two other related ones: the rate of loss and decay of *renewable* resources and the manner in which these losses overlap and support further deterioration. The big problems are the loss of water, trees, fertile soil, clean air, fisheries, and biodiversity *and* the ways the degradation of each of these renewables contributes to the deterioration of the others. In other words, if the planet is seen more like an organism than a machine, with all parts interrelated and interdependent, then after a certain level of decay of its various members, it will, like any "body," become sick at its core, sick to the point of not functioning properly.

To be sure, this process begins with the slow decay or loss of particular parts through clear-cutting of forests, overfishing, water pollution, desertification of land, etc. As long as the world was relatively empty of people, the results of these activities could often be reversed or at least stabilized. Now that the earth is full of people, all of whom are using and overusing these so-called renewables at a high rate, restoration is often not possible. Forests cannot be regrown quickly enough; the fish cannot reproduce at the speed we need; the air cannot be purified when we continue to pour tons of carbon dioxide and other chemicals into it; land that has become desert, while sometimes reversible to an arable state, takes a long time to do so. These so-called renewables are increasingly becoming non-renewables and many of them permanent non-renewables. The problem is not that there is not enough of them, but that we are using them at an unsustainable pace. And for these renewables, there are no substitutes. What can substitute for fresh water, for the microorganisms at the bottom of the ocean's food chain, for fertile land, for the diversity of organisms that give us our food and medicines, for breathable air and a stable climate? These are the *basics* of all human life and all other life as well; these are not "products of nature" that we can purchase, but nature's life-system *in which we all live*. We are forgetting that the carrying capacity of the planet is population times per capita resource use. Neo-classical economics ignores this first rule of planetary living.

This first rule is illustrated, positively and negatively, when we look at the *synergism* of planetary operation. The various parts of the planet as an organism work together both in health and decay to create something both better and worse than the individual parts. When the various members of an ecosystem are healthy, they work together to provide innumerable "free services" that none could do alone and that we take for granted: materials production (food, fisheries, timber, genetic resources, medicines), pollination, biological control of pests and diseases, habitat and refuge, water supply and regulation, waste recycling and pollution control, nutrient cycling, soil building and maintenance, climate regulation, recreation, educational/scientific resources.[44] These services are essential to our survival and well-being; they can continue only if we sustain them. This "list" of services should be seen as a "web": none of them can function alone—each of them depends on the others. These services are the "commons" that are our very lifeblood and that we hold in trust for future generations.

The most important services are not necessarily the most visible ones; for instance, in a forest it is not only the standing trees that are valuable but also the fallen ones (the "nurse logs" on which new trees grow); the habitat the forest provides for birds and insects that pollinate crops and destroy diseases; the plants that provide biodiversity for food and medicines; the forest canopy that breaks the force of winds; the roots that reduce soil erosion; the photosynthesis of plants that help stabilize the climate. The smallest providers— the insects, worms, spiders, fungi, algae, and bacteria—are critically important in creating a stable, sustainable home for humans and other creatures. If such a forest is clear-cut to harvest the trees, *everything else goes as well.* All these services disappear. A healthy ecosystem—complex and diverse in all its features, both large and small—is resilient like a well-functioning body. A simplified, degraded nature, supporting single-species crops in ruined soil with inadequate water and violent weather events, results in a diminished environment for human beings as well. "The bottom line is that for humans to be healthy and resilient, nature must be too."[45]

As we have seen, nature becomes unhealthy gradually and in particular parts and places. But just as the synergism of a healthy ecosystem supports the flourishing of all the parts, so when particular aspects are degraded beyond a certain point, the domino effect toward destruction can be dramatic.

An excellent example of negative synergism is global warming. We choose this example not only because it is among the top three planetary problems (the other two being biodiversity and population/consumption), but also because it illustrates how the top three problems interact.[46] Global warming is the result of emissions from the burning of fossil fuels; this has occurred because of the size and particularly the high-energy lifestyle of the human population; its effects are felt not only by human beings but also by all other plants and animals. Global warming is not just one in a list of environmental issues; rather, since the weather is the largest and most sensitive system influencing the planet, its state is a barometer of earth's health. Moreover, we choose this example because we middle-class Westerners produce three to five times more of the carbon dioxide largely responsible for global warming than do people living in developing counties.[47] While automobiles are the single greatest producer of carbon dioxide emissions, a high consumer lifestyle in general is the culprit. While other countries such as China and India may equal or surpass the West in greenhouse gas emissions in the future, we Westerners have been the preachers of consumerism as the good life. We have not only produced the vast majority of emissions to date, but we export consumerism around the world as the heartbeat of every nation's prosperity. Finally, we choose this example because it is a clear instance of global injustice: the greatest polluters to date have paid the smallest price. When environmental degradation occurs, it hits the poor first and hardest.[48]

What is global warming? It is the warming of the world's temperature due to increase of various gases in the atmosphere, principally but not entirely from the burning of fossil fuels. It is the growing consensus among the world's weather experts that by 2050 C.E. we can expect a 2.5 degree Celsius warming of the worldwide temperature and that this increase is due largely to human activity.[49] Why should this be alarming? Small changes in temperature can have very great consequences on the habitability of the earth. For instance, the earth's temperature during the last Ice Age was only 5 to 6 degrees Celsius *cooler* than it is now; hence, an *increase* of 2.5 degrees Celsius (and perhaps up to 6 degrees by the end of the next century) is substantial. The results would be devastating from the human point of view: desertification of the chief grain-producing lands, scarcity of fresh water, loss of trees, flooding of coastal areas and islands, the spread of tropical diseases, violent weather events, shortage of food, and so on. Global warming will change *life as we know it* and has already begun to do so.[50] Through our high-energy, consumer lifestyle we have triggered fearful, though still largely unknown, consequences for the most important and sensitive system within which we and everything else exists. While even the weather experts do not know how serious the situation will be, many are increasingly afraid of the prospect of a runaway greenhouse effect—the crossing of the line into irreversible temperature increases.[51]

The example of global warming is not a science-fiction apocalyptic scenario. It is the judgment of the best science of our day that it is a coming reality and one that we can do something about. The question, however, is no longer "What if global warming comes. . . ?" but "How much will it be?" At both the United Nations Conference on Environment and Development in Rio (1992) and at the follow-up conference at Kyoto (1997), steps were agreed to by the industrial countries to try to stabilize and eventually cut back carbon dioxide emissions to the 1990 levels by 2012. However, little if any progress has been made, in large part because the consumer worldview is so dominant in all parts of the world and especially in the big emissions-producing countries that few public discussions of the consequences of consumerism on climate have taken place. *All* of us are collaborators in this silence. It is not just "big business" and timid politicians that do not publicly declaim what consumerism is doing to the earth's weather system, but few of us do either. We *enjoy* the consumer lifestyle; in fact, most of us are addicted to it and, like addicts, we cheerfully stay in denial if possible. But we need to overcome this denial. Global warming reveals the failure of market capitalism as presently practiced by most countries to deliver the good life to all and for the planet. Global warming is a spectral figure on the horizon, warning us that unless we change our ways and learn to live all together and sustainably on the planet, the future will belong to the grim reaper. Global warming is the canary in the mine, whose death is the clue that our lifestyle lies outside the planet's house rules.

An Assessment of the Consumer Society

> We are called upon to help the discouraged beggars in life's marketplace. But one day we must come to see that an edifice which produced beggars needs restructuring.[52]

Martin Luther King Jr. questions the unquestionable: he asks whether an economic system that produces beggars deserves to remain unquestioned. The obscurantism and mystification surrounding economics protects it from criticism of its most basic assumptions. While ordinary people cannot enter discussion with economists over complex monetary transactions, we can and should question the taken-for-granted presuppositions of economic theory. The worldview of neo-classical economics has two main faults: its individualistic anthropology and its isolation of the economy from the planet's well-being.

Its anthropology is, strangely, in direct contradiction to twenty-first-century market capitalism's mantra of "globalization." The view of human nature with which it continues to operate is of the eighteenth-century individual who is externally related to others through one's own free choice. But the world that neo-classical economics inhabits—and that it embraces—is one of globalization, of interrelationship and interdependence. The anthropology of neo-classical economics is seriously out-of-date; moreover, it is in stark contradiction with the globalized world in which human beings must operate. Its worldview is making beggars not only of some human beings but of other life-forms and of the planet itself. The central principle of twenty-first-century market capitalism— free trade in a globalized world—means that we must move to an economic theory that embraces a view of human life and other life as compatible with this principle. And that view is not one that satisfies the consumer desires of individuals, but one that recognizes the basic needs of all human beings and other creatures, living in mutual need and reciprocity. Our first critique, then, of the consumer society is that the anthropology undergirding it is contradictory *on its own terms*: a globalized market implies a radically interrelated and interdependent human population. Globalization must be taken all the way.

It must also include the planet—its "resources," well-being, health, and sustainability. Why does market capitalism leave "nature" (loss of non-renewable and deterioration of renewable resources) out of the economic loop? Why does it not see that globalization means that our little economy must fit into the Big Economy of the planet? Again, the mantra "globalization" implies such universal, planetary, holistic thinking. It should be assumed that everything that keeps the economy going would be counted— why, then, the strange hole in the middle, the sustainability of the planet itself on which any and all economies depend? How can any economy suppose that it can keep growing indefinitely when its resource base—planet Earth—is finite? Few ordinary people, I suspect, realize this strange lack in market capitalism—its refusal to face limits. Any responsible householder knows better; you can only live so long on credit—eventually, you have to pay the bills. But neo-classical economics does not acknowledge the limits of the planet: growth with no end is the goal for all economies, regardless of how degraded water, air, forests, oceans, and fertile land become. Again, market capitalism does not acknowledge its own globalization. In fact, in regard to the planet, it is apparently willing to totally disregard the *foundation* of globalization, which is the health and sustainability of the planet itself.

So, we would call neo-classical economics and its consumer society to account on the basis of its own twenty-first-century goal of globalization: neither its eighteenth-century individualism nor its neglect of the planet's sustainability supports such a goal. In fact, they are in direct contradiction to it. If we do indeed live in "one world," all of us, all human beings and other creatures, then we need to embrace a worldview that calls for the just distribution of the world's resources to these many beings as well as the permanent health of those resources. Can market capitalism fit into such a scheme? That question is not for ordinary people to answer, but ordinary people can insist that any economic theory must do so. We, the people, have the right and the duty to decide what the good life is for us and our planet and then to ask the economists to devise ways of allocating scarce resources so as to bring about this good life. If economics is, as we have seen, about this allocation, then it is for society, not economics, to decide the context, the goals, within which that allocation takes place. Economics is a discipline, a field of study, to help people attain their goals; it is not, or should not be, the ideology that sets those goals. But as we have seen, it is: neo-classical economics has an anthropology of individual gratification and a worldview of continual growth. It has overstepped its proper boundaries—it should not decide who benefits from the world's bounty nor be allowed to assume that this bounty is limitless. Issues of distributive justice and the optimal size of an economy should be decided by citizens; the job of economics is to allocate scarce resources once the matters of justice and size have been determined. How to share the planet's goods cannot be left to the vagaries of market capitalism, for, as we have seen, the results are neither equitable nor sustainable.

But who can attend to these issues? As many have pointed out, free trade erases national boundaries making it very difficult for governments to legislate distribution of economic benefits through taxes and welfare or to enforce environmental laws. Big money goes where taxes are low and environmental laws lax.[53] Globalization in trade necessitates globalization in government. This is an enormous problem, but one that many people are working on at many different levels: the United Nations, the European Union, non-governmental organizations, and so on. One hopeful example is the effort called the Earth Charter. The Earth Charter, modeled on the Human Rights Charter of the United Nations, is a "bill of rights" for all people and for the earth itself. It acknowledges that, like it or not, we are faced with a "planetary agenda," of having to think about the well-being of the *whole of the planet*. It proposes that these "rights" begin with an acceptable standard of living for all persons along with the preservation of other lifeforms. Thus, issues of distributive justice and optimal limits are accepted as setting the context within which market capitalism, or any other economic theory, must operate.

In sum, our critique is that we have allowed economic theory to tell us who we are; we have let it become our ideology, even our religion. We have allowed the economy not just to produce things, but people—the people we have become at the beginning of the twenty-first century. We have become consumers—not citizens, or children of God, or lovers of the world, but *consumers*. That is our designation; that is who we are. "We do not exit the womb readymade consumers," as one commentator reminds us.[54] "Consumer" is a social construction; it is a state into which we enter through gradual but relentless formation from the moment of our birth by means of the 150 billion advertisements produced yearly in the United States alone. The liberal view of the freedom of the individual, a view shared by market capitalism and most Westerners, is that we *choose* among all these advertisements what we really want and will fulfill us.[55] But the growing presence of advertising in every nook and cranny of our culture reveals the naïveté of this view. When even school television sets and Girl Scout Cookie boxes carry ads, one realizes that nothing is off-limits to advertising any longer. Do we really believe we *rationally choose* what we "want"?[56] Have we not allowed economics to determine who we are and what we want? Do we not need a reversal: to insist that economics help us fulfill who we are and what we want? Should not economics serve human development, not just individual desires; should it not serve the planet's sustainability, not just consumer insatiability?

These are the crucial questions as we look for an alternative story to the worldview of neo-classical economics. We live within *models* of who we are and what we should do: we have a *choice*. Will we see ourselves as individuals with rights and freedoms, each of us taking from the world all we can get, or as citizens of planet earth, living sustainably and justly with other human beings and life-forms? *Neither* is a description of who we are, but which one do we want to become and which one is closer to reality as we experience it at the beginning of the twenty-first century? Which view should serve as our basic assumption, motivator of actions, and goal? We do not ask which one is attainable, but which picture seems right, true, and good for ourselves, our fellow creatures, and our planet.

5. The Ecological Economic Model and Worldview

> Probably the most challenging task facing humanity today is the creation of a shared vision of a sustainable and desirable society, one that can provide permanent prosperity within the biophysical constraints of the real world in a way that is fair and equitable to all of humanity, to other species, and to future generations.
>
> —Robert Costanza[1]

IF "ECOLOGY IS THE STUDY OF A COMMUNITY THAT WORKS," then ecological economics is the allocation of scarce resources so as to keep that community working indefinitely.[2] Its focus is the well-being of the community, not as in neo-classical economics, fulfilling the insatiable desires of individuals. Moreover, the focus is not principally on human beings; rather, we human beings are seen to benefit when the entire system is healthy. And the way we benefit is not through amassing wealth for ourselves ("exchange value"), but through sharing in the basics of a good life ("use value"). This kind of economics has been called "economics for community": "the management of the household so as to increase its use value to all members of the household over the long run."[3]

The key words in this definition are "household," "all members," and "the long run." Ecological economics is concerned with community, justice, and sustainability. Just as neo-classical economics contains an implied anthropology and view of the world, so does ecological economics. Both are *interpretations,* each based on what is considered important empirical evidence: the first on human greed and the second on human need. Are we *basically* greedy or needy? Probably both, but as our answers veer toward one pole or the other, we will find ourselves embracing an individualistic or a community model of life. Ecological economics claims we cannot survive (even to *be* greedy) unless we acknowledge our profound dependence on one another and on the earth. Human need is more basic than human greed: we *are* relational beings, willy-nilly, from the moment of our conception to our last breath.

These two interpretations of who we are and where we fit in the world are almost mirror opposites of each other on the three critical issues of allocation of resources, distributive justice, and sustainability. Neo-classical economics begins with the unconstrained allocation of resources to competing individuals, on the assumption that if all people operate from this base, issues of fair distribution and sustainability will eventually work themselves out. Ecological economics begins with the viability of the whole community, on the assumption that only as it thrives now and in the future will its various members, including human beings, thrive as well. In other words, ecological economics *begins* with sustainability and distributive justice, not with the allocation of resources among competing individuals. Before all else the community must be able to survive (sustainability), which it can do only if all members have the use of its resources (distributive justice). Then, within these parameters, the allocation of resources among competing users can take place.

Ecological economics does not pretend to be value-free; its preference is evident—the well-being and sustainability of our household, planet Earth. It recognizes the *oikos* base of ecology, economics, and ecumenicity: economics is the management of a community that works for the benefit of all. Ecological economics is a human enterprise that seeks to maximize the optimal functioning of the planet's gifts and services for all.[4]

Ecological economics, then, is first of all a vision of how human beings *ought to live* on planet Earth in light of the perceived reality of *where and how we live*. We live in, with, and from the earth. This story of who we are is based on postmodern science, not, as in neo-classical economics, on the eighteenth-century story of reality. The heart of our current story is a tale of unimaginable relatedness *and* individuality. From the Big Bang some fifteen billion years ago when all matter was one, the entire universe has emerged with its billions of galaxies, stars, and planets. Each stage of the universe's evolution has come about through greater and greater differentiation: individuality (not individualism) is built into the nature of things. All of these individuals are internally, intrinsically, related to one another. About four billion years ago life began on our planet, developing individuality to ever greater heights, but *all* within an increasingly complex network of interdependence. Nothing can be itself (in all its wonderful, radical particularity) except by means of the whole. Everything is an individual but depends on others *to be this individual.* An exquisite alpine forget-me-not only develops in the sparse, dry climate of Northern mountains; the panda's unique digestive tract was designed with the help of bamboo shoots; human beings are also what we are because of where and how we evolved. The earth is not simply the "environment," a scenic backdrop on which the human drama takes place; rather, it is what has made us who we are and what sustains our every second of existence.

We are "mixed up" with it in every way imaginable. Take, for example, breathing: the most basic (and first and last) thing we do. Breath—air—is the invisible essence of life. In the following fine description of the planetary breathing process by David Abram, we begin to see how deep is our immersion in the earth's processes.

> The breathing, sensing body draws its sustenance and its very substance from the soils, plants, and elements that surround it; it continually contributes itself, in turn, to the air, to the composting earth, to the nourishment of insects and oak trees and squirrels, ceaselessly spreading out of itself as well as breathing into itself, so it is very difficult to discern, at any moment, precisely where this living body begins and where it ends.[5]

Each breath we take, which means each moment we live, depends on all these others that silently process the constituents of the air necessary to sustain our lives. It is no surprise, then, that "spirit" should be a primary metaphor for the sacred in many religious traditions. The "breath" of the divine operating in, through, and with the very air we breathe is the most intimate and powerful way human beings have to express their total dependence on the Source of Life. It is no surprise either that global warming (and other forms of air pollution) should sum up and epitomize the deteriorating ability of our planet to support our lives and other life.[6] By our refusal to acknowledge *who we are* (where and how we live), we are ruining the foundation of our very existence. As Abram notes, human beings today look out from an "interior" zone (the self) to a purely "exterior" nature, refusing to recognize the reciprocity, the *respiration*, between the inside and the outside.[7] We erroneously believe we owe little to this outside; what matters is our inside—our precious, unique individuality—which each of us creates and sustains. We need, says Abram, to turn inside-out and realize that our insides are formed by the outside—by the air, the landscape, the plants and animals, the elements and minerals, the events and processes that constitute the earth. We need, in Robinson Jeffers's words, to have "fallen in love outward."[8] If this were to happen, we might realize, as Abram states: "Ecologically considered, it is not primarily our verbal statements that are 'true' or 'false,' *but rather the kind of relations that we sustain with the rest of nature.*"[9] In other words, what we *say about nature*—the words of the human individual, the center of all truth for the Enlightenment and modernity—is less important than the relations we *acknowledge with nature.*[10] "Truth" is not a static fact, but the quality of relationship. Are we in a "right" (appropriate, fitting, proper) relationship with nature? We must ask this question as the direct implication of the postmodern scientific story of who we are: we are the product of relationships with nature—many and complex ones. Thus, truth is recognizing these relationships, honoring them, and helping them to continue and flourish.

We need, then, first of all to *reconceive ourselves.* We need to think differently about who we are. The eighteenth-century individual, isolated from other people except through contracts and from nature except as the resource base from which to amass wealth, is false *according to the picture of reality current in our time.* The postmodern picture sees us as part and parcel of the earth, not only as dependent on it and its processes, but since we are high on the food chain, as *radically* dependent. If all human beings disappeared from the earth tomorrow, no plant or animal would miss us; on the contrary, everything would be better off. But we cannot live for a few minutes without air, a few days without water, a few weeks without the plants or other animals. We simply are *not* who the reigning economic model says we are, so says our current story. We may be greedy, but more basically, we are needy, terribly needy.

Having said this—and underscored it—we must also say that, like it or not, we have become, in a strange and perverse way, the dominant species on the planet. Ironically, the very air, water, trees, soil, forests on which we depend now depend on us to manage them *economically,* that is, for the long-term well-being of the whole household of planet Earth. Our very success as a species has landed us in the position of having to care for the rest of nature in order to continue as a species, in order to survive ourselves. But we have achieved another success as a species that can help here. We do not simply live in, with, and from nature: we have gained some distance from it as self-reflexive beings—we know that we know. Our peculiar ability for symbolization and thus language (and all that follows—the entire human enterprise) gives us some control over nature, for good or for ill. We have choices. One of the greatest insights of the Enlightenment was the realization that we *know* that we know; that is, naïve realism ("I know the truth") gave way to critical interpretation ("I know one version, one view, of the truth"). We began (and have never stopped for the past two hundred years) in seeing ourselves and our world in different ways, through different glasses, from different perspectives. We are no longer embedded unknowingly *in* nature; in fact, over the last two centuries we have developed the peculiar view that we are scarcely related *to* it. But now we must, as Paul Ricoeur puts it, return to nature, not with the "first naïveté" of the hermeneutically innocent, but with the "second naïveté" of those *who know that they know.* And what we know most profoundly (if we accept the interpretation of postmodernity) is that *we belong to the earth.* Other interpretations, such as neo-classical economics, will tell us a different story about who we are. We have a choice, and we will make it, either by changing our relations with each other and with the planet to fit with nature's house rules, or by continuing to believe we are free individuals with permission to do what we wish and have the ability to achieve.

We begin, then, with our most *basic* sense of who we are. Just as neo-classical economics assumes the unquestionable importance of the individual and his or her desires, so ecological economics rests on the presupposition of our inalienable membership in the earth community. These are fundamentally different paradigms: the one supports a self-interested view and the other an extended view of the self.[11] At the one extreme of the continuum are societies that stress individualism to the point of libertarian anarchy; at the other end is complete communitarianism. The goal is to balance individual freedom with the community's integrity. Ecological economics claims that neo-classical economics fails to do so by focusing on individual desires alone apart from issues of distributive justice and sustainability. "Modern economics typically continues to assume that society is simply the sum of its individuals, the social good is the sum of individual wants, and markets automatically guide individual behavior to the common good."[12] As we have seen, neo-classical individualism has become increasingly libertarian, freed as it now is from traditional religious and political communities. The eighteenth-century model of the individual *in* community has becomes the twenty-first-century model of the expressive or utilitarian individual *outside* community.

Can the model of the individual-in-community from ecological economics give us a new and better way to achieve a balance of the individual and community? The key feature of this model, as we have seen, is its stress on both radical individuality and uncompromising community: the individual exists only within the community and the community is composed entirely of these individuals. Postmodern cosmology solves the "one" and the "many" problem very differently than does the eighteenth-century view. According to the contemporary view, an individual does not enter into relationships but exists only within them; however, the community does not erase individuality—on the contrary, the community can continue to exist only if the individuals that compose it are healthy. This is a view of the individual that necessitates community and a view of community that demands individuality. The individual and the community are not in conflict with each other; rather, they need and thrive on one another.

For example, an old-growth forest is composed of thousands of different species of plants and animals (millions, perhaps billions, of individuals representing these species). It is a mind-boggling bonanza of individuality and yet, at the same time and because of the intricate ways these individuals are interrelated and interdependent, it is a highly impressive functioning community—the community being nothing more than the sum of the activities of all the billions of individuals. If this forest is clear-cut and replanted with a single species of tree, it will contain less individuality and be a less healthy community. In the natural world, well-being goes with differentiation and complexity: "oneness" is the goal *only* if it is the product of differences.

While no model of the individual and community will fit us perfectly (we recall that models are interpretations, not descriptions), the ecological model is an attractive, interesting one for human beings to consider as we try to understand who we are in the scheme of things. Its equal stress on individuality and community, but on each only in relation to the other, suggests that we cannot have the one without the other. Thus, sustainability of the community, of the whole, is a preeminent necessity, but this cannot occur except through the health and well-being of individuals; hence, the just distribution of common resources must take place. This model is as concerned with individuals as is the neo-classical view; the main difference is that the ecological model claims that individuals cannot thrive apart from the well-being of the whole—and the whole will not thrive unless the individuals are provided for.

We see, then, why issues of sustainability and distributive justice must precede the allocation of resources. The allocation of resources is a decision made on the basis of what it takes to achieve a just and sustainable society. Let us delve more deeply, then, into what a just and sustainable society involves. Whereas in neo-classical economics the goal is the satisfaction of the desires of individuals through constant growth, here the goal is the maintenance of a healthy community so that all its members may flourish.

The Ecological Economic Worldview and the Ecological Society

Who Are We? We Are Members of the Household

Whereas neo-classical economics begins with human desire, the desire to amass wealth, ecological economics begins with human need, the need for a productive and permanent dwelling in which to live. Ecological economics begins with *sustainability* as the preeminent and irreplaceable *sine qua non*. That we must maintain the health of the planet that gives us everything we need to live—from breathable air to food, clothing, shelter, as well as the means for all emotional, intellectual, and creative experience—seems too obvious to bear mentioning. It is, however, the big hole in neo-classical economics. Contemporary economics does not recognize the Great Economy, the household of planet Earth, as the overall reality within which all other functions—and economies—must fit. At most, it considers nature as "natural resources"—in terms of their availability and cost. The big picture is lost; it is as if the human economy takes place in a vacuum, in isolation from any setting, any limits, any laws other than its own.[13] Hence, the difference of "who we are" in these two economic paradigms is striking: the one begins with individual human beings and their desire for material goods, while the other begins with human beings as a species, a very needy one, dependent on a complex but vulnerable living space. The first view says we are consumers of nature's wealth; the other view, that we are members of nature's household.

Assessing who we are in the scheme of things is one of the most important judgments we make, because from that judgment everything else follows. We have seen the implications of neo-classical economics' judgment; we now turn our attention to the significance of ecological economics' position. It means first of all that the design principle for economics changes from a line (of "progress") to a circle (of sustainability). We see ourselves now not as striving in a linear fashion toward a golden future of material comfort that each of us must reach on our own, but as living within a circle composed of networks of interrelationship and interdependence with all other beings, human and otherwise. These two pictures within which to imagine our lives—an upward line that we each must climb versus a closed circle within which we all must live—are not only fundamentally different understandings of human life, but they also *feel* different. Since a sense of who we are at this deep level is felt as much as (or more than) thought, it is important that we note how different these pictures are at this level. In the first, each of us feels alone to find our own way and rewards; in the other, we are forever with others for whom we are responsible and to whom we can turn for help.

This circular design principle means, then, that we focus on *sustainability*. What is "sustainability"? Some of the synonyms for "to sustain" are suggestive here: aid, bear, befriend, carry, comfort, continue, defend, feel, foster, help, keep alive, lend a hand, nurse, nurture, relieve, save, support. These are words we might use among family members, among those who live in the same household. Environmental economist S. Viederman gives us a rich, suggestive definition of sustainability.

> Sustainability is a community's control and prudent use of all
> forms of capital—nature's capital, human capital, human-

created capital, social capital, and cultural capital—to ensure, to the degree possible, that present and future generations can attain a high degree of economic security and achieve democracy while maintaining the integrity of the ecological systems upon which all life and production depends.[14]

There are several things to note here. First, sustainability is a social vision—it is "a community's control and prudent use of all forms of capital." In other words, the community makes the basic decisions concerning how to maintain the good of the community; economic decisions are for corporate good, not for individual benefit (or, to phrase it differently, the individual's benefit can only occur within corporate good). Prior to allocation of resources must come the community's conception of the good life, the overall goal for the whole. This is a political vision in the broadest sense: What is for the good of the polis, the cosmos? It is an envisionment of how we would *like* to live, given how we *can* live. Thus, the second and equally important implication of our definition is that *all* forms of capital must be considered in the notion of the good life and first in the list is "nature's capital." The good life is not, as neoclassical economics maintains, dependent only on human capital and its products, but more fundamentally on nature's capital.[15] Thus, physical limits combine with social vision to suggest the kind of good life we would like and can have. Whatever we may want and however clever our technology, human-made capital cannot substitute for nature's capital: what good is a fishing boat if there are no fish or a saw if there are no trees?[16] What is increasingly limited and precious is not human know-how, but the health of nature's basic resources and processes.

A third insight from our definition of sustainability is that while the physical base (nature's capital) is essential, it is not enough. Our definition of sustainability as the principle that grounds the good life includes *all* kinds of capital—whatever it takes to make the good life good for all. For human beings, this includes not only a decent basic standard of living and a democratic form of government, but also opportunities for cultural, technological, educational, social, and spiritual development. The good life is not limited to economic efficiency in the narrow sense of economic security, but includes as well social, emotional, and creative growth both for ourselves and for future generations. This comprehensive vision of the good life—one that is based on "maintaining the integrity of ecological systems upon which all life and production depends"— is cultural, sociopolitical, and inclusive of all human beings alive now and in the future.

Is this vision of the good life attainable? Is it merely a pleasant utopia, idealistic and naïve in its assumptions of cooperation and responsibility? Perhaps—but all interpretations are: the neoclassical vision assumes that all individuals will be able, by their own efforts, to realize "the American dream." What is seldom factored into this interpretation are issues of class and privilege or race and gender. Visions are seldom entirely realistic or attainable, but they *do* matter: we become, in part, who we think we are. If we are persuaded that we are isolated individuals with insatiable desires in a dog-eat-dog world, we are likely to act that way. If we become convinced and begin to feel that we are, willy-nilly, all in this together, marooned on a finite planet with limited resources, where cooperation and responsibility are not just nice but necessary traits, we might also begin to act within these terms. We can only act individually and concretely—no one can change the world—but how we act individually and concretely rests to a large degree on our deepest feelings about who we are. One of the purposes of this book is to persuade readers that the ecological image of the good life is both "good" and "good for you." The first critical dimension of that image is *sustainability*: a vision of the good life that sees our good as within the good of the planet, now and always.

Therefore, embracing sustainability rests on a kind of self-interest. Just as the neo-classical economic worldview depends on a kind of self-interest—consumer aggrandizement—so does the ecological economic worldview. In fact, it recognizes both long-term and short-term self-interest. The good life certainly depends on the indefinite viability of the planet, but it also claims that its vision of satisfactory living is more desirable than consumerism.

But sustainability is only possible if there is also distributive justice. This follows logically; for the planet and its various life-forms to continue indefinitely in a healthy state, all must have access to the earth's resources upon which survival—and flourishing— depend. Thus, the second critical economic component we must deal with is distributive justice.

Distributive justice is a contentious issue between neo-classical and ecological economics. Conventional economics believes that the distribution of material goods will "trickle down" from the jobs created by entrepreneurs to the workers who will eventually benefit. "Distribution" is covered by the "invisible hand" of market capitalism, which guarantees that everyone will profit, though to different degrees. The two fallbacks for any inadequacies in the system are taxes and philanthropy. Ecological economics takes a different view on distributive justice. Because sustainability is its goal, it sees the sharing of material goods (nature's resources) as a necessity; it is the principal means *to* sustainability. To have a sustainable economy, there must be limits to inequality in terms of minimum and maximum incomes and also in terms of how much of nature's wealth we use now versus hold available for future generations.[17] In other words, since both poverty and excessive wealth destroy nature (for example, the poor denuding their environment for cooking fuel and the rich polluting the air with greenhouse gases), a median lifestyle for all human beings is desirable. While one billion of us live too high on the energy scale, another billion live too low; we all need to move toward the middle. But that is not happening; in fact, the opposite is true. The income gap between the richest fifth of the world's people and poorest fifth, measured by average national income per head, increased from 30 to 1 in 1960 to 74 to 1 in 1997.[18] Or, another telling statistic is that the world's richest 200 people more than doubled their net worth between 1994 and 1998 to one trillion dollars.[19]

Distributive justice does not mean that all (or even most) people would have the same income; a scale is necessary to recognize the *individual*-in-community. An extreme communist anthropology would insist on absolute parity in material goods, while an extreme individualistic anthropology—as we increasingly have in the global market economy—resists all forms of limits to inequality.[20] An ecological anthropology opposes these extremes, believing that the best way for individuals and the community to thrive—or, to put it more accurately, the best way for the community that is composed of billions of individuals of all species to thrive—is to assure that all have the basics to survive and flourish. Sustainability is not possible if people devastate nature either through excessive wealth or excessive poverty. Nor is the good life possible if

some have too much and others too little (remember Goldilocks!). As we have seen, the good life is not necessarily the high-
consumer life; in fact, happiness does not seem to correlate with
excessive consumerism.

But *can* "all have the basics to survive and flourish"? Of course
all life-forms cannot. However questionable the truth of the Dar-
winian phrase "the survival of the fittest," it is painfully evident that
in the natural world, most individuals do not survive and those that
do experience vast differences in justice. However, until our numbers and lifestyle became the dominant force, nature was in a more
or less sustainable condition. Can all of *us* survive and flourish?
Certainly not at the level of consumption we desire nor at the level
of our projected population. So, what does it mean to have a goal
of distributive justice in which "all have the basics to survive and
flourish"?

From a theological perspective, it means a picture of reality that
we believe is desirable and right. It is not an "economic plan" that
can be attained, any more than the fulfillment of the insatiable
desires of all individuals can be. Both are images of *how things should
be;* both are goals toward which societies and persons can work;
both are ways of criticizing our present and envisioning a different
future. To be sure, economists who embrace one or the other picture have devised strategies and suggested laws that will help us
reach these goals, but the more basic issue for all of us is the question, "Which one do we *want*"?[21] Which vision of life on our
planet are we willing to work *toward,* realizing that it will never be
reached but that approximations are possible?

To sum up: who are we? As members of the household called
Earth, we are relational beings, defined by our needs that make us
dependent on others and by our joys that make us desire one
another. We are not just self-interested individuals; in fact, according to the ecological economic picture of reality, we are basically
and primarily communal beings who become unique individuals
through help from and response to others.[22] Each baby, if fortunate, is born into communities of love and guidance that not only
are necessary for her to become a human being but also the particular human being she becomes. Each of us, if fortunate, takes
from nature not only our food, clothing, shelter, and other physical
gifts too numerous to mention, but also the very words we use to
describe our emotional and spiritual lives: the lion as an image of

courage; the phoenix as a glimmer of hope; an ancient tree as the model of perseverance; the sea as a symbol of eternity. We would not even know that we are individuals if it were not for the similarities and differences we see with all other life both human and non-human, in which we are immersed. If, then, we are *beings-in-community* at every level—physical, mental, emotional—how can my good not be related to your good or your diminishment not diminish me? Can I flourish alone? Will I not suffer if you do?

> Communal relations are mutual relations in which the norm is not that one loses when another gains, but that each loses in the other's losses and gains in the other's gains. . . . The proper service of community in this case is not sacrificing one's life but enriching the community through means that enrich oneself as well.[23]

The implications are clear: our joy and sorrow, our gain and loss, our "for better or worse," are tied to our need and our responsibility for one another. This brings us, then, to the question of whether the ecological society is the good life, good for all of us and for the planet.

The Ecological Society: The Good Life?

Money isn't everything. This is the first counter-cultural statement that the ecological society makes. And the second is that the purpose of money is to help people have productive, creative lives. The 1990 United Nations *Report on Human Development* makes this point.

> The real wealth of a nation is its people and the purpose of development is to create an enabling environment for people to enjoy long, healthy and creative lives. This simple but powerful truth is too often forgotten in the pursuit of material and financial wealth.[24]

In the ecological society the good life is defined not by the individual accumulation of money, but by the use of money to help people have decent, fulfilling lives. The good life is not having "more and more," but "enough." "Enough" of what? Not money as such but what money can give people: adequate food, clothing, shelter, education, medical care, creative and spiritual opportunities, fellowship and leisure time and space. Money is here being redefined in terms of its *use* value to the well-being of the whole community, all human beings, and the planet itself. The good life epitomized by Bill Gates's infamous fortune makes no sense from the perspective of the ecological society; it is not so much wrong as meaningless. Money is not the end but a means to an end: the end is the healthy development of human beings on a sustainable planet. By "development" is meant whatever it takes for different forms of life and the earth's processes to flourish in a sustainable fashion. Development does not mean "progress," but fostering or nurturing. It is not a linear process of changing something into something else (a forest into a parking lot), but a maturation and fulfillment of people and processes. Money is for the purpose of realizing possibilities: the possibilities within a human child and within communities of people living sustainably in nature.

If money is a means to an end in an ecological society, then we are also, in this model, *consumers*. Since money is the substitute for goods in contemporary culture—the means of obtaining what the planet and its inhabitants need to flourish—then we are necessarily consumers. "Consumption" is not a bad word: it is at base the energy we must have to continue in existence and to fulfill our potential. If there were no money, we would still be consumers: either we would hunt or grow the basics or barter for them. Consumption is not the problem: excessive consumption of luxuries by some while others (and the planet) deteriorate for want of basics is the issue. The United Nations *Human Development Report* (1998) sums up the necessity and purpose of consumption.

> Consumption clearly contributes to human development when it enlarges the capabilities of people without adversely affecting the well-being of others, when it is as fair to future generations as to the present ones, when it respects the carrying capacity of the planet and when it encourages the emergence of lively and creative communities.[25]

We see here a whole new perspective on consumption: it is an inclusive notion for planetary well-being; it is not the right of privileged human beings to amass luxury goods.

But is human development in this sense of enlarging the capabilities of all (while maintaining the integrity of nature) the good life? Would it make us happy? Is it something we must do in order to survive, or is it *good* as well as good for us? This is a difficult question to answer, because no society on earth lives this way; we have little empirical data (nothing comparable to the research on consumer-oriented lifestyles in the neo-classical economic paradigm). But there are a few sources that might help us imagine what life in the ecological society would be like.

There are the utopian communities from history (and science fiction): these are the dreams and longings of people who have wanted to "live differently," who have imagined and, for short periods of time, constructed communities that were egalitarian, focused on basic needs, non-materialistic, and sustainable. The dream was to create a way of living that allowed people to grow and develop in an atmosphere of simplicity and natural beauty. These communities were also, however, overly optimistic about human nature; naïve concerning dark, repressed urges and power struggles; often absolutistic in terms of customs and culture; and usually short-lived. The point is not that they failed, but that they symbolize a deep sense in many human beings that *things are not right*. We are not living as we should, as we could. We are not just self-interested beings who are satisfied by consumer culture; there is some other need in us that is profoundly dissatisfied by the neo-classical economic model.

Another source and a more down-to-earth one that might help us imagine an alternative good life is the United Nations Human Development Index (HDI). This was conceived as a corrective to the GDP—the Gross Domestic Product, which is the sum of all the stuff (goods and services) produced in a country. The assumption of the GDP is that economic growth inevitably brings other benefits as well—education, good health, and well-being. But that assumption has proved wrong—at least for all people. Some countries with a high GDP allow wealth to concentrate among a small elite, while others with less money distribute it more evenly. Thus, the HDI does not consider just economic growth (or per capita income), but two other indicators as well: life expectancy and education. While the HDI is a crude gauge and has several failings, nonetheless, by including life expectancy and education, it attempts to measure how well a society provides the basics (people do not live long without adequate food, clothing, shelter, and medical care) and also the "extras" that make life worth living (education provides people with the means to fulfilling work as well as creative and emotional opportunities).

Interestingly, a very ordinary country—Canada—has been named number one in the HDI ratings for the past six years because, as the 1999 report states: "it has been very successful in translating income into the well-being of its people."[26] Canada is no utopia, and it has a capitalist economy, but it acknowledges that "money isn't everything," that what matters more is how money is distributed so as to help people have productive, fulfilling lives. Since the HDI does not take the environment into account, it is by no means an adequate indicator of the good life in an ecological society. It does suggest, however, that something like life in Canada is a glimpse of the direction in which we need to go.[27] At the very least, it suggests that the good life is not primarily about excessive wealth for some, but the quality of life for all.

Have we answered the question whether the ecological society can give us the good life? Each of us must answer that for ourselves. It would be a different good life than we middle-class, North Americans presently have. For us it would mean consuming less (perhaps even making some sacrifices), but I find it attractive. It is not just that we need to change our notion of the good life, but for me, the possibility of living on the planet with the knowledge that most other people are also living decent lives and that the planet itself is doing well is deeply satisfying. In fact, I would find it exhilarating. I could get out of bed each morning free of the guilt and fear I now feel. It would be liberating.

The Ecological Society: The Good Life for All?

"Why should the South control its population if the resources saved thereby are merely gobbled up by Northern overconsumption? Why should the North control its overconsumption if the saved resources will merely allow a larger number of poor people to subsist at the level of misery?"[28]

The telling truth in this statement is its basic contradiction: the consumer paradigm of the good life for all is unworkable. It is a loser. We need a different model of who we are, one that understands well-being in collective terms. A fundamental shift to community values is mandatory in order for the necessary economic reform to take place. What the particulars of that reform would be we must let the economists figure out for us. What *we* (the people) must decide is the kind of society and planet we want: do we want the good life for everyone or just for the fortunate few?

Having sketched the good life in the ecological paradigm as one of sustainability and justice—"the capacity of the natural and social systems to survive together indefinitely" (sustainability) and the promotion of mutual well-being through the sharing of resources (justice)—we privileged North Americans must now ask whether we are willing to allocate resources so as to come closer to a just, sustainable planet.[29] This is not to claim that what *we* want will occur, but to ask the more modest question of where we want to put our energies, passions, and commitments. *Approximations* are possible: the gulf between the wealthy and the poor can be more or less, the health of the ecosystems of the planet is a relative matter. A conversion to the ecological paradigm is not a magic bullet: in the foreseeable future the population of the planet will not revert to one billion people, nor will all the Edenic landscapes we have destroyed bloom again. The ecological paradigm for the good life is aimed precisely at the "middle way": the assumption is that we must live on a planet full of human beings, all of whom will continue to consume, and on a planet that has fewer natural resources and less beauty than we wish. In other words, the ecological economic model is a sober, realistic one, aware that the good life must be a moderate one in every respect—in terms of our numbers, our lifestyle, and our expectations.

But, in spite of its sobriety, the ecological model is not all stick and no carrot. In fact, it is neither stick nor carrot. It does not function by punishing or enticing individuals; rather, it suggests a different way of being in the world that finds pleasure from something other than consumer goods and sees obligation as mutual responsibility. The individual-in-community model claims human happiness does not derive principally from possession of things (beyond the basics), but from community, nurture, friendship, love, and dedication to higher purposes. It also claims that once this communal mind-set begins to take hold, people, while still needing laws to make them good, will also *desire* their fellows' fulfillment, for they will see it as their own as well. It is not, then, carrot *or* stick or even carrot *and* stick, but a view of life operating from a different set of assumptions about who we are in the scheme of things.[30]

Would the middle way—moving the billion privileged and the billion impoverished toward each other—be the good life for all? Again, the economists must figure out the ways and means for all of us to share the planet's resources in a just, sustainable way, but there is little doubt that it would be an improvement for the poor and a *different* good life for the privileged. James Nash sketches this out for us in his comments on the virtue of "frugality."[31] He notes that frugality is an instrumental virtue—a means to an end—and the end is a better society. From its monastic and Protestant roots to Max Weber's description of it as "worldly asceticism," frugality has been for a *social* purpose, not for self-denial or world-denial.[32] Nash claims that frugality is "an alternative to the American Dream, a competing vision of the future—one that promises full-ness of being in solidarity."[33] At base, frugality "denotes modera-tion, temperance, thrift, cost-effectiveness, efficient usage, and a satisfaction with material sufficiency."[34] It is having a "sense of enough" and the willingness to live within material limitations so that others may also have enough. In other words, frugality is a response to solidarity, an affirmation of the truth of the ecological model that our lives are interdependent. It is not a saintly virtue reserved for the pious, but simply an honest acknowledgment that we are all in this together and others have needs. At the very least, it is a different attitude toward the physical world: as Alan Durning says, frugality is "a true materialism that does not just care about things but *for* them."[35] Frugality is a conservative virtue, concerned to use the world's goods sparingly and carefully, both in order to preserve them and to share them with others. Nash sums up the point nicely.

> Frugality is an earth-affirming and enriching norm that delights in the non- and less-consumptive joys of the mind and flesh, especially the enhanced lives for human communi-ties and other creatures that only constrained consumption and production can make possible on a finite planet.... Fru-gality minimizes harm to humans and other life-forms, enabling thereby a greater thriving of all life.[36]

Needless to say, frugality is not a popular contemporary virtue: Nash calls it the "subversive virtue." It is not only unfashionable but unpatriotic, since our economy depends on consumption. But for us privileged North Americans it may be the one thing need-ful: a world-affirming sense of restraint, of enough, because our very constitution as ecological beings demands it and because it is the way to our true happiness.

Finally, for North American middle-class Christians, the refusal to practice the subversive virtue of frugality describes sin. No lesser term will do. If we are called to love God by helping all to flourish—our human and earth neighbors as well as the planet itself—then sin is living in a manner that thwarts this. For *us*, the high consumer lifestyle is sinful; indeed it is evil, for it lies at the root of the systemic structures that make the wealthy richer and the poor more impoverished. Sin and evil are not static concepts; they change according to the attitudes and accompanying institutions that undermine flourishing in different times. For *us*, sin is not so much committing "bad" deeds or even "not believing in God" as it is living in a way that undercuts God's desire that all thrive. Christians, in our time, should see market capitalism as presently practiced as one of the most explicit and recognizable forms of sin. Sin for twenty-first-century North American middle-class Christians is simply "living the way everyone does"—in silent complicity with the structures of evil that grow from the insatiable desires of millions of privileged individuals.

In sum, then, the ecological economic paradigm gives us a picture of the good life very different from that of the consumer society, and it is one that most (if not all) of the world's peoples might attain. It is more realistic than the consumer model in facing squarely the planet's limits on both population and lifestyle, and it issues a special call to us, the privileged, to live with a sense of restraint, of frugality. It is not a utopia but merely a picture to help us move in the right direction. Many other fields of expertise, institutions and laws, programs and policies are needed before we can progress very far down this alternative road.

The Ecological Society: The Good Life for Planet Earth?

We have been considering the ecological society as a candidate for the good life, not just for the privileged, but for all human beings. It has been shown to have some merits, if the good life is seen in community rather than just individualistic terms. But what of the planet itself? Would the ecological economic paradigm be good for it?

From the perspective of the ecological model, what is good for us is also good for the planet and vice versa. We recall a statement quoted earlier, "The bottom line is that for humans to be healthy, nature must be also."[37] Nature does not permit "apartheid thinking," the falsehood that we can have a good life apart from nature or contrary to its own limits and health.[38] Just as the good life for human beings rests on distributive justice—all must have the basics—so also the planet must have the basics. The earth itself must have the conditions necessary to support us and, increasingly, this means we must live so that these conditions are possible. In other words, the good life for all human beings and for the planet is a whole—it is one good thing. It is intertwined (like the recycle symbol): the well-being of humans is dependent on the health of the earth's ecosystems, but these ecosystems depend on us preserving them. In a curious way, we have become the keepers of our own life-support systems; we have become responsible for the foundations of our society.[39]

This foundation, what provides the possibility of the good life for us, needs to be recalled and recited often, because we constantly overlook or forget it. We engage in "apartheid thinking," believing that our lives and our economy exist apart from nature. We forget that nature's so-called "free services" are beyond value: the maintenance and composition of the atmosphere, the amelioration and stabilization of climate, flood control and drinking water supply, waste assimilation, recycling of nutrients, generation of soils, pollination of crops, provision of food, maintenance of species and a vast genetic library, scenery and landscape, recreational sites, aesthetic and amenity values.[40] Many of these important services are not immediately visible: habitat, canopy, watershed, insects and plants, ocean plankton, root systems, climate control. Many of the most important providers are the smallest ones: insects, worms, bees, birds, microorganisms. We rely on these services for our good life, but we are cavalier about maintaining them. "We are willing to pull the threads of nature's safety net"; we have gone from living off the interest to spending down the capital.[41]

From the perspective of the ecological model, we see immediately how perverse this is: by destroying the health of nature, we are undermining our own. The ecological model does not support either/or thinking: *either* my good or yours, *either* our good or nature's. The good life for nature—a resilient, complex nature—is what we must have for our good life, but our good life rests on our caring for nature's well-being.

An example of this cyclical notion of the good life is seen in how "land" is understood in the neo-classical economic paradigm and in the ecological economic model. In the conventional view land is property; land is another form of capital.[42] Land (which includes all of nature) is interchangeable with money. Neo-classical economics is not concerned with nature "for itself" or even for the many visible and invisible services it provides to us. Since our economy is seen as an isolated system of abstract exchange value with no opening to the planet, "land economics" is not necessary.[43] We can do as we will with the land; it is just another form of property, of money.

Ecological economics sees land very differently: it is more like our "mother" than our "property." It is the source of our being, the one from whom we can never be weaned, and the one that we must now care for. These two ways of thinking—of land as property and as mother—suggest the total mind-shift necessary if we are to move from the one to the other: a conversion from a narrow, self-centered consumer mentality of abundance for the fortunate to an earth-centered, inclusive, long-term vision of the good life for all, including the planet. Both are images of the good life, both are models or paradigms or utopias—neither is a description of how things are. One is not reality and the other fantasy; both have elements of reality (human greed or human need) and fantasy (individual material satisfaction or inclusive community well-being). Both are candidates for our affirmation, commitment, and hard work.

But how, one asks, could a change to an ecological economic model occur, even if we wanted it? The task seems monumental, global, impossible. Nonetheless, worldviews have changed many times in human history; the difference now is that we can be more self-conscious about it. First of all, attitudes must change; in a democracy laws and policies do not change by fiat or because a few people want them to. People, ordinary people, must want something else, and to want it they must be able to imagine it. Theology can make a contribution to envisioning this alternative worldview; the last two chapters are an attempt to sketch two such different ways of being in the world. The embodiment and realization of the ecological way, however—should we choose it—must take place in the same comprehensive, detailed, multidimensional way that the neo-classical model is presently embedded in our society. Everything must change—from where we grow our lettuce (nearby, not thousands of miles away) to how we drive our cars (by fuel cell, not combustion engine), from how we educate our children (to be ecologically literate) to who gets medical care (everyone), from how we use the land (sharing it with other species) to how we envision God (as the source of the good life for all). There is no aspect, no dimension, no detail that would remain untouched. Just as we are defined now as consumers and see our planet in terms of consumption, so if we lived within the alternative model, we would define ourselves as household members and would see our planet as the home within which we all must live now and in the future. Who we think we are matters, both for our own good life and for planetary well-being.

An Assessment of the Ecological Society

"That happiness is to be attained through limitless material acquisition is denied by every religion and philosophy known to humankind, but is preached incessantly by every American television."[44]

We have been considering two economic paradigms with two different notions of happiness. Each rests on a view of who we are in the scheme of things and what human fulfillment means. In assessing the neo-classical economic anthropology and good life, we criticized it for its excessive individualism as well as for isolating our economy from the planet's economy. We suggested that in both these matters it did not follow its own dictum of globalization; in fact, its individualism and isolationist thinking contradict globalization.

As we turn now to an assessment of the ecological economic paradigm, we must ask a similar question: Does this model address the emerging reality of globalization? Does it suggest an agenda for planetary well-being, the well-being of all people and the earth itself? It appears to; at least its motto, the "individual-in-community," suggests it might. The motto, however, is too general, too nonspecific, for us to be certain that it would move us toward greater happiness for most people and better health for the planet. The "individual" must be specified; the non-specific individual is the one embraced by neo-classical economics who, by their own efforts, can reach consumer satisfaction. The non-specific individual often serves as a mask for the privileged individual. We must ask whose "standpoint" we assume when we speak of "the human individual": is it from above or below, from the winners or the losers, from the rich or the poor? There is no such thing as "the human individual"; each of us is characterized by the many concrete circumstances in which we actually live.

The "global village" exercise might help us decide the standpoint we should assume. If we could shrink earth's population to a village of precisely one hundred people, with all the existing ratios remaining the same, it would look something like this. There would be:

57 Asians
21 Europeans
14 from the Western Hemisphere
8 Africans

52 would be female
48 would be male

70 would be nonwhite
30 would be white

70 would be non-Christian
30 would be Christian

89 would be heterosexual
11 would be homosexual

6 people would possess 59 percent of the entire world's wealth
    and all 6 would be American
80 would live in substandard housing
70 would be unable to read
50 would suffer from malnutrition
1 would be near death; 1 would be near birth
1 would have a college education
1 would own a computer.[45]

However we read this data, "the human being" emerging from it is not one of us—that is, a privileged, North American, middle-class person. The standpoint of the majority of human beings is non-Western, non-white, and poor. She (52 percent are female) would also, at most, have a minimal education. If we were to stand in this person's shoes, it would not be because her condition is the one that the ecological model recommends for all of us. On the contrary, we need to stand there in order to judge which model makes for greater human happiness and planetary well-being. We need to stand there in order to understand better what it means to live in the "global village." Globalization is not the opening of markets to free trade so that the six people who possess 59 percent of the world's wealth can get even more. Globalization in the ecological model means a decent life on a sustainable planet for all human beings.

As we imagine ourselves living in the global village, we become aware of new house rules. To assess the ecological model—to see what living within this model would entail—we need to recall that its basic image is members of a household. Whereas the neoclassical economic model's rules are for individuals—you are free to amass whatever material goods you lawfully can—the rules of the ecological economic model are for housemates. Economists express these laws in technical language: classical economists insist on the importance of comparative advantage among different trading units, the efficient allocation of resources, and environmental externalities, while ecological economists hold to the Second Law of Thermodynamics, the planet's carrying capacity, and the need to internalize the cost of pollution. We lay people need not know the laws in their technical detail, but we do need to know how they function as unquestioned assumptions and hence influence our behavior.

In lay language, the ecological model claims that housemates must abide by three main rules: take only your share, clean up after yourselves, and keep the house in good repair for future occupants. The first rule—as in any household—is to take no more than your share (do not raid the fridge). My share or your share is what we need for a decent life: food, shelter, clothing, medical care, education. If each of us has these things, we have the *possibility* of a reasonable chance at happiness (i.e., a long, healthy life with personal fulfillment). Following this rule will not guarantee that all will prosper, but it does help to level the playing field. The second house rule is to clean up after ourselves, to take care of our waste and to recycle it so that its energy can be used again. The house is a sphere (the planet itself) that functions by a process of energy input and output. We cannot survive in a throw-away society where pollution (output) overtakes energy sources (input). The house will be unlivable: it will become full of hot, noxious gases instead of the clean air and food we need. The last rule is that we keep the house in good shape for the kids and the grandchildren. We don't own this house; we don't even rent it. It is loaned to us "free" for our lifetime with the proviso that we obey the above rules so that it can continue to feed, shelter, nurture, and delight others. These rules are not laws that we can circumvent or disobey; they are the conditions of our existence, and they are intrinsic to our happiness.

If we were to follow these rules we would be living within a different vision of the good life. We would begin to accept what Robert Costanza calls our greatest calling.

> Probably the most challenging task facing humanity today is the creation of a shared vision of a sustainable and desirable society, one that can provide permanent prosperity within the biophysical constraints of the real world in a way that is fair and equitable to all of humanity, to other species, and to future generations.[46]

This is a one-sentence summary of the ecological economic paradigm. Do you find it satisfying? Would it be the good life in your view? If you can answer yes with enthusiasm and commitment, then you have begun to shift to a new way of being in the world—the way of the ecological society.

 **Part III**

The Content of
Planetary Theology

Introduction

THE CONTENT OF THEOLOGY IS GOD; theology is about God. There can be no other subject, no other focus, no other concern. Nothing else matters except God or, to phrase it differently, everything else matters as it is related to God. God is not an object or abstraction added *to* the world, but the ground and source *of* the world. God is not a being in whom we should believe, but the breath of life in every being that exists. God is not a possibility within reality, but reality itself. To say yes to God is simply to trust reality; it is to acknowledge that reality is good. This sounds simple, but it is not easy. It means affirming the basic trustworthiness of things in spite of all evidence to the contrary. Faith in God is nothing more or less than this.

Apart from and beyond all specific, historical contexts within which theology is done, then, *the* context is God. But this context, while serving as both the possibility of saying anything about God as well as the critique of all we do say, is not available to us directly. We cannot "speak of God," but only of God from this or that perspective, this or that worldview. In the preceding chapters we have outlined two worldviews that provide very different contexts for speaking of God. We shall now sketch theologies from the perspective of these worldviews—the neo-classical and ecological economic ones. We will develop the latter in much greater detail, since the dominant economic model and its accompanying theology is well-known as the context for current popular religion. We will be looking at how three interrelated topics—God and the World, Christ and Salvation, and Life in the Spirit—are understood from within these worldviews.

As we begin this process, let us recall that its goal is to help middle-class North American Christians develop a *working* theology, one that emerges out of experience, makes sense in terms of reality as understood today, is consonant with the Christian tradition, and will liberate us from our role as oppressors. I have used my own theological journey as a case study, as an example of one path toward such a theology. What I have written so far and what the rest of the exercise contains is nothing more than that: an illustration of a working theology for twenty-first-century planetary living. It is an interpretation of Christian faith as channeled through my own experience—my religious autobiography—and seen within the ecological economic worldview. It is a theology that functions in my personal and public life, and one that I believe will be good for other people and the planet. It is also, I would claim, in continuity with the Scriptures and the tradition.

I invite you, then, to "pass over" to my theology in order to work out your own. I cannot pretend that this is a neutral or objective project, that I am encouraging whatever theology seems "right" to you. I have suggested criteria in chapter 3 that I believe all good theology should live up to, but there is a wide range of options within those criteria. I will argue for my theology as a worthy working theology for our time, but it is by no means the only one or even the preferred one. It is what *I* have come to hold as true and necessary. I can only give my reasons for this commitment.

The briefest version of the "relative absolute" on which my theology is based is this: *The glory of God is every creature fully alive and, therefore, we live to give God glory by loving the world and everything in it.* The particular, historical context for interpreting what this means for us today is an economic one. The last two chapters have insisted that our self-definition must be economic: who we are should be understood in terms of how much we consume of the planet's bounty, both in terms of its health and of justice to other inhabitants. We cannot "love the world and everything in it" unless we take the economic context with utter seriousness, since economics means the allocation of scarce resources among users. Love without economics is empty rhetoric. The primary anthropological question is no longer, as it was in the Protestant Reformation and still is for many Christians, "How can the individual come close to God?" but the more mundane "How can we all survive and prosper in God's world?" The question is not how each of us can win salvation, but how all of us can give God glory by living together as God's creatures.

This means, then, that theology for middle-class North American Christians must be *liberation theology.*[1] Liberation theology is about economics, about living sustainably and justly. As Susan Thistlethwaite comments, "Unless you do your economic homework, you can't pretend to be doing liberation theology."[2] Liberation and economics are inextricably linked, unless one buys into the dualism of body and spirit, seeing salvation as having to do only with the spirit. A holistic anthropology, one in which the good life includes body and spirit, insists that liberation *is* about economics. And this is doubly so for us well-off North Americans: we not only need economics to achieve our own well-being, but we also need it in order to realize how we are hampering others from achieving their well-being.

Theologian Joerg Rieger captures this double perspective in his definition of liberation theology as "common interest" theology: "Liberation theology is common interest theology, identifying common pain and seeking the liberation of both the poor and the rich, oppressed and oppressors."[3] He goes on to explain that common interest theology addresses the common good from a new angle, *from the standpoint of the oppressed.* In other words, common interest theology is about the well-being of the entire community, but for this to occur, the privileged must look at things differently. *We,* the privileged, will only be able to see what the common good is if we pay attention to where the pain is the greatest. Our own standpoint does not tell us much, or rather, it tells us everything is fine: the view from middle-class America is that life is good and getting better. If we stay with this standpoint, we will not liberate others or ourselves from the injustices and planetary deterioration of the consumer paradigm. We need to stand in a different place, in the shoes of those where the pain is the greatest. In choosing the appropriate standpoint, Rieger suggests, "A rule of thumb might be that context . . . which hurts" or as Paul puts it in 1 Cor. 12:26: "If one member suffers, all suffer together with it."[4]

We cannot understand our collusion in systemic suffering, in the suffering that the assumptions and institutions of the neo-classical economic model entail, unless we take the standpoint of those—the poor and the planet itself—that are being devastated by it. We will then see that loving others does not mean giving one's excess to the poor, but rather, working to overcome structural injustices that allow and encourage poverty. It means not charity but a different set of institutions to avoid the need for charity. Even the poor must choose to assume this standpoint, for simply being poor does not insure one against an individualistic view of the good life.[5] Many poor people want nothing more than to "advance" into the consumer lifestyle, leaving their needy sisters and brothers behind.

The standpoint of the poor, then, must be a choice, both for the well-off and the poor (but especially for the well-off). Therefore, liberation theology, common interest theology, is not a fad that middle-class North Americans might join. It is a necessity for us; it is what we need in order to do theology at all. As Frederick Herzog tellingly asks, "Are we using our commitment to Christ merely to legitimate our life politically and economically? Or does Christ open a way for critical spirituality?"[6] A "critical spirituality" is no small task, and it will undoubtedly be uncomfortable; it will be especially uncomfortable when the critical lens is an economic one. We would much prefer that lens to be religious or even political, as Joerg Rieger suggests as he asks a probing question:

> At a time when the market has finally become God, how seriously does contemporary theology . . . address economic issues? While the Protestant Reformers of the sixteenth century still dealt with a human being that was primarily religious, the Enlightenment deals with the political human being. Today, however, while much of the First World theology is still caught up with the *homo politicus's* dream of autonomy and control, the globalizing world of the twenty-first century is moving on to the human being as economic animal, *homo economicus.* Whether we like it or not, economic relationships now determine much of our lives.[7]

As we turn now to the substance of theology—God and the World, Christ and Salvation, Life in the Spirit—we do so through the critical lens of economics. The ecological economic model will be the interpretive context for my attempt at a planetary theology for twenty-first-century North American Christians. Since this economic model is about the just and sustainable allocation of resources among all planetary users, the framework for speaking of God, Christ, and ourselves becomes worldly well-being. Or, to phrase it in more traditional terms: "The glory of God is every creature fully alive." Dietrich Bonhoeffer called it "worldly Christianity": he said that God is neither a metaphysical abstraction nor the answer to gaps in our knowledge—God is neither in the sky nor on the fringes, but at "the center of the village," in the midst of life, both its pain and its joy.[8] An ecological economic model means an earthly God, an incarnate God, an immanental God.

As we look, then, at the big picture, the general outline of this theology, we find it basically different from theology implied by the neo-classical model. Broadly speaking, the differences can be suggested as a movement toward the earth: from heaven to earth; from otherworldly to this worldly; from above to below; from a distant, external God to a near, immanental God; from time and history to space and land; from soul to body; from individualism to community; from mechanistic to organic thinking; from spiritual salvation to holistic well-being; from anthropocentrism to cosmo-centrism. The ecological model means a shift not from God to the world, but from a distant God related externally to the world to an embodied God who is the source of the world's life and fulfill-ment. The neo-classical economic model assumes God, like the human being, is an individual; in fact, *the* super individual who controls the world through the laws of nature, much as a good mechanic makes a well-designed machine operate efficiently. This God is at the beginning (creation) and intervenes from time to time to influence personal and public history, but is otherwise absent from the world. The ecological model, on the contrary, claims that God is radically present in the world, as close as the breath, the joy, and the suffering of every creature. The two views of God, then, are very different: in the one, God's power is evident in God's distant control of the world (transcendence is external); in the other, God's glory is manifest in God's total self-giving to the world (transcendence is immanence).

Likewise, the understanding of Jesus Christ will be different from the perspective of the two models. In the neo-classical view Jesus is the redeemer of sinful individuals (those greedy, insatiable beings from Bentham, Hobbes, and Adam Smith), whose sacrifice on the cross is the way back to God. The focus is on individual human beings (not all of creation), who need the help of Jesus Christ in order to appear righteous before God. In the ecological model, Jesus is the embodiment of God's love and power, the man-ifestation of the source from which everything comes, the goal toward which everything yearns, and the presence in whom every-thing exists and flourishes. Jesus Christ is "God's heart" made known to us as being *on our side* no matter what. Jesus Christ is

God's prophet and incarnation, preaching a ministry of liberation to the oppressed and embodying this ministry in his death and resurrection (by accepting the consequences of his total identification with the world's pain and in manifesting God's glory in, through, and in spite of it).

Finally, in this sketch of the big picture suggested by our two models, human life and its mode of discipleship is also dissimilar. In the neo-classical model, the individual, freed from his or her sins by Christ, is expected to live a moral life, being generous to the poor and a good steward of the natural resources that we need. Human life is basically individualistic; hence, following Jesus means personal rectitude, fair dealing, payment to others for work done and the hope of rewards for good deeds performed. In the ecological model, human life is basically communal—sin is therefore a relational matter, being out of appropriate relations with God and neighbor (which includes non-human neighbors). As communal, sin creates institutions that perpetuate unhealthy relations with neighbors and the earth. Therefore, in this model, sin is principally systemic evil. Right relations with God and the world are made known to us in Jesus' ministry, death, and resurrection; therefore, discipleship means deification, becoming like the God we see in Christ. It means also creating institutions and structures that embody the kind of relations among all beings that promote their flourishing. Discipleship means that "we live to give God glory by loving the world and everything in it." This is what God does in Christ; this is what we do as followers.

6. God and the World

All things shall be well. . . . You shall see for yourself that all manner of things shall be well.

—Julian of Norwich[1]

Some Preliminary Reflections

AUGUSTINE WROTE THAT GOD IS THE BELOVED, the lover, and love itself.[2] If so, then who are we and what is the world? Where do we fit in? If God is the One who is loved and the One who loves, as well as defining love, what is left for us? If the source of all reality is love and this source is the goal, agent, and definition of reality, then how does one talk about the world at all? What does it mean to say "God *and* the world"?

It can only mean that our creation and fulfillment are included *within* God, that "God" is not an object, an explanation, or even a being, but the good news that reality is not indifferent or malevolent; rather, reality is with us and for us—on our side. God is good news about reality: God is not something in addition to reality, but the claim that reality is good. To say, "I believe in God," means "I trust, at the deepest level, in the goodness of things."[3] There is nothing special about this trust—it is not something reserved for mystics or religious types—and it does not take a sacrifice of the intellect as does believing in God as a supernatural being. All it involves is the awareness that I did not create myself and the gratitude toward what did. It is the awareness that life, my life and all other life, is included within God's life, and God's life or reality is defined by love. Life, then, is a gift of love, and therefore, whatever happens in life will be "well." Needless to say, being able to make that statement, let alone live it, is close to impossible—for most of us, it is impossible. Thus, back to Augustine: *God* must be the lover as well as the beloved. *We* become lovers of God, of the beloved who is reality itself, only as we become one with God. We become "deified"; we return to where we came from as we grow into the fullness of the image of God in which we were created. We come from God, we return to God, and in the interim we live in the presence—the power and love—of God.

This is the God who has come to me through my own experience. But it is by no means merely my opinion. It is one interpretation of the classical view of God in the Hebrew and Christian traditions. What is the classical view of God? Langdon Gilkey gives a definition:

> the word or symbol "God" has generally referred to one, supreme, or holy being, the unity of ultimate reality and ultimate goodness. So conceived, God is believed to have created the entire universe, to rule over it, and to intend to bring it to its fulfillment or realization, to save it.[4]

This definition veers in the direction of deism, of imagining God as a being ("one, supreme, or holy being"). How, then, is God as beloved, lover, and love itself an interpretation of the classical view? The difference between deism and God as love is where the emphasis falls—on God's distance from and rule over the world or on God's presence to and support of the world. David Tracy puts the continuum well when he writes: "In sum, God and God alone as the Wholly Other One, is both *transcendent* to all reality and totally *immanent* in all reality."[5] The Hebrew and Christian traditions have affirmed both, but more often and more successfully they have underscored God's transcendence at the expense of immanence. Thus, a primary question in the West has been whether God "exists," whether or not there is "one supreme, or holy being" who is "transcendent to all reality"? It was easier to believe in such a God when the reigning worldview was of a three-story universe with heaven as real a place as earth. It has become increasingly difficult to do so. It is also not very important to believe in such a God. This God does not have much to do with the world; in fact, one could accuse this image of God as being responsible for the strange silence about God in our culture. Most people can go through entire days, weeks, perhaps even years without needing to think about or speak of such a God. The more God's transcendence is stressed at the price of divine immanence, the less relevant God becomes. If, however, God is the love that creates, sustains, and transforms everything that is—if God is the declaration that reality is good—then all is changed. It is not, then, so important that "I believe in God" as it is that I align my life with and toward this reality. I must try to discover what it means to live in reality that is defined by love.

As we attempt to answer this question, we will do so from several angles. First, where should we begin finding out how to live in reality as defined by love? As Christians, this means asking whether we begin with God, Christ, or ourselves? Is there a right or better place to begin? Second, what is the range of ways to understand God as love—should we be theists, panentheists, or pantheists? Is God's love transcendent or immanent, or is it both, and if so, how? Third, what does it mean to speak of God's love as creating, liberating, and sustaining reality? Is God "three" or "one," or is that question even important? If we speak of God in terms of creator, liberator, and sustainer, we imply that God acts in and toward the world. So, a fourth question would be: What does it mean, can it mean, to speak of God's love as active in the world? Finally, the question that looms over all the others: How can we possibly speak of reality as good, of God as love, when we have just lived through the most violent century in history—when more people have been killed in war and by genocide as well as more of nature destroyed than at any other time? All evidence seems contrary to Julian's statement, "All things shall be well."

The questions we will be considering are standard ones in any Christian doctrine of God. However, we will be asking them from the perspective of our two economic models, reminding ourselves that there is no such thing as *the* doctrine of God, but only interpretations. We begin by repeating our definition of theology: Theology is reflection on experiences of God's liberating love from various contexts and within the Christian community. The subject of theology is God; the medium is our own experience as interpreted in various contexts and guided by the Christian community.

Beginning with God

So, where should we begin—with God, with Christ, or with ourselves? Where can we start finding out what it means to live in reality as defined by love? John Calvin put the issue bluntly when he noted that we could start with either God or ourselves, but we had best start with God lest by beginning with ourselves, we overestimate our importance. Not bad advice. If reality is defined by God, it makes sense to begin with God: we are less likely, as Calvin suggests, to go astray. But how *can* we? What do we know of God? How can we know God—reality—is love? Many have insisted that we do not and cannot know God: hence, we must start with the revelation of God in Christ—here we learn who God truly is. The difficulty with this advice is that "revelation" for Christians usually means the Bible, and the Bible is a collection of peoples' experiences of God. So, we are back to ourselves and our own experience.

Or, are we? One of the oldest and most abiding insights of the Christian tradition is that everything is from God, even our experiences of God's love. These too are gifts, not human works; all knowledge of God, whether "natural" or "revealed" is from God's initiative, God's grace. We can only know God because God makes this possible for us. We were created to know God: intimacy with God is part of our birthright—it comes with our creation, so to speak.[6] In one sense, then, it does not matter where we begin—whether with God, Christ, or ourselves, we are always beginning with God. But *how* we begin with God does matter. Dorothee Soelle says, "We can only speak *about* God when we speak *to* God."[7] What she means is that prayer precedes theology; being in relationship with God (acknowledging this as one's actual state) comes before the conceptual, systematic task of talking about God. She is not claiming that we must each have mystical experiences of God or even affirm the "existence" of God; rather, we must, as many other liberation theologians have also claimed, acknowledge *the presence of God in the world*.[8]

What does this mean? Many things to many people, surely, but at base I believe it means becoming aware that reality is good. It came to me through nature: a sense of unity with the natural world, of give and take with it, of pulsating life of which I and everything else is a part. I felt I belonged and I gradually came to name this sense of belonging as God's love. Nature was the route by which I came to knowledge of God's presence in the world—or, more accurately, the existence of everything within divine love. There are many other routes. Since, for the Christian, God is always incarnate and present, there is no place on earth, no joy or wish that any creature experiences, no need or despair that they suffer, that is not a possible route to God. Wherever reality is seen as hopeful, joyful, and loving, God is there; whenever reality is experienced as despairing, cruel, and hopeless, God must be there also. If God is love, then where love is, God is; where love is not, God must needs be. In nature's health and beauty, I see God; in nature's deterioration and destruction, I see that God is here also. In the first case as a Yes and in the second as No: in the first case as a positive affirmation of God's glory through the flourishing of creation; in the second, as a negative protest against whatever is undermining God's creation.[9]

"Beginning with God" means, then, daring to trust the tiny smidgen of God's liberating love that has come to you, but doing so in light of some criteria—whether it is consonant with Christian faith and whether it would be good for all people and the planet. We come to God through becoming *aware* of God's presence in one or more of its infinite forms in the world. God is always there (or here); *we* need become so.

Beyond the necessity of starting with God—our experiences of God's love—is the *desire* to do so. The experience of reality as love is one of great wonder and gratitude. It is an experience of worship. We start with God because the realization that love (and not indifference or malevolence) is the heart of reality is overwhelming. The *sanctus* is our response: the deepest religious emotions are awe and thanksgiving. If God is not a being or even just being-itself, but reality as good, then our astonishment and gratitude knows no bounds. It is more than we could ask or imagine; it is complete satisfaction and fulfillment. And we are called to be part of this amazing web of life and love: to praise God by helping all God's creatures flourish.

Now, then, how does all this fit with our two economic models? Can we start with God from both models, and what does it mean to do so? It is very difficult to begin with God from the neoclassical economic worldview. For the most part, God is absent from the world in this model. To be sure, God designed and set the world in motion, as one does a machine, but God is not a ubiquitous presence in the world. The deist God of the model allows for "acts of God" in terms of natural calamities (causing or preventing them) as well as intervention on behalf of individuals in pain, but most of the time, this God can be forgotten—and is. The deist God—otherworldly, distant, uninvolved—suits a worldview of individual aggrandizement. The secularization of the world—the dismissal of God's presence from it—is a necessary by-product of seeing life in terms of individual pleasure and profit, especially if this entails the impoverishment of other people and the planet. The neo-classical economic worldview begins with *us*, we human beings of insatiable desire: this is its primary sense of reality. "God" must adapt to this "relative absolute," this primary commitment of the model.

The ecological economic model, however, is open to beginning with God, because at the heart of this worldview is the individual-in-community: everything *is* because of relationships of interdependence. Individuality emerges in community and the community is nothing but the interaction of individuals. The sense of life intrinsic to this economic model is that our very breath, each breath, depends on others. We live within an unimaginably vast and intricate reality of which each one of us is a part and to which each of us contributes. Is it, then, a great leap to the supposition that this reality is good, rather than indifferent or malevolent? We are not being asked to believe in an otherworldly being, but in the trustworthiness of the whole process that has created and sustains us. In this worldview, starting with God almost comes "naturally"; at the most basic level, it is simply acknowledging that while we are part of the web of life, we are not its creator, its center, or its means of continuation or transformation. We are recipients of a gift.

God Is Love: The Many Ways to Say It

Beginning with God, then, means beginning with that scrap of our own experience of God, our "relative absolute," as understood from various contexts and as congruent with Christian faith. My "relative absolute"—the glory of God is every creature fully alive—means that reality is good. "I believe in God" is what we say when we rest on this assumption, the assumption of the goodness of reality.

But what does it mean to say that reality is good? Is this the same as saying that God is love? I believe it is one way (the best way) but certainly not the only way. The ways of speaking of God's love range from the deistic and monarchical to the dialogic, the agential, and the organic.[10] On the one end of the continuum, the deistic model sees God's love as radically transcendent over the world, so transcendent that God and the world are only externally and occasionally related. At the other end—the organic model—

God's love is radically immanent in the world, so immanent that it is difficult to say how God and creation are separate. The monarchical view, God as King and Lord, is also a highly transcendent understanding of God, but with suggestions of greater relatedness, for a king cares for his subjects. The dialogic model is more personal, proposing that God and the individual have an I-Thou relationship: this model allows for divine immanence, but only with human beings. The agential model, a variation on the dialogic, broadens God's transcendent love to embrace history, both human and natural, but the agency is all on one side—God's. None of these models is adequate, needless to say. "God and the world" is not a subject we *can* model accurately. The question is which one or ones is/are closer to the Christian paradigm (as understood in our time) and better for the planet and its inhabitants?

The monarchical model, while deep in the tradition and still popular in many quarters of both church and society, has come under severe criticism from philosophers and feminist and other liberation theologians, as well as process theologians.[11] From the perspective of an ecological economic worldview, it is especially problematic because it sees the God-world relationship as entirely one-sided: God is an imperial, patriarchal figure whose transcendence is manifest in his total control over the world and whose immanence is shown by divine sacrifice for the sins of the world. The model views power as control, is anthropocentric to the neglect of the rest of creation, understands relationships externally, and removes responsibility from human beings. God's love *is* transcendent—as is a king's or absent father's—but it is not immanental: we do not live and move and have our being in this God.

The dialogic model has been an attractive way of modeling God's love, especially during the twentieth century, though the model is also ancient, going back to the earliest Hebraic roots where God speaks with human individuals. It is a way of talking of God's immanental presence as close to us (we pray to and are addressed by God), while at the same time insisting that this conversation partner is pure spirit and hence not overly interested in the world. From the perspective of our ecological economic model, it is even more anthropocentric than the monarchical model, limiting divine concern to the inner joys and fears of individual human beings.

The deistic model is, as I have suggested, the one that fits best with the secularized, consumer-oriented economic worldview: it so emphasizes, *over*emphasizes, the transcendence of God that God becomes irrelevant. The last thing this worldview needs is a "sacred universe," the sense that God is in, with, and through all that is. This model is often joined with the dialogic one, creating at least one place—the inner individual—where God and the world meet. This meeting place, however, is protected from the physical needs of either other people or the planet. It is bodiless and individualistic: the sins confessed here are mainly personal failures and the love given mainly a forgiving, comforting one.

Is this enough? Should God's love be no more than radical transcendence mitigated by care for persons? Is this what we mean, should mean, by "God"—that God is the One who designs and starts the world, controlling it through natural laws while intervening now and then to aid needy individuals? The ecological economic model says no: God is much more than this. God is radically transcendent *and* radically immanent: God's love is the power that moves the galaxies and that breathes in our bodies. One way to imagine this relationship between God and the world is with the metaphor of the world as God's body.[12] This metaphor is a combination of the classical agential and organic models. It suggests that we might think of God's transcendence as radical immanence; that is, God's love is totally, though not exhaustively, incarnated in the world. The world, the universe, is the "body of God": all matter, all flesh, all myriad beings, things, and processes that constitute physical reality are in and of God. God is not just spirit, but also body. Hence, God can be thought of in organic terms, as the vast interrelated network of beings that compose our universe. The "glory" of God, then, is not just heavenly, but earthly: we can praise God by marveling at and caring for people as well as everything else. But God is not only the universe; God is also (and primarily) the breath that gives it life, the spirit that transforms it. Just as we are not primarily our bodies (though we are thoroughly bodily), so also God is not reduced to the body of the world but is also and primarily, the life and power, the breath and love, that makes the universe what it is. By combining the agential and organic models, we have a way (a feeble, inadequate way, of course) of expressing what it means to say that reality is good, that God is love.

It is a way that combines being and goodness: if we say only that God is being-itself and exclude goodness, then perhaps reality is indifferent or malevolent; if we say only that God is good but not being-itself, then perhaps God is just a being—a good one—but what about the rest of reality? With the metaphor of the world as God's body, God as the agent or spirit in and through all that is (as our spirits are the energizers of our bodies), we can imagine a unified view of God and the world, which does not, however, identify them. Moreover, this view gives us a way of imagining reality as good, as having value: every creature, thing, and process in the universe has value because it is an aspect of God, it is part of God's body. Another way to express this is to say that since everything derives its existence from God, everything has value. H. Richard Niebuhr says that seeing being and value together is "the assurance that because I am, I am valued, and because you are, you are beloved; and because whatever is has being, therefore it is worthy of love. . . . In [God] we live and move and have our being not only as existent but as worthy of existence and worthy in existence."[13]

The world as God's body or the agential/organic model of God and the world is a form of panentheism. Whereas deism is an extreme form of theism (God as external to and distant from the world) and organism is an example of pantheism (the identification of God and the world), panentheism is an attempt to speak of God as both radically transcendent to *and* radically immanent in the world. It is a corrective to the classical view, which, while affirming both divine transcendence and immanence, has tended to emphasize the former, undercutting the sense of God's presence in and to the world. While the world as God's body tends in the other direction, toward highlighting God's immanence, it is an emphasis that we need, given our long history of transcendence understood as divine distance from the world. We recall that *no* models are adequate; they are not descriptions, merely an attempt to express something of God's being and nature. Moreover, many, if not most, contemporary doctrines of God are, to one degree or another, panentheistic.[14] Monarchical or deistic theism, even when softened by the dialogic model, results in a supernatural being who wields power in unilateral and oppressive ways. This is not a model of God that most people today can believe in, nor is it a model that is good for the earth and its people. Its credentials as Hebraic and Christian

are also doubtful, for the God of both traditions is Emmanuel—
God with us—the compassionate, available, and caring source and
renewer of life.

We are suggesting, then, that the understanding of God that is
compatible with an ecological economic worldview (and one that
is consonant with Christian faith) is not the popular image of God
as a supernatural individual, the designer of the world and
redeemer of human individuals, a God who can be forgotten most
of the time and who is mainly concerned with "religious" or personal moral matters. This God, while a caricature of the Enlightenment and Protestant legacies, is nonetheless a powerful force in
civil society and the model of God that fits best with the conventional economic worldview. On the contrary, in the model of God
for an ecological economic view, God is radically present in and to
the world and is concerned with everything that goes on in it,
especially with bodily needs and pain. This is a "God of the basics,"
a God who cares about those things that keep beings alive, healthy,
and flourishing. This is, in other words, the God who cares about
the *oikos,* the management of the entire planetary household, so
that all will have a fair share and the house will be in good shape
for future inhabitants. This God cares so much about the *oikos,* the
inhabited world, that we are allowed to think of it as God's *body.*
It is an outrageous thought, but both the Hebrew and Christian
traditions suggest it is a better way to think than of God as a heavenly spirit who is indifferent to the world. It is better, say these
traditions, to err on the side of God loving the world "too much,"
than of not loving it very much.

If, then, we were to accept the agential/organic model, the
world as God's body, as a helpful way to speak of God and the
world from an ecological economic context, what would our basic
response be to both God and the world? I suggest we would
address both as "Thou," as living subjects who have being and
value; not as "objects" that we can manipulate or use, but ends in
themselves to be honored.[15] In other words, our primary stance
toward God, other people, and nature would be one of appreciation
and gratitude. We would value each being—and the source of all
being—in itself, for itself: we would value each just because it is. We
would also be grateful for these others whom we desperately need
and in whom we take joy. If we are individuals-in-community, then

we live and flourish with and by means of all these others, as well as the Other. In summary, this way of saying that God is love or that reality is good places us in a position of reverence toward God and the world: in the model of the world as God's body, there is no way to separate them.

God as Creator, Liberator, and Sustainer

The "God of the basics," the God who cares about the management of the household, is its creator, liberator, and sustainer. The radically transcendent *and* radically immanent God is the source of everything that is, the power that frees creation from what would destroy it, and the love that nourishes it in every moment. The God whose glory is every creature fully alive cannot be a solitary, distant being. The "trinity" is a *model,* a way of speaking of God, that tries to express God's profound involvement in, with, and for the world.[16] It claims that the universe originates in God, owes whatever signs of hope and goodness appear in it to God, and depends on God continuously for all forms of nourishment. The trinity is certainly about God, but just as important, it is about God and the world; it is a way of talking about God's transcendence and immanence in relation to the world.[17]

The notion of the trinity has been a source of misunderstanding and mystification for most of Christian history: How can three be one or one be three? Which of the three is responsible for what actions? We are not interested in such puzzles, but rather in the way the trinitarian model of God gives us a language for speaking of what we know from our own experience and what the Christian tradition upholds; namely, that God is our ground, our savior, and our nurturer. The trinity is an attempt to express the full dimensions of the experience of God as the One in whom we live and move and have our being; the One from whom we come, to whom we return, and in whose presence we live every minute; the One who is no more alone than we are—as Martin Buber puts it, "In the beginning is relationship."[18] From the "beginning" God is relational as we are, all the beings and things God has created. As we are not solitary individuals, neither is God: in the ecological, economic worldview and in Christian faith, beings are individuals-in-community. We *are* because of relationships. The trinity, then, is not a conundrum or theoretical obscurantism; rather, it is the most basic affirmation we can make about God. The trinity is about rela-tionship, about God with us in every way, at every level, in every moment.[19] In Catherine LaCugna's words, the trinity "expresses the one ecstatic movement of God whereby all things originate in God and are returned to God."[20] The trinity, so understood, is a way of speaking of creation, incarnation, and deification; that is, our beginnings from God, our salvation in God, and our move-ment toward God. The trinity, then, far from being irrelevant, is central to Christian faith: it expresses the entire God-world dynamic. This dynamic graphs the movement of God with us and us with God as a going out and a return: as God goes out to the world in creation/incarnation, so the Christian life is a return to God. Since God's life penetrates ours in creation and salvation, so Christian life becomes a participation in the divine life: ". . . ortho-praxis means right practice, right acts, in response to God's life with us."[21] The trinity, so understood, is not a Christian doctrine in a narrow sense. It is not the claim that Jesus of Nazareth is "the sec-ond person of the trinity," although, as we shall see, for Christians Jesus is an affirmation, deepening, and clarification of the trinity. More basically, the trinity is about God's love for the world and the world's response.

Let us look, then, at the substance of this doctrine—God's activ-ity as creator, liberator, and sustainer—to see how they fit with and illumine the ecological, economic worldview. These three "activi-ties" of God spell out what the God-world relationship is from our side, the world's side. Most broadly, these divine activities mean that God does everything for us: we owe our existence, our happiness, and our daily nourishment to God. These are not, however, one-time events, nor do they conflict with or replace scientific expla-nations. They are ways of speaking of our radical dependence on God for life, for love, for all the things we need to exist and flour-ish. They are a doxological statement, not a scientific one. They are perfectly compatible with an evolutionary view of the universe; in fact, the Big Bang creation story *enhances* our praise to God. To remythologize Christian faith from that perspective is to make God all the greater, as Job would have well understood.[22]

Understanding God's love in creator/liberator/sustainer terms is especially relevant to us today if we want to live within an ecolog-ical economic worldview. These three divine activities are about creaturely flourishing; they are concerned with the gift of life, its maintenance, and its liberation from forces that would destroy it. The ecological economic model is similar: it is a vision of planetary living in which justice and sustainability are priorities. Both are radically relational understandings of existence; neither sees either human beings or God in solitary, individualistic terms. They are commensurate, though by no means identical, perspectives. The ecological economic worldview and the understanding of God we have been depicting are compatible and mutually enhancing.

How is this the case? The creator/liberator/sustainer God—the One whose glory is every creature fully alive—is concerned about the well-being of all creatures, not just the moral rectitude of human beings. This is a radically physical, inclusive, democratic God who gives religious backing to the ecological economic model. This God cares that those to whom she gives birth have enough to eat; that those who are sculpted by the divine hands retain their beauty; that those whose existence he calls into being with a word continue to flourish.[23] God the creator is fiercely protective of his/her creation, just as any parent or artist. We, all of us, belong to God: we are the precious creations of God's hands and words, and we are the fruit of God's body. No metaphors are too strong or too intimate to express the loving relationship between God and creation: parenthood and artistic creation can give us only a *glimmer* of how God the creator feels about all of us. Just as human parents would give their life for their children (and sometimes do), so God's love for creation is particular, boundless, and total. Just as artists feel that they are embodied in their work, that who they are is expressed in their creations, so also God's glory is reflected in each and every creature, from the mite to the whale, from the acorn to the mountain, and in each one of us human beings. The doctrine of creation is not primarily about whether God produced matter from nothing, nor is it about a moment in time when the universe appeared. The doctrine of creation is about God's total graciousness in the gift of life and total commitment to the life so created.

God as liberator and sustainer does not tell us something new or different about God. God as liberator underscores that God is there for us no matter what. God the savior does not mean that in the incarnation, ministry, death, and resurrection of Jesus of Nazareth,

God does a new work, something different from God's work in creation. God as savior or liberator continues the work of God as creator; it is God's sign and seal that *nothing* can separate the world from God's love, not even the most perverse and evil acts of human beings. The creator God *must* also be the liberator God, for since creation in the ecological economic model is an infinitely old and infinitely complex reality, it is an ongoing event that meets with all sorts of natural, historical, and increasingly human forces that would destroy it. God the liberator is always Emmanuel, God with us, as the Hebrews well know in their exodus from Egypt and the long journey toward the promised land. God the creator has to be God the liberator; the parent will do whatever is necessary to protect from danger the products of its own being.

Likewise, God the sustainer is a further elaboration of how the creator and liberator God operates to insure planetary well-being. The sustenance—breath and food and all needful things—that creation must have to survive are provided daily and concretely by God. God the liberator will not only protect us against great evils and dangers—whatever would enslave and undermine us, but God the sustainer will also give us the most mundane, basic things we need to thrive.

This God—the creator, liberator, and sustainer of everything—is a down-to-earth householder. This God cares about just and sustainable planetary management, so that all creatures may flourish. This God will judge harshly those who do not consider the lilies or who kill a sparrow or who take extra helpings at the table when others are hungry. Economics and God are interrelated topics: an ecological economic worldview demands an understanding of God such as we have been sketching. Likewise, this view of God enhances the ecological economic worldview, providing depth and a sense of appropriateness to it. The ecological economic worldview helps us see how we can serve God, for it means that we do *God's work* as we labor to incorporate this economic view on our planet. The ecological economic model also benefits because we can now see that it is not just an idealistic fantasy, but a partial reflection of God's will for the world. This economic view is closer to the love that God has for the entire creation than are some other economic views.

And this brings us to the neo-classical economic worldview. How does it fit with the model of God as creator, liberator, and

sustainer that we have been sketching? Are they mutually compatible and enhancing? Not likely, since one's view of God and of the
world go together. The neo-classical economic worldview high-
lights the importance of the individual and his or her desires. It is
atomistic and dualistic. It understands reality as composed of discrete, individual units and beings that are externally related, either
as parts of a machine or by human decisions and contracts. Reality
so understood is divided into mind and body, spirit and flesh,
humanity and nature. Individuality and not relationality is basic in
this picture; likewise, mind—not body—is primary. The *sensibility*
of this worldview—its basic awareness of who I am, who we are, in
the scheme of things—is very different from that of the ecological
economic worldview. In the neo-classical picture each creature and
thing is alone, independent, and whatever has "mind" is superior
to all bodily functions and needs. Whereas in the ecological economic model the basic awareness is of a spirit-filled bodily existence that all people, creatures, and things share (even God!), in the
neo-classical picture the basic awareness is of disembodied, solitary
individuals over against a purely physical world composed of animals and matter.

Where does God fit into this picture? God is the super-individual,
the utterly transcendent designer and creator of the world-
machine, who, like humans, is disembodied, a mind/spirit who is
external to the world but in charge of it. This God is creator, the
One who originates the world process; and also savior, the
redeemer of human beings who fall into sin by not loving God and
neighbor; but this God is only marginally sustainer, for this God is
not continuously and constantly in and with the world. Rather, the
deistic God is at most present just once: in Jesus of Nazareth whose
death was a sacrifice for the sins of the world and whose life was an
inspiration for all to follow. This is not the God in whom we live
and move and have our being; this God is to be worshiped on Sun-
days and provides some ethical guidelines for treating other people
fairly and even for conserving natural resources for future generations. But unlike the understanding of God that accompanies the
ecological economic worldview, this God is not a statement about
reality. Believing in this God does not mean that one trusts that
reality is good; rather, it means that one enters into a contract with
the supernatural divine force that is the mind behind the world
machine, a contract to live decently and virtuously with other

rational beings and in a world composed of matter. This God is distant from worldly events, both physically and emotionally; it is a detached God who views the world from "the sky," protected from the mundane agonies of starvation, persecution, pain, war, and death.

It would, in fact, be impossible for the God of the ecological model to fit with the neo-classical worldview. That God is constantly, annoyingly present in the world and concerned with basic and ordinary physical well-being. That God cares about lilies and sparrows and hungry stomachs, not just about mental anguish or spiritual alienation—or even moral peccadilloes. That God is the busy householder, insisting that all family members deserve a fair share at the table and that the house must be kept in good order for others. That God is intrinsically and permanently worldly. Such a God is very difficult to escape or forget, for this God is always present.

How Is God Present in the World?

This simple question is, among all other questions about God, one of the most difficult. It did not used to be. Until the Enlightenment, many events were seen to be "acts of God," from unwanted babies to illnesses and earthquakes. Until the scientific revolution, people did not ask *how* God could act in the world, but simply assumed that unexplained events as well as extraordinary ones, whether good or bad, were from God. Moreover, before scientific empiricism insisted that only matter is real, spiritual acts and actors were seen to be just as real. In other words, God was a presence in the personal and public lives of people as well as in nature in ways we can scarcely imagine.[24]

But those days are long gone. For many if not most contemporary people, God's *absence* is a far more common experience. This is not necessarily felt as an absence; it is not the experience of the loss or "death" of God, so much as it is the experience of the irrelevance of God or simply the lack of any experience of God.

The neo-classical economic worldview, the reigning paradigm of our time, suggests how this has come about. As we have noted, the deistic God of this paradigm is absent from the world. This God resides elsewhere and has little connection with worldly pains and pleasures. Apart from starting up the world as creator and intervening now and then, mainly in the inner life of individuals, God is not a factor to be reckoned with in world events. Everything, or almost everything, goes along just fine without God—the scientific, economic, and public worlds. No explanations or interference from God is necessary; in fact, it would be inappropriate and intrusive. "Religion" is one discrete area of life that deals with personal issues of morality and mortality; it is not part of economic or public life. The scientific revolution and the Enlightenment dealt with religion by compartmentalizing it; God was no longer always and everywhere present as had been true in medieval times. Now God was pushed to the margins of the world and especially into the inner person.[25]

The deistic view of God is a convenient one for a consumer society that does not want interference in matters of the distribution of necessities or the sustainability of the planet. This God stays out of the political arena, finding its only abode in the inner recesses of human beings. This God is not a householder, butting into every nook and cranny of the planet, concerned about its well-being at every level. To the householder God, nothing is off-limits, and especially not politics and economics.

So, how *is* the householder God present in the world? We recall that the God who fits with the ecological economic view is the world's creator, liberator, and sustainer, the One upon whom everything is dependent for everything: each creature's first and last breath, the billions of species of living things and billions of electrons and quarks that constitute all things, the stars and galaxies, and so on. "God" is the source of all power, all love, all good in and with and for everything, at all times and places. This is the "ubiquitous God" *par excellence;* this God is never absent. If this God were absent, nothing else could be present: everything would collapse or disappear, for God is being-itself, the source of all being without whom nothing else is. This God is also the source of all goodness and love: reality is good because God is the "direction" of reality, its direction toward love and goodness. "God" means reality is good.

The radical intimacy of God and the world in the ecological model means that we can experience God's presence anywhere and everywhere. There is no place where God is not. Is this pantheism? Are we saying that God and the world are identical? No, they are not, but we are suggesting that one needs "double vision" to distinguish them. By "double vision" I mean that God is always present in mediated form, through something or someone else.[26] We do not meet God directly "face to face," but we do meet God in the world. As the body of God, the world is a sacrament, *the* sacrament, the incarnation, of God, so that while each thing is itself in all its marvelous particularity and uniqueness, *it is at the same time and in and through its own specialness,* the presence of God.[27] This is not pantheism because the world is not simply a manifestation of God; on the contrary, by means of each being's uniqueness, each rock's concrete contours, each tree's particular form, each galaxy's unique constellation, God is glorified. The God whose glory is each creature fully alive revels in differences, not in sameness. The God that fits with the ecological paradigm is the God for whom oneness is only achieved through the infinitely complex interrela-tionships and interdependencies of billions of different constituents, beings, and events. So, it is in and through this world, the very one that lies before us, that God is present, if God is present at all.

We have found it helpful to think of this relationship of God and the world in terms of agent and body, in terms of a body (the world) inspirited by God, a body made alive, kept alive, and pro-tected from destruction by God. One can imagine these processes of creation and its fulfillment occurring in many ways. Contempo-rary theologians have suggested some of these ways with the help of evolutionary and process thought.[28] The effort in most of these cases is to suggest how God's presence can be imagined in light of an evolutionary, ecological worldview without identifying the two or even necessarily suggesting that evolution is guided or directed by God.[29] Rather, the intent is to remythologize the world's story from the perspective of a particular religious tradition. That is, given belief in God as love, how can this belief be seen in terms of the current evolutionary worldview? Evolution does not prove or disprove the "existence of God" or the "goodness of reality." Rather, we ask, if one does so believe, can the ecological paradigm fit with such belief? We have here suggested that it not only fits, but that this view of God enhances the ecological, economic world-view even as this worldview gives concreteness, meaning, and detail to the belief in God's worldly presence.

In addition to God's presence in and through the natural processes of the world—as incarnated in everything—we can also

speak of this God, the agential/organic God, as particularly present
wherever and whenever creatures are helped to flourish. And this
places a special vocation on us human beings as the self-conscious
part of creation who know when we help others to flourish and
when we participate in their destruction. (Here is this view's definition of right action and of sin: helping others to flourish versus
participating in their destruction.) If God's presence is to be found
sacramentally everywhere, it is to be found especially in those
human beings who, as God's co-workers, improve the well-being
of some aspect of creation. Liberation theologies have been especially insightful on this point, insisting that God cannot do all the
work of salvation (that is, helping the world and especially the
oppressed to flourish). *We* human beings are the hands and feet of
God, manifestations of God's loving presence. If God is absent from
the world, it is because we are; made in God's image, as agents of
our own bodies, we are also God's auxiliary agents in and for the
body of the world—our lifework is to further the divine purpose
of planetary prosperity.

This means, of course, that we love God by loving the world,
but such loving can only be done in public, political, and economic
ways. The well-being of the planet is not a private, personal, or
"religious" matter; it has to do with public debate, political laws,
and economic policies. Theologians—and all religious people—
who accept this understanding of how we should love God will
become public advocates for political and economic policies that
promote fair distribution of necessities and the sustainability of the
planet. Theology is about these matters, about the well-being of
the earth, not about how to win eternal salvation or even how to
find personal peace and serenity.

Is Reality Good?

H. Richard Niebuhr claims that our most immediate awareness of
"the Transcendent or the Unconditioned or the Enveloping" is
negative, an awareness of distrust that manifests itself as hostility,
fear, and isolation.[30] And why shouldn't it be? To suggest that reality is *good* as one looks back over the twentieth century seems
absurd, if not immoral and outrageous. One does not need to
rehearse the horrors: the Holocaust and Hiroshima sum up the
depth and breadth of death and destruction that we have heaped

upon one another and the earth. It has never been easy to justify belief in God in light of history, but our century—and the one that looms before us—make the task seemingly impossible.

The classic form for discussing this issue is called "theodicy," which Webster's dictionary defines as "a vindication of God's justice in tolerating the existence of evil."[31] Or, more simply, How can an all-powerful, all-good God permit evil to exist? The question in theodicy is focused on defending God's justice. It has not proven to be a very successful venture; at most, two principal defenses have been proposed: an aesthetic one in which the magnificent panorama of the entire world-picture justifies the spots of evil here and there or a character-building justification in which the evil we experience on earth molds us into better people, fit for heaven.[32] Neither of these answers, however, encourages trust in reality; neither speaks to our basic distrust. They are rationalizations to save a particular view of God: God as the supernatural, super-individual who is all-powerful and all-good. This form of theism is close to deism: God is the being who can—and therefore should—manage all things so that evil does not have such a sway on earth and in our lives.

The neo-classical economic worldview is compatible with this view of God and evil. The relationship between God and evil is basically one of "management," of God, and we as God's viceroys, accenting the positive and diminishing the negative. The Protestant and Enlightenment views of human nature, as we have seen, are basically progressive and optimistic (curiously, given the Protestant emphasis on sin): the individual must take hold of his or her life and become successful by making things better through the acquisition of goods. Evil, both in its natural and moral forms—earthquakes and selfishness—are certainly part of existence in the neo-classical economic paradigm, but neither is insurmountable. Technology can diminish destruction from natural disasters and philanthropy helps to lessen the gap between the haves and the have-nots brought about by human selfishness. The neo-classical economic worldview is basically positive: human beings, made in the image of God, have power and goodness; hence, they can do much to diminish evil in the world. This is undoubtedly true, as statistics such as the Human Development Index indicate. Through technology, foreign aid, and charity, millions of poor people have received basic medical care, some education, and a better standard of living over the past century.

The difficulty with the foregoing view of God and evil—and ourselves and evil—is that it is "lightweight": it does not take evil seriously enough in two ways. First, it does not take human suffering seriously enough. Because the neo-classical economic view of human beings is focused on the successful individual, it does not see the depth of pain and suffering that most people living within this paradigm experience. The widening gap between the wealthy and the poor globally and the depths of despair that poor people experience in their daily struggle just to survive is not factored into the neo-classical view. It is not *felt*. If we are to say that "reality is good," it must be said in the face of the suffering of the most miserable human beings, not the favored. The affirmation that "reality is good" is not a comment on the serendipity of existence for the well-off; it must be, if said at all, a hard-won acknowledgment by the worst-off. Thus, from the perspective of the ecological economic paradigm, the place to stand for us middle-class North American Christians is not in our own shoes but in those of the most destitute human beings. The point of view from which we must be able to say "reality is good" is theirs, not ours.

Second, this view of evil is lightweight because it does not take our participation in evil seriously enough. It fudges on the blame issue: it tends to put the burden for evil on God, not ourselves—especially we better-off ones. It asks how *God* can permit bad things to happen, rather than what is increasingly the case, how can *we?* That is, from the perspective of the ecological economic worldview, the neo-classical paradigm puts too much emphasis on natural evil and not enough on moral evil.

One often hears in the aftermath of floods, hurricanes, or tornadoes, "Why did God let this happen?" One of the few places where God-talk emerges in contemporary society—absent as God generally is from it—occurs in regard to what the insurance companies call "acts of God." These are, presumably, "natural" disasters. The interesting point about them, however, is that they are increasingly human-generated disasters, not entirely natural and certainly not from God. If one understands that belief in God is parallel to saying that reality is good, then God could never be actively involved in the death of people in a tornado or from starvation.

But *we* are involved—increasingly. The link between "natural" disasters and our behavior is growing stronger—from the effects of global warming on weather crises and the way that global starvation is a matter of unjust distribution to the loss of species due to the expansion of the human population—we can see the finger of blame pointing at ourselves. While natural disasters are by no means human-caused—there have always been such events—even *they* are now at least partially our fault.[33] The line between natural and moral evil, between what we cannot help and what we can, is getting fuzzier all the time. Moreover, the greater evil is not even the worst of natural disasters, but the ordinary poverty, illiteracy, illnesses, and despair that a high percentage of the human population experience every day: more people die from malnutrition and starvation each year than in all natural disasters combined.[34]

So, *is* reality good? From the perspective of the ecological economic worldview, we would say, "Yes, but. . . ." The qualification is due to two factors. First, the evolutionary, ecological understanding of reality is so complex in terms of causes, changes, and intents among the billions of animate and inanimate constituents and forces that compose the universe that one has to ask, "good for whom?" What is good for the mosquito is not for the naked arm; the heart transplant that saves my life comes at the cost of another's life; the flood that destroys homes may benefit the crops. This is just the ways things are. If we want a world in which nothing bad happens to any person, tree, or elephant, then nothing could happen at all. The price of our infinitely complex, changing, beautiful, and diverse world is events that will be experienced by some as evil. The only alternative is robotization—everything and everyone programmed to act in simple, set ways. Thus, the first "perhaps" in our answer is that reality is necessarily "good" and "bad" depending on one's perspective. For this very reason, the ecological economic worldview insists that we take the perspective of those who suffer the greatest from the blind forces of evolutionary change and ecological interdependence.

But the second factor is even more important. "Reality is good" *if* we help it to become so. This is an acknowledgment that God is not the supernatural being who can control what happens, either at a natural or a personal level, but rather is the direction toward flourishing for all creatures. "God" is the belief that hope and not despair, life not death, laughter not tears are deep in the nature of things and that while despair, death, and tears are a necessary part of reality (as we have just seen), they are not the dominant part. But this is said, if said at all, in a small voice and with a "perhaps." Empirical evidence does not support this analysis; it is claimed in spite of the facts. The reason, however, why some people hold to it is because of the glimmers, partial incarnations, theophanies, flashes of goodness and love and beauty in the earth and in each other. It is the "double vision" possible when attending to ordinary things and people that prompts some to hope and believe. It is those moments of illumination when one has a glimpse of something better: another possibility, another way to live, another reading of reality beyond the usual one of distrust, fear, and hostility.

We realize then that if we are to say that reality is good, we must help those glimmers and glimpses become stronger: we must help reality to be good. The embodiment of God in the world is both an illumination of hope and a call to heal the pain of the suffering world. The affirmation that reality is good means that God is with us and that we must therefore be with God. Divine incarnation combined with our response of prophetic action on the side of the oppressed is the way that we can say, "Yes, reality is good."

We return in the end, however, to Julian of Norwich and her insistence that "all things shall be well," not because of confidence in ourselves or our efforts, but because of God. She does not mince words here. She claims that God attends to the simplest, smallest of things ("the least thing will not be forgotten") as well as the greatest of evils—the ones of which it seems "impossible that they should ever come to a good end." The smallest things and the greatest evils lie within God's care. She concludes with the boldest possible claim: "Take heed now in faith and trust, and at the last end you will see it truly in the fullness of joy." Our response can only be to say, "Amen—so be it."[35]

7. Christ and Salvation

An ecological economic Christology can be summarized by the phrase 'God with us.' . . . An ecological economic Christology means that *God* is with us—we are dealing with the power and love of the universe; it means that God is *with* us— on our side, desiring justice and health and fulfillment for us; it means that God is with *us*—all of us, all people and all other life-forms, but especially those who do not have justice, health, and fulfillment.

—Sallie McFague

Christ and the Neo-Classical Economic Worldview

ONE ANSWER THAT CHRISTIANS HAVE GIVEN to the question "Is reality good?" points to Jesus' death and resurrection as the confirmation that God conquers evil and gives eternal life. In conventional theology Jesus Christ takes the sins of the entire world—past, present, and future—upon himself. Through his sacrificial death he achieves forgiveness for all our sins; through his resurrection we are assured of eternal life. Since Jesus Christ is "fully God and fully human," the second person of the trinity, according to the orthodox position, he *can* accomplish our redemption: as God he has the power to do so and as man he stands for and includes all human beings in his saving death and life-giving resurrection. Through the sacraments, especially the eucharist, and the reading of Scripture, we become active participants in God's saving deed in Christ. For these gifts of forgiveness of sins and eternal life, we should show our gratitude by loving God and neighbor.

This Christology is very satisfying psychologically: it is aimed at releasing individuals from the burden of their sins. The slate is wiped clean, and we can start over with a clear conscience and the desire to live better, more charitably, more compassionately. This Christology has its merits as a religion of comfort for the spiritually afflicted and of guidance for right living.

Personally, I have never been able to believe it. Nor does it answer for me the question of whether reality is good. However, like millions of other North American Christians, I was brought up on this Christology. But early on I had "trouble with Jesus"; in fact, many troubles. I mention this because having trouble with Jesus is one of the common reasons why people drop out of the church. A Christian (and a Christian theology) stands or falls with Christology. Being a Christian means identifying with, taking the name of Christ. There is no way for Christians to avoid Jesus.

So, what is wrong with the conventional picture of a mythological savior who descends from heaven and, as the God-man, shows us how to live, forgives our sins, and wins eternal life for us? While this may sound like a caricature of Christology, it is the bare-bones version that is deep in Western Christianity and even in Western culture. It is the picture, the image, of Christ that we sing about in Christmas carols and recite in the church's creeds and that has been embodied in Western sculpture, novels, poetry, and music. The Christian iconography of Western art is imbued with the story of a king who became a servant to die on a cross for the sins of the world that we might all be forgiven and have eternal life. The story begins and ends in heaven: with God the Father sending his only Son down to earth, that through his death and resurrection all human beings might finally, at the story's close, be united with God in heaven.

So, once again, what is wrong with this story? I would suggest two things: it is not believable, and it is bad theology. Perhaps not much needs to be said on the first point: the traditional story, the product of first-century Mediterranean and early medieval culture, is no longer credible within the postmodern scientific understanding of reality.[1] The three-story universe, the descending and ascending preexistent Christ, the Aristotelian terminology that claims Jesus to be "of one substance" with God as well as fully human and so forth, are *barriers* to believing in the reality of God, let alone in divine goodness. This Christology is a scandal to the intellect, which Christology should not and need not be. It is *right* to find this Christology *wrong,* because it puts the offense of Christ at the wrong place. Christ is not merely or mainly an assault on the mind; believing in Christ is not a matter of religion versus science.[2]

But the deeper issue is the bad theology that lies behind this picture. It is, of course, only "bad" from a particular context of interpretation and set of criteria. Given the criteria I am using and the context of the ecological economic paradigm, it is bad theology. But it is "good" from the perspective of the neo-classical economic worldview because of three of its central features: it is a form of "Jesusolatry"; it is individualistic and anthropocentric; and it understands salvation in purely spiritual terms. These three characteristics fit well with the conventional economic paradigm.

On the first point, since Jesusolatry means the worship of Jesus, in this Christology "Jesus does it all"; it is an interpretation of Christianity in which Jesus is the focus of attention. In the traditional picture, the incarnation of God occurs at one point and one point only in the world—in the man Jesus.[3] God is not everywhere all the time, for, apart from creating the world, God enters it just once. The incarnation of God in Jesus is a "miracle," something unlike anything else we have ever known.[4] Moreover, not only is Jesus entirely different from the rest of us, but what he accomplishes, especially his death and resurrection, is total salvation on our behalf. The sacrificial, substitutionary atonement and its variations assert full and complete redemption by Jesus Christ in place of and for all humankind.[5] Salvation, or liberation, is not a joint project in which we join with God in Christ to help all creatures flourish; in fact, since the Reformation, the primacy of grace over works has been emphasized in all forms of traditional Christianity. The resurrection also is understood as concentrated on Jesus; it is new life given to Jesus, and to us only as we are joined to him.

These characteristics of Jesusolatry mean God's focus and ours is on Jesus: he is God's unique incarnation, sacrifice, and resurrection, and for these services human beings must turn to Jesus. Essentially, all this takes place outside and apart from us; God is not always and everywhere with us and we with God. This theology is bad, I believe, because it limits God and excuses us. If God is present only in Jesus and if Jesus "does it all," then we do not have to meet God in the face of a starving person or in the remains of a clear-cut forest, nor do we have to help that starving person or that devastated forest. We can confine God to Jesus and to Jesus' work of forgiving human sins. This theology is convenient for an economic paradigm that does not want religion intruding into economic matters: here God is concerned primarily with individuals and their personal failings.

We have already touched on the other two reasons that the traditional christological story is bad theology (at least from the perspective of the ecological economic worldview): its individualism and spiritualism. The traditional story focuses on human beings, not the whole cosmos, and on human beings as individuals, not as beings-in-community. To be sure, traditional theology has at times also been cosmological and political, but its contemporary, conventional form is neither. Rather, it is psychological. Salvation is not for the well-being of the whole planet and all its peoples, but is focused on a narrow slice of creation—just us, and moreover, us as individuals. Whether in its evangelical or New Age form, current Christianity is therapeutic, oriented to making human beings better and happier. As in the limitation of God to Jesus, here we have the limitation of God's concern to us. Again, it is a convenient Christology for the neo-classical economic paradigm because it focuses divine interest on the personal and moral failings of individuals. If divine care extended to the liberation of the entire earth, then cosmological and political concerns would be seen as "religious matters" or, stated in the reverse, religion would be involved, deeply and permanently, in ecological and political questions. And, as we have seen, ecological and political questions are intrinsically also economic questions—the management of the well-being of planet Earth and all its creatures. Hence, religion would be especially concerned with economic policy.

Finally, the traditional story of salvation is spiritualistic, not physical. This is mystifying, since the story is about incarnation, the Word becoming *flesh,* but the ascetic, anti-world perspective is old and deep in Christianity.[6] Needless to say, this is also highly convenient for an economic worldview that gives priority to individual desires rather than to the just distribution of necessities or the sustainability of nature. The neo-classical paradigm is strangely blind to the state of the physical base on which all its profits rest as well as to the physical needs of the majority of individuals whose desires it claims to be concerned about. It is oriented, rather, to unlimited growth and especially the growth of consumer goods for those who can afford to buy them.

In sum, this picture of contemporary Christianity, while not the product of the neo-classical paradigm, is the version of Christianity that best fits with it. It is a docile, non-threatening partner.

Ecological Christologies

As we have seen, contemporary Christianity is psychologically oriented rather than politically or cosmologically. Liberation theologies have widened the context to the political realm, insisting, with a good deal of biblical support, that Christian faith has a "preferential option for the poor." These theologies question the limitation of God's action in Christ to the individual and his or her sins and serenity. They insist that God in Christ cares for all people and especially for the poor and oppressed, and particularly for the physical needs of these people. Liberation theologies have radically questioned the basic assumptions of conventional theology that the neo-classical paradigm finds convenient. They question its Jesusolatry, individualism, and spiritualism. Christian faith, they claim, is about God acting through Christ and with us for the well-being of all people, especially the oppressed. Jesus does not do it all (we must help); salvation is not just to alleviate individual sins; liberation must be for the body as well as the spirit. But liberation theologies, at least until recently, have been mainly political: God's concern is limited to human beings, albeit needy ones. So, we must ask, can Christianity be ecological? It has been shown to be concerned with oppressed peoples, but is its central and distinctive doctrine—Christology—capable of being interpreted authentically as "ecological"? Is such an interpretation *Christian* as well as timely?

Thirty years ago when Lynn White, in a now-famous essay, accused Christianity of being ecologically bankrupt, he revealed ignorance of theological history.[7] To be sure, for the last few centuries Christianity's celebrated "turn to the self" has meant a neglect of nature and, as liberation theologians have pointed out, millions of oppressed human beings as well. But it was not always so. From the earliest days of Christianity, the cosmological context was a major interpretive category along with the psychological and the political.[8] The renewal of creation, the salvation of the individual, and the liberation of the people were all seen as necessary components of the work of God in Christ. The cosmological context—the assertion that the Redeemer is the Creator—is deeply rooted in Hebrew faith and surfaces in John's incarnational Christology, the Pauline cosmic Christ, Irenaeus's notion of Christ recapitulating all of creation, as well as in sacramental motifs in Augustine and Thomas. Christianity is not entirely anthropocentric, although it was substantially so from the Enlightenment until recently, and therein lies the justification for White's indictment.

Since Christology is the heart of Christianity, we must ask whether Christology can be ecological. This question cannot be answered simply by citing Christianity's cosmological roots. What creation meant in the first or third or twelfth century cannot answer the question how Christians can act responsibly toward nature in the twenty-first century.

Jesus' enigmatic question to Peter, "Who do you say that I am?" must be answered differently in every age. Is there an ecological answer? This is not a frivolous question; in fact, it is one of the central questions that recent theologians have tried to answer, and it is one that cannot be avoided. To be a Christian is to deal with Jesus; Jesus is, for Christians, Emmanuel, God with us. Hence, current issues of oppression needing God's saving grace provide the contexts for christological interpretation. In our time ecology is one such important context. Christologies written since White's essay appeared thirty years ago acknowledge this context and reveal a wealth of ecological potential.

A typology of some of these Christologies includes the following motifs: prophetic, wisdom, sacramental, eschatological, process, and liberation. While a theologian's Christology might embrace several motifs, a typology can only lift up the ecological assets and limitations of each. Thus, like all typologies, it will be artificial but can at least suggest the rich ecological potential of contemporary Christologies.

Prophetic Christology

Prophetic or covenantal Christologies focus on Jesus' ministry to the oppressed—his inheritance of Hebraic concerns with justice, evident in his parables overturning conventional hierarchies, in his healings to the suffering, and in his practice of eating with outcasts. Jesus is paradigmatic of a way of life that ends on the cross, since the rights of the oppressed will usually be opposed by the powerful. For the disciples who practice this way, life will be cruciform, characterized by justice for the oppressed and limitations on the oppressor. This Christology is easily extended to nature: nature is the "new poor"; nature deserves justice; other life-forms have rights that must be acknowledged; human beings are in a covenantal relationship with God to protect nature even as they should care for other human beings.[9] The ecological value of prophetic Christologies is the insistence that Jesus' message of justice is relevant to nature: other life-forms are not means to our ends, but like human subjects, have intrinsic worth and should be considered as deserving ethical consideration. Prophetic Christologies give a firm base for extending *rights* to other life-forms, countering the supposition that sentimental attachment to nature is sufficient. A limitation of this position is its possible deformation toward individualism; for example, total emphasis on the rights of particular animals rather than focus on the well-being of an entire ecosystem.

Wisdom Christology

Wisdom Christologies understand Jesus as the embodiment of *Sophia,* God's creative and ordering energy in both the human and natural worlds.[10] Connecting the Jesus of the Logos tradition (which is largely anthropocentric) to the Hebraic Wisdom trajectory allows his work to include nature. As Elizabeth Johnson writes, "As the embodiment of *Sophia* who is fashioner of all that exists, Jesus' redeeming care extends to the flourishing of all creatures and the whole earth itself."[11] A form of incarnationalism, Wisdom Christologies understand the divine in Jesus (and in his followers) in a natural, everyday way—wherever justice, care, and respect for others, including nature, occur—rather than focused on "once-for-all sacred deeds in history."[12] The ecological value of this Christology is its turn to the earth, a turn that contemporary Christians profoundly need. The rich textual resources of the Hebrew Scriptures for reinterpreting Jesus' work and person in Wisdom imagery has ecological potential for both liturgy and ethics. The considerable assets of this tradition in supporting everyday life point to a limitation: it says little about the cross that is integral to Christian faith.

Sacramental Christology

Sacramental Christologies are characterized by divine immanentalism, the incarnation of God in Jesus (and often in the world at large).[13] Whether the form of divine incarnation is the Logos, Wisdom, or the Spirit, the direction of these Christologies is toward immanentalism, overcoming the traditional emphasis in Christianity on divine transcendence—often God-world dualism. These Christologies can see Jesus as the explicit expression of what is implicit everywhere: divine presence. As Gerard Manley Hopkins expresses the sacramental perspective, "The world is charged with the grandeur of God."[14] While a narrow incarnational Christology—Jesus alone as embodying divine presence—is anthropocentric, a wider incarnational interpretation is very hospitable to ecological concerns: God is in nature as well as in Jesus. And all of nature, human beings included, is knit together organically. This wider view was the basis for the oldest Christian affirmation of nature, seen preeminently in Augustine and his love of "light and melody and fragrance and food and embrace" as ways to God.[15] Incarnationalism affirms the flesh, the body, and hence, by implication, nature. But as we are all well aware, Christianity's extraordinary verbal affirmation of the body—bread and wine as the body and blood of Christ, the resurrection of the body, the church as the body of Christ—has not resulted in appreciation for bodies (especially the female body), or until recently, great concern for starving, tortured, or raped human bodies. And it certainly has not resulted in a love of nature. Hence, while sacramental Christologies find God in nature, do they respect nature itself? Do they pay attention to the other or do they use it, however subtly, as a way to God?

Eschatological, Process, and Liberation Christologies

The three other types of Christology—eschatological, process, and liberation—can be dealt with more briefly, for in significant ways they overlap with prophetic, wisdom, and sacramental Christologies. However, each of them offers one or more significant notes for an ecological Christology.

Eschatological Christologies, such as those of Jürgen Moltmann and Catherine Keller, underscore renewal and hope: God's Spirit working in Christ re-creates, transforms, the entire universe toward reconciliation and peace. As the firstborn of the new creation, the resurrected Christ symbolizes the power of life over death. Nothing, no scrap of creation, will be excluded from this new life: "the body of Christ is the whole cosmos."[16]

Eschatological Christologies speak to one of the most difficult issues in ecological praxis: despair. The slow unraveling of the earth's living networks permits human beings to be in a state of denial concerning the seriousness of the deterioration. Those who wake up to reality often experience hopelessness: Can anything be done? The eschatological images of a resurrected creation speak to this despair.

Process Christologies also provide ecological motifs; specifically, those of nature's intrinsic worth and its interrelationship and interdependence.[17] Similar in some respects to sacramental Christologies in their stress on organic unity, process Christologies differentiate the subjects in this unified body more adequately. In process thought, since everything, from an atom to God, is both subject and object, the intrinsic worth of all beings, including those in the natural world, is affirmed. The process view of the one and the many, of unity and differentiation, is close to the ecological view: unity is characterized by radical individuation in networks of profound interrelationship and interdependence. Process thinking offers a contemporary way to speak of the subjecthood or intrinsic worth of *all* life-forms.

Finally, a word about the contributions to an ecological Christology from the very broad and diverse category called liberation theologies.[18] To a significant degree, most liberation Christologies fall under the prophetic type, focusing as they do on Jesus' ministry to the oppressed and his death as a consequence of this solidarity. Initially, most liberation Christologies were not cosmological; in fact, they were militantly political, concerned with the liberation of oppressed people and often only of people with a particular oppression. But increasingly, liberation theologies have recognized the intrinsic connections between human oppression and nature's oppression. Thus, Leonardo Boff speaks of social ecology as "the study [of] social systems in interaction with ecosystems," acknowledging the way human and nature's well-being are mutually dependent.[19] Likewise, Chung Hyun Kyung invokes the Spirit through the spirits of all the oppressed, from the murdered "spirit of the Amazon rainforest" to the spirits of exploited women and indigenous peoples, victims of the Holocaust and of Hiroshima, as well as Hagar, Jephthah's daughter, Malcolm X, Oscar Romero, and all other life-forms, human and nonhuman, that like "the Liberator, our brother Jesus," have been tortured and killed for greed and through hate.[20] Thus, recent liberation theologies make an essential contribution to an ecological Christology: they point to the intrinsic connection between all forms of oppression, and especially between that of poor people and degraded nature.

From our brief overview of recent Christologies, we can appreciate the ecological potential they offer. Specifically, the following points emerge as needed dimensions of a Christology that both fits with and goes beyond the ecological economic worldview: the appreciation of the intrinsic worth of all life-forms, not just of human beings; the need to turn to the earth, respecting it and caring for it in local, ordinary, mundane ways; the acknowledgment that human salvation or well-being and nature's health are intrinsically connected; the insistence on justice to the oppressed, including nature, and the realization that solidarity with the oppressed will result in cruciform living for the affluent; the recognition that God is with us, embodied not only in Jesus of Nazareth but in all of nature, thus uniting creation and sanctifying bodily life; and, finally, the promise of a renewed creation through the hope of the resurrection, a promise that includes the entire cosmos and speaks to our ecological despair.

An Ecological Economic Christology: Prophetic and Sacramental

Can these various motifs be united into an ecological economic Christology? I am sure there are many ways they might be; I will attempt just one. Needless to say, my attempt will be from my own context as a white, North American, middle-class feminist. Its limitations and partiality will be obvious.

My attempt at an ecological economic Christology can be summarized by the phrase "God with us." I will try to unpack this phrase in several stages of increasing detail. An ecological economic Christology means that *God* is with us—we are dealing with the power and love of the universe; it means that God is *with* us—on our side, desiring justice and health and fulfillment for us; it means that God is with *us*—all of us, all people and all other life-forms, but especially those who do not have justice, health, or fulfillment. This Christology would then be very "high" and very "low": it will acknowledge that in Jesus we see nothing less than the presence of *God,* but that God's presence is embodied, paradigmatically, in a mere human being. However, such a Christology, centered as it is on *God's* presence with *all* of us, is not Jesusolatry: Jesus is the finger pointing to the moon.

An ecological economic Christology summarized by the phrase "God with us" focuses on the ministry of Jesus of Nazareth for the content of our praxis toward oppressed people and deteriorating nature and on the incarnation and resurrection for its range and promise. What is a Christian ecological, economic praxis? How inclusive is it? Can we practice it without despair?

Prophetic Christology

The first question is answered in the prophetic ministry of Jesus and his death on a cross. While there is little in the New Testament about nature (and it is futile to rummage about with fig trees and hens, trying to make Jesus into a nature lover), his ministry to the oppressed can be extended to nature. His parables, which overturn conventional human hierarchies, should include the hierarchy of humans over nature; his healing stories can be extended to the deteriorating ecosystems of our planet; his practice of eating with outcasts is pertinent to the extinction of species and loss of habitats due to human overdevelopment and consumption. Who the oppressed are—those to whom Jesus' message of hope and renewal is preached—has changed over the centuries. The circle has also widened to include the poor, as well as those suffering due to gender, race, sexual orientation, physical and mental challenges. From an anthropocentric perspective, the inclusion of nature as the "new poor" may seem sentimental or even ludicrous, but it does not seem so from either a theocentric or a cosmocentric point of view. If the Redeemer is the Creator, then surely God cares for the 99 percent of creation, not just for the 1 percent (actually, less than 1 percent) that humans constitute.

Hence, I am suggesting that all the language about justice, rights, care, and concern that Christians believe the human neighbor, especially the oppressed neighbor, deserves should be extended to the natural world. What this will mean in practice is complex, varied, and costly—just as love for the needy neighbor is—but the principle that Jesus' ministry is focused on God's oppressed creatures must, in our day, include the deteriorating planet.

To say that Jesus' ministry to the oppressed should be extended to nature is the same as suggesting that the Great Commandments should be. We are told to love God and neighbor as "subjects," as valuable in and for themselves, as ends rather than means, but we are given no instructions concerning nature. Should we not extend that model—the model of loving others as having intrinsic worth and hence deserving of justice and care—to the natural world?

Jesus' ministry to the oppressed resulted in his death on a cross. Solidarity with the oppressed is likely to end this way, as many of his loyal disciples over the centuries have discovered. This suggests a theology of the cross: reality has a cruciform shape. Jesus did not invent the idea that from death comes new life. We see it in nature; for instance, in the "nurse logs" on the ground in old-growth forests, which, in their decaying state, provide warmth and nutrients for new saplings. Some must give that others might live. Raising the cruciform shape of reality to the central principle for human living is Jesus' contribution.

But it is not easy to live this way, especially for the well-to-do. Cruciform living has particular relevance to today's affluent Christians, whether of the first or third worlds, in regard to their praxis toward nature. Our consumer culture defines the "abundant life" as one in which "natural resources" are sacrificed for human profit and pleasure and "human resources" are the employees who will work for the lowest wages. Both nature and poor people are means to the end of consumerism. The World Council of Churches in several of its recent publications has stated that it is crucial to redefine the abundant life in terms that recognize the limits of our planet, that encourage sustainable communities, that embrace a philosophy of "enoughness."[21] For affluent Christians this should mean a different understanding of abundance, one that embraces the contradiction of the cross: giving up one's life to find it, limitation and diminishment, sharing and giving—indeed, sacrifice.

Sacramental Christology

"God with us" also suggests the range and promise of divine concern. In prophetic Christology we considered what it meant ecologically and economically to say God with us; now we consider the inclusivity of justice to and care of people and nature as well as its possibility. In sacramental Christology we move from the anthropological to the metaphysical: from the human Jesus and his distinctive ministry and death to issues of divine scope and power. This metaphysical move is necessary because Christology is not just about a prophet, even a unique prophet, but about *God*. This move avoids Jesusolatry and anti-Judaism; it also means salvation is not just for me or for humans, but for all of creation, and it gives hope for the well-being of all. In other words, sacramental Christology underscores that it is *God* with whom we are dealing (and who is dealing with us) and that this God cares for the entire creation. And since *God* is with us, we need not despair of the outcome. We are, then, concerned here with the incarnation and the resurrection, with the embodiment of God in creation as well as the hope of a new creation.

The incarnation is a crucial feature of an ecological economic Christology for two reasons: inclusion and embodiment. By bringing God into the realm of the body, of matter, nature is included within the divine reach. This inclusion, however, is possible only if incarnation is understood in a broad, not a narrow fashion; that is, if Jesus as the incarnate Logos, Wisdom, or Spirit of God is paradigmatic of what is evident everywhere else as well.[22] In other words, nature, not just Jesus, is the sacrament of God; the entire creation is *imago dei,* as Thomas Aquinas suggests when he claims that the whole panorama of creation is needed to reflect the divine glory.[23] The scope of God's power and love is cosmological; it must include every scrap of creation: atoms and newts, black holes and elephants, giant redwoods and dinosaurs. Otherwise, God would not be God. The logic of divinity pushes to the limits; a God of history is a lesser God than the God of nature, since human history is embraced within nature. Christianity has expressed this inclusivity with the phrase "the cosmic Christ."

In addition to inclusivity, incarnational Christology underscores embodiment. The tradition has expressed this in John's phrase "the Word became flesh," as well as in its rich body language. But often, Logos Christologies are narrow, validating only Jesus' flesh. Recent Spirit and Wisdom Christologies widen the range: both can include other life-forms—the Spirit of God can dwell in spirits other than human ones, and Wisdom makes her home in creation.[24] Incarnational Christology valorizes matter; moreover, it focuses the justice and care of the prophetic dimension of Christology on physical needs and well-being. Incarnational Christology means that salvation is neither solely human nor spiritual; it must be for the entire creation and it must address what makes different creatures and ecosystems flourish. Incarnational Christology says that God wants all of nature, human beings and all other entities, to enjoy well-being in body and spirit. Incarnational Christology, then, expands the ministry and death of Jesus, the model for

Christians of "God with us," to envelop the entire universe. The metaphysical dimension of Christology is its Big Bang, exploding that gram of matter to the limits of the universe.

Sacramental Christology adds one more crucial note to an ecological Christology: in addition to inclusion and embodiment, it adds hope. There are few contemporary issues that engender more despair than ecological deterioration: global warming, the extinction of species and habitats, clear-cutting of old-growth forests, the pollution of streams and lakes—the problems are overwhelming, seemingly infinite, and deeply saddening. To be sure, many people deny that there is ecological decay because they fear the costly personal and commercial changes that are necessary to reverse it. But others, even those who feel ready to live in a cruciform way so that other people and creatures can survive, feel despair over the immensity and complexity of environmental issues. Needless to say, the resurrection will not solve our ecological crisis; it will not tell us what to do with regard to either small or large problems.

But it can give us hope. Whatever else the resurrection might mean, it certainly symbolizes the triumph of life over death. As Dante knew a long time ago when he wrote *The Divine Comedy*, Christianity is not a tragic vision. The resurrection claims, as a woman in labor knows and as we also see in nature, that new life is hard; it is usually preceded by diminishment and pain; it sometimes involves death. But it is a sign of hope. Christians see the resurrection of Christ as the first day of the new creation; his resurrection is emblematic of the power of God on the side of life and its fulfillment. We are not alone as we struggle to save our planet: *God* is on our side.

In summary, an ecological economic Christology characterized by the prophetic and the sacramental, claims that "God is with us." This Christology looks Godward through Jesus: Jesus is the model for Christians of what "God with us" means. God is with us in Jesus' particular ministry of justice and care as well as in his death, which gives us a pattern for cruciform living. God is also with us through inclusive divine embodiment, valorizing physical well-being as well as divine victory over the powers of death and despair. Both of these dimensions—the prophetic and the sacramental—are necessary in an ecological, economic Christology: the one tells us how to live with others and with nature; the other informs us that all of creation is within divine love and power, as is our hope for creation's well-being.[25] Together, they suggest an ecological economic Christology summarized by "God with us." The focus of this Christology is not on Jesus except as the lens through whom we see God. Hope for our world lies not only in what Jesus tells us to do, but also, and more deeply, in Christian belief that God is with us as we attempt to do it.

Ezekiel's valley of the dry bones, one of Scripture's most haunting and lovely resurrection texts, comes to mind when we reflect on our partnership with God. When God leads Ezekiel to the valley and asks him, "Mortal, can these bones live?" Ezekiel answers (with, one imagines, a bit of despair), "O Lord God, you know." God then undertakes a second creation story, forming sinews, flesh, and skin onto dry bones, bringing life out of death, but God does not do it alone, as in the first creation story. Now God has two helpers: a human being and nature. Ezekiel is the mediator of God's word, told by God to prophesy to the bones, which he does, and they come together, bone to bone, forming a whole being. The body, however, is still dead—there is no breath in it. So God calls on a second helper, nature, the "four winds," to supply the breath. Then the new beings became alive and stood up. The power of life can override the reality of death with the help of God's partners, human beings and nature itself. The passage says that with God all things are possible, even the reconstitution of dry bones.

In my mind's eye I see huge mounds of elephant bones, remnants of the ivory trade, the spindly remains of an old-growth forest after a clear-cut, and the visible skeleton of a starving child. Can they also live? Those who trust in the God of creation and recreation, the God of the resurrection, answer Yes—even these dry bones can live. But, remembering the cruciform reality of Christian life, we must add, only if we, as partners of God, turn from ecological selfishness and live a *different* abundant life.

Christ and the Ecological Economic Worldview

Aye, here's the rub: how *can* we live a different abundant life? The ecological economic worldview gives few instructions and even less hope. We have suggested that an ecological economic Christology not only fits with this worldview but goes beyond it. How is this the case? How can Christology help us live a different abundant life? As a dramatic and concrete way of answering this question, let us look at some of the interesting results of recent scholarship on the historical Jesus.[26]

The figure who emerges from these studies is peculiarly fitted to help us embrace the ecological economic worldview. More than that, this figure goes beyond and intensifies what living within this worldview means. The conventional image of Jesus (the one we have suggested fits with the neo-classical economic model) and the emerging one are summed up in the two following statements:

> Jesus was the divinely begotten Son of God, whose mission was to die for the sins of the world, and whose message was about himself, the saving purpose of his death, and the importance of believing in him.[27]

> Rather strikingly, the most certain thing we know about Jesus according to the current scholarly consensus is that he was a teller of stories and a speaker of great one-liners whose purpose was the transformation of perception. At the center of his message was an invitation to see differently.[28]

In the conventional view, Jesus does something for all the rest of us—he dies for our sins—and our role is to believe in him. In the second scenario, Jesus invites us into a different way of seeing—a transformation of perception—and our role is to follow him. We are to see as he sees and live accordingly.

And what is it that he sees? According to a number of contemporary New Testament scholars, Jesus was a social revolutionary—he saw a different way of living in the world. He was not primarily interested in political upheaval, but, as is evident in his parables and wisdom sayings, he was opposed to the various forms of domination and domestication that cast some people in a superior position and others in an inferior one, whether from purity laws, eating customs, gender discrimination, economic disparities, or ethnic/racial divisions.[29] Above all else, he invited people to imagine a different life, one centered in God and inclusive of all others—and then to live it. It is a revolutionary vision because it goes against the conventional hierarchies and dualisms (however these are understood in different cultures) and invites us to see the world in a radically new way—a way that has some similarities with the community model of ecological economics. It is a vision of the world opposed to an individualistic, merit-centered view of human life with insiders and outsiders, haves and have-nots. It is just as clearly on the side of a community-oriented, egalitarian view of human life, inclusive of all living beings.

How is this portrait of the historical Jesus relevant to a Christology for an ecological, economic worldview? If all contemporary understandings of Christ should be grounded in historical judgments about Jesus of Nazareth—if there should be continuity between the Jesus of history and the Christ of faith—then we need to see if the ecological economic context is an appropriate one for reconstructing Christology for our time.[30] Who is the Jesus that grounds our discipleship for planetary living in the twenty-first century?

Let us look at the vivid portrait of Jesus by New Testament scholar John Dominic Crossan. "The open commensality and radical egalitarianism of Jesus' Kingdom of God are more terrifying than anything we have ever imagined, and even if we can never accept it, we should not explain it away as something else."[31] For Jesus, the Kingdom of God was epitomized by everyone being invited to the table; the Kingdom is known by radical equality at the level of bodily needs. Crossan names the Parable of the Feast as central to understanding what Jesus means by the Kingdom of God. This is a shocking story, trespassing society's boundaries of class, gender, status, and ethnicity—as its end result is inviting *all* to the feast. There are several versions (Matt. 22:1-13; Luke 14:15-24; Gospel of Thomas 64), but in each a prominent person invites other, presumably worthy, people to a banquet, only to have them refuse: one to survey a land purchase, another to try out some new oxen, a third to attend a wedding. The frustrated host then tells his servants to go out into the streets of the city and bring whomever they find to dinner: the poor, maimed, blind, lame, good and bad (the list varies in the three versions). The shocking implication is that everyone—*anyone*—is invited. As Crossan remarks, if beggars come to your door, you might give them food or even invite them into the kitchen for a meal, but you don't ask them to join the family in the dining room or invite them back on Saturday night for supper with your friends.[32] But that is exactly what happens in this story. The Kingdom of God, according to this portrait of Jesus, is "more terrifying than anything we have imagined" because it demolishes all our carefully constructed boundaries between the worthy and the unworthy and does so at the most physical, bodily level.

For first-century Jews, the key boundary was purity laws: one did not eat with the poor, women, the diseased, or the "unrighteous." For us, the critical barrier is economic laws: one is not called to the just or sustainable allocation of resources with the poor, the disadvantaged, the "lazy." To do otherwise in both cultures is improper, not expected—in fact, shocking. And yet, in both cases, the issue is the most basic bodily one—who is invited to share the food—in other words, the issue is who lives and who dies? In both cases, the answer is the same: everyone, regardless of status (by any criteria), is invited.

We North American middle-class Christians may not be terrified by the unclean, but we are by the poor. There are so many of them—billions! Surely we cannot be responsible for all of them! Yet, this historical Jesus appears to disagree: he is not, it seems, interested so much in "religion," including his own, as in human well-being, beginning with the body: feeding the hungry and healing the suffering. Moreover, his message, according to Crossan, had less to do with what Jesus did for others than what others might do for their neighbors.

> The Kingdom of God was not, for Jesus, a divine monopoly exclusively bound to his own person. It began at the level of the body and appeared as a shared community of healing and eating—that is to say, of spiritual and physical resources available to each and all without distinctions, discrimination, or hierarchies. One entered the Kingdom as a way of life and anyone who could live it could bring it to others. It was not just words alone, or deeds alone, but both together as life-style.[33]

The body is the locus: how we treat needy bodies gives the clue to how a society is organized. It suggests that correct "table manners" are a sign of a just society, the Kingdom of God. If one accepts this interpretation, the "table" becomes not primarily the priestly consecrated bread and wine of communion celebrating Jesus' death for the sins of the world, but rather the egalitarian meals of bread and fishes that one finds throughout Jesus' ministry.[34] At these events, all are invited, with no authoritarian brokering, to share in the food, whether it be meager or sumptuous. Were such an understanding of the eucharist to infiltrate Christian churches today, it could be mind changing—in fact, perhaps world changing.

At the very least, it is indeed terrifying. It is also absurd, foolish, and utopian. But, as we have suggested, there appears to be a solid link, a degree of continuity, between this reconstruction of society and what we have described as the ecological economic worldview. This worldview is closer to that terrifying picture than is the neo-classical economic model. If this is the case, then for us middle-class North American Christians it may well mean that *sin* is refusing to acknowledge that link, that continuity, explaining it away because we will not accept the consequences for our privileged lifestyle. Sustainability and the just distribution of resources are concerned with human and planetary well-being for all. This is, I suggest, the responsible interpretation of the Parable of the Feast for us. It demands that we look at the structural institutions and systemic forms separating the haves and the have-nots in our time, those invited to the table and those excluded. And it demands that we name them for what they are: evil. They are the collective forms of "our sin." They are the institutions, laws, and international bodies of market capitalism (often aided by the silence of the church) that allow some to get richer and most to become poorer. Our sin is one of commission but perhaps more damningly of omission: our greed camouflaged by indifference and denial—and even by our "charity."

This picture of the historical Jesus suggests some directions for us: it gives us some guidance as we seek a liberation theology for middle-class North American twenty-first-century Christians. It does so in three ways: it suggests what to do, how to do it, and when and where to do it. It gives us a message, a ministry, and marching orders. At the center of Jesus' message as prophet and wisdom teacher is the vision of a world as an egalitarian commu-nity of beings, not a hierarchy of individuals. His parables and aphorisms disorient our conventional expectations and suggest a way of being in the world where all are valued, especially the vul-nerable and outcast. He shows us *how* to live this message by doing so himself: his unsettling parables and sayings are embodied in his own practices of living among the marginalized and siding with those considered inferior by conventional standards. He tells us also when and where to do it: now and here. Recent interpretation of

Jesus' notion of the kingdom of God shifts it from an otherworldly, existentialist, individualistic abode to a this-worldly, public, and communal vision of new life now for all.[35] The message, ministry, and marching orders that emerge from current historical Jesus research are summed up by Marcus Borg: "As a charismatic who was also a subversive sage, prophet, and renewal movement founder, Jesus sought a transformation in the historical shape and direction of his social world."[36]

This evangelism or good news, however, is not offered as an imperative or as an accomplished fact, but rather as an invitation: it is not telling us to believe something or accept something but inviting us to live differently. It does not appear to be principally a matter of the intellect or the will, but of the heart. The alternative to the conventional hierarchical, dualistic paradigm of life is, according to Jesus, the way of death to the old life and rebirth to the new.[37] At the center of this new life is love to God and others: not just a moderate or "sensible" love, but God-intoxication and compassion for others that knows no limits.[38]

How is this possible? Would such a person be human? Can we be totally engrossed by God and totally and empathetically involved with others?[39] There have been some people who approach this ideal—we call them saints and they appear in all religious traditions. For Christians, Jesus' life is of course the prototype, but it is sometimes easier to argue from the reflection rather than the model (the latter being too overlain with god-like trappings). One of the consistent characteristics of the Christian disciples revered as saints is precisely this combination of God-intoxication and universal compassion for others. Those who have followed Jesus most radically, regardless of their other errors and failings— people like Paul, Augustine, Teresa of Avila, Julian of Norwich, John Woolman, Pierre Teilhard de Chardin, Dorothy Day, Dietrich Bonhoeffer, Sojourner Truth, Martin Luther King Jr., Mother Teresa, and many others less well known—passionately loved both God and the world (and everything in it). Their spirituality and their ethics emerge from excessive dual love, as Teilhard de Chardin puts it, plunging them into God and into matter.[40] These people seem to know no limits, either in their outrageous intimacy with God nor with their borderless love for all living things. They saw things differently because of being grounded in God and practicing compassion for all others, especially the oppressed. The new heart gave them a new mind and a new will: knowing the limitless depths of divine love as that in which all live and move and have their being—including themselves—opened their hearts to others, all others. Here we see examples of human lives lived as reflections of the life we cannot describe but only speak of metaphorically: the life of the historical Jesus who invited us into a new way of seeing, a new way of living.

It is, quite simply, the way of "deification." It is a reflection of God's life and the attempt to become like God.[41] In this way of thinking, Jesus became like us that we might become like him—a human being totally open to God and others. Being God-like is our destiny, but it is not an otherworldly goal. As John Dominic Crossan remarks, "The Kingdom of God is what the world would be if God were directly and immediately in charge."[42] Deification, then, is a worldly matter. We see glimmers and shadows of it here and there, even in something as mundane as the ecological economic paradigm. That model, which underscores the importance of every individual creature, which understands unity only in terms of interrelationship and interdependence, which insists on distributive justice to all beings and sustainability of the earth, is a template ready and open to receive the radicalization of "deification"—the limitless and universal love of God reflected in human lives. This radicalization is expressed by Jesus' cross and resurrection, death to the old way of life and rebirth to a new way, a way that will often involve sacrifice, pain, and diminishment.

The picture of Jesus emerging from recent scholarship and the lives of myriads of his followers over two thousand years give us a sense of the *way* to the new life: it is only possible by relying utterly on God and, by so doing, developing the capacity for selfless love to others. The way to the new life is not by believing something nor by willing something, but by practicing the presence of God in daily communal life. It is not an imperative but an invitation: the invitation to live in God and with others, to live from and toward God here and now with all others, especially the needy.

What, then, of the cross and resurrection as "saving us"? In the traditional, otherworldly, individualistic view, Jesus' sacrifice on the cross for the forgiveness of sins and his subsequent resurrection is the salvific event: it is done for us, and we need only accept it. In the view supported by recent scholarship on the historical Jesus, we are invited into communion with God and partnership with Jesus to bring about a social transformation of life on earth for all creatures.[43] This will involve both cross and resurrection, both sacrifice (especially from us well-off people) and new life (especially for the not-so-well-off creatures). Should we, the favored ones, want to be part of this new way of being in the world? Only if we want to be able to say that reality is good—because, on this reading of Christian faith, we must help to make it so.

Annie Dillard, in her book *For the Time Being,* lays out a grim picture of human existence—from "bird-headed dwarfs," AIDS, and childhood leukemia to tornadoes, earthquakes, and floods. Life is a mess and a misery (but she doesn't indict God—things just are this way, she claims). Now and then, however, to those who seek God, God grants that they see "an edge" of the divine. This gift is so overwhelming that "Having seen, people of varying cultures turn—for reasons unknown, and by a mechanism unimaginable— to aiding and serving the afflicted and poor."[44] These people can say that reality is good, because they have experienced, however briefly, that it is so, and also because they help to make it so.

Finally, then, what does it mean from the context of an ecological economic Christology to say that reality is good? First and most important, reality is good because *God* is with us (Jesus points beyond himself to the source of love and power in the universe); God is *with* us (on our side, working with us, not instead of us, to bring justice and fulfillment to all); and God is with *us* (all of us, not just privileged human beings, but all people and all other life-forms, especially the needy). This Christology allows us to say reality is good because it claims that *God is with us* and it claims this in spite of evidence to the contrary—overwhelming evidence. It makes this claim in a strange, involuted way: the claim embraces its opposite. Ecological economic Christology claims that reality is good by way of the cross and cruciform living. It makes the claim by way of diminishment, sacrifice, solidarity with the oppressed, limitation of desires, standing compassionately in another's place. Christianity is not sentimental or naïve: it does not claim that the world spread out before us—the one of inequality, intolerance, greed, genocide, discrimination, and even innocent indifference— is good. Reality can be said to be good only through joining God in trying to make it so. This way was shown by the prophetic, historical Jesus (and his many disciples) to demand such solidarity with all people and the earth itself that it is called "the way of the cross." Here the cross is not the substitutionary, sacrificial death of Jesus of Nazareth for the sins of the whole world, but the *way* of God in the world, always. Jesus is paradigmatic of God's eternal and constant siding with the outcasts and hence the inevitable meeting with diminishment and death that such association involves.

The claim that reality is good does not, however, end with cruciform living: it says also that life conquers death. From the perspective of ecological economic Christology, the resurrection does not say that God raised Jesus from the dead—and us with him—to eternal life. Rather, it claims that the forms of death (physical starvation, mental and emotional deprivation, discrimination, rape, poverty, genocide, ecological destruction) are not the last word. The resurrection is a promise from Reality Itself—from God— that life and love and joy and health and peace and beauty are stronger than their opposites—if we will help make it so, if we will follow the way of Jesus, the way of cruciform living.

What is emerging, then, from ecological economic Christology is a different notion of the abundant life, not the abundance of consumer goods, but the possibility, the promise, of a new life in God for all. This abundant life uses the template of an ecological economic worldview in which individuals live in community on a sustainable earth and with the just distribution of necessities for all. But it goes beyond this worldview, insisting that the *way* to this new life will be difficult, painful, and sacrificial, especially for those who are presently taking more than their share and thus depriving other people and the earth of a good life. But how could the way not be cruciform for us privileged middle-class North American Christians if this new life is "what the world would be if God were directly and immediately in charge"?[45]

Theology, Christology, anthropology: God, Christ, and human life are not three topics but one interrelated matter. Human life under God—the way the world would be if God were directly in charge—is made known to us and made possible for us by Jesus Christ, God with us. Who we are in the scheme of things is defined by God being with us. The prophetic and the sacramental, the historical and the incarnational, the Protestant and Catholic emphases in Christology together declare that God is with us: the glory of God is every creature fully alive. And it is our task to help this happen. In the life, ministry, and death of Jesus we see concretely what is entailed in helping all creatures live fully: it involves, at the very least, distributive justice and sustainability, goals unattainable apart from significant changes by the most privileged human beings. This is the prophetic, historical, Protestant dimension of what God with us in Christ means. The sacramental, incarnational, Catholic side promises all creatures that God is in the world and on the side of the world. In the incarnation and resurrection of Jesus we see more clearly what is the case everywhere and always: *God is with us, with all of us, with us* in our struggle to give God glory by working for the fulfillment of all creatures. We are not alone as we seek to grow into the image of God—into the image we see in the face of Jesus. "Having seen, people ... turn ... to aiding and serving the afflicted and poor."[46]

8. Life in the Spirit

> The market ideology wants us to believe that *the world is profane.*
>
> —Walter Brueggemann[1]
>
> Christians believe *the world is hidden in God.*
>
> —Hans Küng[2]

"AT THE CENTER OF [JESUS'] MESSAGE was the invitation to see differently."[3] How do we see the world—and ourselves? As we see, so we believe, or in Erich Heller's chilling reminder, "Be careful how you interpret the world; it *is* like that." We live within our world constructs and act out of their assumptions. If we see the world as profane, as a place to buy and sell, use and discard, control and possess, we will treat it differently than if we see it as hidden in God. If we see ourselves and everything else as having its being and fulfillment in, through, and with God, we can no longer treat each other and the earth itself in a utilitarian way. We belong to God: everyone and everything does. We are "hidden in God," poised to emerge as reflections of divine glory. All creatures, other than human ones, do so intrinsically just by being; we alone must be shown the way to reflect and grow into the image in which we were created. *The glory of God is every creature fully alive.*

In chapters 4 and 5 we looked in some detail at how human life and the world were interpreted from the neo-classical and ecological economic worldviews. We saw how each understood the good life, the abundant life, and our place in the scheme of things. We concluded that the ecological economic paradigm was by far the preferable one for the well-being of humanity and the earth. In fact, we suggested it is not only better, but a necessity if we are all to survive and prosper.

But does Christian faith add anything to the ecological economic model? What is its distinctive contribution to this paradigm? How should Christians live in the world? Surely as advocates and examples of a just and sustainable planet, but what does this mean, especially for middle-class North American Christians? We have been asking how we can have a liberation theology, one that will help release us from being oppressors of the poor and of the planet. What must *we* do to be "saved"? What is the evil in which we participate that is damning ourselves, our neighbors, and the earth itself to destruction? These are painful questions for us, the most comfortable, privileged people in the world. We do not seem evil to ourselves or especially in need of salvation; most of us behave lawfully and decently, do our bit for the common good, and often give generously to the needy from our surplus. But is *this* "the invitation to see differently" that lies at the base of Jesus' life and message? That invitation, as Walter Brueggemann puts it, involves "an entirely different kind of economy, one infused with the mystery of abundance and a cruciform kind of generosity."[4]

People like us might wish this were not so; I wish it were not, but I suspect it is. In fact, everything that I have come to know about God and Christ tells me it is so: a different kind of economy, one of surprising abundance and sacrificial generosity, is the *oikos*, the household, in which we are all called to live. Christianity is not just support for the ecological economic worldview, but a radicalization of it, especially for the well-off.

Human existence within the theology sketched in previous chapters tells us why this is so. A Christian theology is about God, Christ, and the world: these three topics form a coherent whole. Therefore, to discover who we are—what the world is—we must see ourselves *within* God in Christ. Hence, we need to look at what "life in the Spirit" means for individuals, for the church, and for public institutions. We begin, however, with a retelling of the Christian story of God and the world, a retelling with the model of the world as God's body, a retelling that is, I believe, commensurate with the contemporary cosmological and ecological worldview.

Human Existence in the Spirit

"Christians believe the world is hidden in God."[5] This is the same as saying that human existence takes place within God's Spirit. The world does not have a separate existence for Christians. Ontologically, we live from, toward, and with God. I did not used to believe this; in fact, I fought it. I wanted the world to stand on its own; I feared that otherwise it would be sucked up into God—shades of

Hegel and Barth! But believers are always mystics (even if they are not philosophical idealists). One (or, at least I) cannot believe in God as a being, no matter how infinite, eternal, ubiquitous, good, powerful, or supernatural. God is either everything or nothing, or to phrase it more carefully, God is reality (or being-itself)—if not, there would be something "beyond God" or "more than God" that would be *God*.

So, how are the world and we human beings differentiated from God? In this story, we are the body of God, we are God "spread out," we are God incarnate.[6] We (the universe) come from God and return to God, and in the "interim" we live in the presence of God—even when we do not know or acknowledge it. We are created in the image of God (the entire universe reflects God's glory, each and every creature and thing in its particular, concrete, unique way). Creation is a panoply of mind-boggling diversity, a myriad of outrageously extravagant species and individuals who all together make up the body of God—God going out, God enfleshed, God become matter. Each creature—except us, it appears—praises God by simply being itself, by being fully alive. The whole universe, in this story, desires to grow back into God: the beloved longs to return to the lover. It is the deepest desire of creation to do so: eternal life, as Julian of Norwich says, is being "oned" with God, being "knitted" up with God.[7]

In this story there is nothing but God: God in God's self (the Spirit) and God going out from God's self (God embodied). God incarnate means God going out from the divine self to create "another," the world, which in a sense is over against God: the billions of particular, different creatures and entities that constitute it. But the world's "being" and its "well-being" and even its "reason for being" is to live in intimate relationship with God, which, of course, means living in intimate relationship with all other parts of divine embodiment as well.

What, then, of sin and evil? Sin and evil are pretending that we can live outside reality, this reality of interrelationship and interdependence of all things with one another and with God. Sin is refusing to grow into the image of God in which we (and everything else) is made. Sin is refusing to reflect God, become like God, by imagining that we can exist outside of relationship with God and others, living as if one's life came from oneself. Sin is *living a lie*. If God is reality and if reality is good, then sin and evil are a turning away from the ground of our being and our hope for happiness; sin and evil, as Augustine claimed, are *not*. They are a turning away from reality, from the radical, intimate relationships that constitute life and its goodness. Sin and evil are a denial of reality in their false belief that we can live from and for ourselves.

My exegesis of the statement, "Christians believe the world is hidden in God" is, I have suggested, a "likely story" of God and the world for our time. It is not a description, but neither were the medieval or deist stories of how God and the world are related. Rather, all three are Christian retellings of the relation of God and the world in terms commensurate with, appropriate to, different times. The story of God's embodiment and return, of all things evolving from one source that is reality, is congruous with the Big Bang of contemporary cosmology and the resulting unimaginable diversity and interdependence of matter—from the billions of galaxies to the DNA in bacteria, and everything in between. It is a creation story that gives God greater glory than any other that human beings have ever told. It is a retelling of the creation story that underscores God's awesome magnificence and power (God *is* reality) and our total dependence on God (as God's body created to reflect God's glory, each in our own way). It is a story that can be imagined without sacrificing one's intellect, although contemporary cosmology and evolution do not give special support to this religious tale. But this tale can "accompany" the contemporary worldview with minimum strain.

At an important point, however, this story makes a claim that the cosmological, ecological worldview does not: it makes a claim concerning the direction of the universe. This claim, for Christians, is focused on Jesus of Nazareth as the lens or model of God. His life, ministry, death, and appearances are the way that Christians look Godward, the way they dare to speak of the world not as a tragedy, but as a "divine comedy." All of creation, this story says, reflects God, but at one place that reflection is seen (by Christians) in an especially illuminating way. In Jesus of Nazareth, Christians believe they see *what we are meant to be,* and by implication, what we are not meant to be. If the purpose of all of creation is to reflect God, then the story of Jesus is the message and the means for how human beings can do so.

Life as it should be—salvation—is then, for Christians, christo-morphic. It is becoming like God by following Jesus. "Following

Jesus" is not principally a moral imperative, but a statement of *who we are*. We learn what it means to say human beings are created in God's image for God's glory by looking at Jesus Christ. "The importance of the confession 'Jesus is the Lord' is not only that Jesus is divine *but that God is Christlike*" (italics added).[8] The focus of salvation, then, becomes living in a new way, the way of God's abundance.

This is a deification, not an atonement understanding of salvation. It is an incarnation rather than a cross emphasis, a creation rather than a redemption focus, from the Eastern Christian tradition rather than the Western. It claims that we were created to be with God: creation is the pouring out of divine love toward that end; the incarnation in Christ is the reaffirmation and deepening of that love; the cross is the manifestation of the suffering that will occur, given sin and evil, if all creatures, especially the most vulnerable, are to flourish; and the resurrection is God's Yes that, in spite of the overwhelming forces of sin and evil, this shall be so. We will, all of us, be one with God and with each other. It is an understanding of salvation, of the good life, that reflects and deepens the ecological, economic worldview, for it is communal, physical, and inclusive. It imagines God's work for and with us as the enrichment and fulfillment of all forms of life, with special emphasis on the basics that creatures need for survival and well-being.

This is a different notion of salvation than is typical in most Western theologies. In the West salvation has usually been seen as redemption—God in Christ paying a price for our sins, or ransoming us from the forces of evil, or sacrificing the Son as a substitutionary atonement for us. The focus of these theologies is on redemption from our sin, not on our creation for the abundant life in union with God and others. The focus is on human individuals who are saved from evil (which is often equated with the world), rather than on the whole creation being invited into fuller communion with God and all others. The focus is on "Jesus doing it all" rather than on us, in partnership with God by following Christ, working toward a different way for all of us to live together on the earth.

While the deification view may at first glance appear to take sin and evil less seriously than the atonement view, it actually takes them more seriously. It views them not simply as individual failings for which human beings need forgiveness, but rather as all the forces—individual, systemic, institutional—that thwart the flourishing of

God's creation. "Sin" is not mainly or only a personal problem, the solution for which is divine forgiveness. Rather, sin is *living a lie,* living contrary to the way the christic lens tells us is God's desire for all of us. "Evil," in this understanding, is the collective term for the ancient, intricate, and pervasive networks of false living that have accumulated during human history. In the atonement model sin and evil are mainly individual, personal matters; in the deification view they are principally communal, worldly matters: one focuses on individual redemption from sin, the other on the forces, whether individual or institutional, that keep creation from flourishing.

This means, then, that the point of Christology for the deification view is not personal redemption but a "a conversion to the struggle for justice."[9] It means becoming "conformed to Christ" since he is, for Christians, the lens by which we know God. If, however, the goal of salvation is God's glory—every creature fully alive—then becoming christomorphic will involve very mundane work. "Work, land, housing, health, food, and education become the very expression of the glory of God. Likewise, the glory of God is trampled underfoot in any person who suffers hunger, destitution, and oppression."[10] Deification, becoming like God or following Christ, means, then, becoming involved in such matters as ecological economics, the just distribution of resources on a sustainable basis. Deification, becoming like the incarnate God, means making the body of God healthier and more fulfilled. Salvation is worldly work. Human existence "in the Spirit" means working "in the body" so that it may flourish.

Do we do this? *Can* we do this? Some do, and they can do so only by being deeply, personally, profoundly grounded in God. The "saints" who work tirelessly for justice are spiritually alive. Persistent, lifelong cruciform living appears possible only through immersing oneself in God's presence. Justice work and mysticism seem to be companions. To live this way is very difficult; it is, however, what I believe we middle-class North American Christians are called to.

The Life of Discipleship: John Woolman and Dorothy Day

I do not myself live this way, but I know some people who do, and it is from them I have learned what I would rather deny: that the abundant life, for us, is the cruciform life. These are the people I have studied for thirty years in my course on religious autobiography. In the stories of these deeply committed individuals who live their beliefs in concrete, persistent and, by conventional standards, ridiculously excessive ways, I find an unnerving authenticity. They are, like Jesus himself, walking parables of a new way of life. Like him, they are disturbing, disorienting presences in our midst, upsetting our plans and projects. Are they "answers" to our planet's dilemma? Scarcely, but they serve two purposes in regard to a liberation theology for oppressors: they are cautionary tales reminding us of our profound assimilation to our economy's pervasive and alluring power, and they are models of how we might see and act differently.

I will share my reading of the lives of two of these remarkable Christians—John Woolman and Dorothy Day—both middle-class North American Christians, one a Quaker and the other a Roman Catholic, who found that to live the abundant life in their own times involved doing so in a cruciform way. This exercise is not so that each of us will simply "go and do likewise" (most of us could not or would not); rather, it is to suggest what lies at the heart of the Christian understanding of life in Spirit: a different economic vision for God's household on earth. This will certainly have implications for our lives as individuals, but also, as we shall see, for our ecclesiastical and public institutions as well.

Woolman's *Journal* and Day's *The Long Loneliness* are classic Christian texts of disciples who lived what they believed. Woolman's understated remark sums it up: "Conduct is more convincing than language."[11] Easy to say, but seemingly impossible to live—but not for Woolman and Day. They attempted in everything they did to bring faith and practice together. By conventional standards, it often resulted in outrageous or ridiculous behavior. Robert Coles, commenting on Day, asks: "As for Jesus Christ, who of any importance in the West's intellectual or political world now pays any real attention to His teachings?"[12] Woolman and Day did. They were social revolutionaries who accepted Jesus' invitation to see differently and having seen differently, they ventured on a life-long journey to embody that new vision in everything they thought and did.

For many years I found them hard to take—not because they were perfect, for they were not. In fact, both of them come across as somewhat rigid ideologues who were not easy for family and colleagues to deal with. Nonetheless, their prophetic, no-nonsense, unflinching identification with the poor and their lifelong struggles to reverse the effects of oppression on the most vulnerable were an indictment of my own detachment and willingness to rationalize. I did think language was more convincing than conduct; at least, it suited me much better. I could persuade myself that it was my vocation to teach about such "saints," not to try to be one.

John Woolman, eighteenth-century Quaker, sold his grocery business because it was too profitable and spent a lifetime traveling on foot (because the post-horses were cruelly treated) around eastern United States preaching against slavery, excessive wealth, and the mistreatment of Indians. He was a rather absurd figure, easy to dismiss. He wore only white clothing because the trade in dyes depended on slave labor; he was a walking parable of his beliefs; he was excessive and often annoying. Dorothy Day was a kindred spirit who spent her life after conversion in middle age living in the slums of New York City running soup kitchens for Bowery bums and editing the leftist newspaper *The Catholic Worker*. Her influence was not great during her life and is less so since her death. Both she and Woolman, while saintly, seem relatively unimportant when faced, as we are, with the need for massive institutional planetary change.

But I find I cannot dismiss them so easily. For them, Christianity was "wild space," a place to stand in order to see the world differently, and having seen differently, they acted on it. Both of them had a vision of *another* abundant life than what they saw around them. At the heart of this vision was economics. Although their circumstances were as dissimilar from each other as both are from the current North American situation, the issue in all three cases is the same: How can we all live together in God's household, planet Earth? Neither of them would have expressed it this way, but each saw the need for a thorough-going restructuring of society's present economic arrangements as central to their religious vision.

In other words, these "wild," marginal, radical prophets on behalf of society's outcasts—especially the poor—saw something so remarkable that it changed them completely, down to the nitty-gritty of where they lived, what they ate, how they dressed, how they spent their time and money. They were not being dutiful, or giving generously to the poor, or helping the less fortunate through their writings or volunteer work. They saw the world *differently,* they saw it as hidden in God, and then everything else followed.

Over the years as I have read and reread Woolman and Day, I have felt less condemned by their amazing consistency of belief and lifestyle (though still mightily impressed by it) and more intrigued by what they *saw.* What changed them? What did their Christian "wild space" give them? What was the other possibility, the other abundant life? Let us take a few moments to look at this question, because I believe it holds a key to our own situation: How can we imagine another possibility for the good life in our time? How can we restructure our society's economic arrangements so as to reflect the new way we see the world?

John Woolman sums up his credo, what he saw differently, at the beginning of his *Journal.* He writes that early in life he became convinced

> that true religion consisted in an inward life, wherein the heart doth love and reverence God the Creator, and learns to exercise true justice and goodness, not only toward all men, but also toward the brute creatures; that, as the mind was moved by an inward principle to love God as an invisible, incomprehensible Being, so, by the same principle, it was moved to love him in all his manifestations in the visible world; that, as by his breath the flame of life was kindled in all animal sensible creatures, to say we love God as unseen, and at the same time exercise cruelty toward the least creature moving by his life, or by life derived from him, was a contradiction in itself. . . . I looked upon the works of God in this visible creation, and an awfulness covered me. My heart was tender and often contrite, and a universal love to my fellow-creatures increased in me.[13]

This amazing passage—so modest, logical, and simply stated—says that nothing short of universal love to all creatures is "true religion." To live such a credo consistently would involve a person in situations ranging from the awkward to the painfully sacrificial. And this is exactly what happened to Woolman. The vision may be glorious, but the practice is inconvenient to say the least: he insulted hosts by refusing to drink from silver vessels because they came from the slave trade; he was ready to pay a higher fare than asked on a trip to the West Indies because the slave trade subsidized the lower fare;

he was willing to take medicine only if it did not come "through defiled channels or oppressive hands." At the close of his life Woolman had a dream in which he heard a voice saying, "John Woolman is dead." He interpreted this to mean the death of his own will, that he was so mixed up with the mass of human beings in their greatest misery that henceforth he could not consider himself a distinct being. His credo of universal love ended with his disappearance as a separate individual.

We North American individualists surely will cringe at his fate, but what is crucial is to understand why he interpreted his dream as he did. John Woolman had an ecological sensibility before such a thing had a name: after killing a mother robin in his childhood, he realized that he must also kill her babies. He saw how interrelationship and interdependence worked: he saw how the intricate network of increasing needs and desires resulted in the oppression of others, even to the point of slavery. "Every degree of luxury hath some connection with evil. . . ."[14] After visiting in the homes of wealthy slaveholders, he realized the connections between the desire for luxuries and the "necessity" of having slaves. By "unencumbering" his mind—that is, by simplifying his own lifestyle, his needs and desires—he was able to see clearly what was plainly before him: that slaves were a rationalization for greed.

The two main features of Woolman's life that enabled him to see clearly another possibility—the possibility of adequate food and clothing for all people as well as care for other creatures—were simplicity of lifestyle and empathy toward others. He disciplined himself to need and want less so that his eye could remain "single," and he put himself in situations where he would concretely experience the oppression and pain that others were undergoing. He visited Indian villages to experience the dismal conditions under which these formerly proud people were living, having been deprived of their inheritances by the whites. He needed to experience their misery in order for his own vision to come clear, in order to see differently. As he remarks at the close of his visit, "People who have never seen such places have an imperfect idea of them. . . ."[15] A typical Woolman understatement, and it was the reason he also chose to sail steerage to Europe: so he could experience—and hence empathize with—the misery of the poorest and most oppressed.

Woolman undertook his simple lifestyle and his arduous journeys not from asceticism or perfectionism, but so that he could see clearly what it meant in his time to follow Christ. "The gift is pure; and while the eye is single in attending thereto, the understanding is preserved clear; self is kept out. We rejoice in filling up that which remains of the afflictions of Christ for his body's sake, which is the church."[16] The new life he sees, the abundant life in Christ, is one in which all God's creatures are knit together through economic sharing, none having too much but each having enough. Woolman's witness to this vision involved him in cruciform living: he could not even *see* it, let alone live it, until he had unencumbered himself and opened himself to experience the misery of others. Frugality and exposure, personal limitation and openness to others, simplicity and empathy: these were the keys to seeing differently and living differently.

John Woolman was not a wandering ascetic dressed in sackcloth and ashes trumpeting a life of poverty in order to win eternal salvation. He was, on the contrary, a tough-minded, keen-eyed realist concerned with the psychological power of greed and its networks of "necessities" that resulted in destruction of other people and animals.

Two centuries later another middle-class North American Christian who saw the world differently—as hidden in God—attempted also to live a different abundant life. Dorothy Day writes that from childhood on she felt that God intended for people to be happy, and this meant that all should have the necessities of life.

> I wanted life and I wanted the abundant life. I wanted it for others too. I did not want just the few, the missionary-minded people like the Salvation Army, to be kind to the poor, as the poor. I wanted everyone to be kind. I wanted every home to be open to the lame, the halt and the blind, the way it had been after the San Francisco earthquake. Only then did people really live, really love their brothers. In such love was the abundant life and I did not have the slightest idea how to find it.[17]

She was to spend her entire life trying to find it—for herself and for others. In a moving postscript at the close of her autobiography, she realizes that it is not poverty that is at the center of the Catholic Worker Movement (as some say), but community:

> We are not alone anymore....We cannot love God unless we
> love each other, and to love we must know each other. We
> know Him in the breaking of bread, and we know each other
> in the breaking of bread, and we are not alone any more.
> Heaven is a banquet and life is a banquet, too, even with a
> crust, where there is companionship.[18]

It would be difficult to find a fuller or more satisfying vision of
the alternative Christian vision of the good life than the one
sketched and lived by Dorothy Day. It is not a life of self-denial, of
regret and loss, of charity toward the less fortunate. On the contrary, it is one of joy and fulfillment. In this same postscript, Day
writes, "I found myself, a barren woman, the joyful mother of children."[19] Her delight is not only in her own natural daughter, but
also in all the others within the community where she discovered
the alternative abundant life. The remarkable thing about Day's
reenvisionment of the abundant life is its embrace of the prophetic
and the sacramental dimensions of the life, ministry, cross, and resurrection of Jesus Christ. It is as if she somehow "got" the whole
story: losing one's life *and* finding it. Hers is a Protestant and a
Catholic sensibility. It contains a prophetic blast against the systemic and institutional forces oppressing the poor, and thus her
commitment to communism and the radical Gospel imperatives to
side with the poor. But her sensibility also knows something of the
new life that is possible now: heaven is a banquet, but so is this life.
It embraces sex, children, food, community: it is the good life now,
shared with all others.

It is this rare combination of relentless personal and professional
identification with the poorest and most destitute people combined
with delight and joy in an alternative abundant life that is distinctive about Day. Her days were spent in soup kitchens that fed these
people and campaigning against the capitalist economics that created their destitution. One does not expect such a person to claim
delight and joy as characteristics of her life. But Day did; in fact, it
was *in* the life of poverty and protest that she discovered the abundant life. Hers is not a dour spirit: life is a banquet as long as there
is bread to share and a community with which to share it.

But Day, like Woolman, was a picaresque saint. She did not fit a
politically correct mold. She was neither a feminist nor a post-
Vatican II Catholic; she prescribed motherhood for women and

was doctrinally orthodox. Nonetheless, she did not herself follow conventional family values: she had several love affairs as well as an abortion, and she never married the father of her child although her love for him was deep and strong. She claimed that she was an "obedient" daughter of the church but added that she was also an "angry" one.[20] In other words, Day's traditionalism on issues of women and orthodoxy was due to a deeper radicalism, an alternative vision of the good life that neither feminism nor the church had grasped or practiced. She saw physical love, children, and the banquet of a shared communal life on a continuum; as she claims, she came to God out of great natural happiness, not out of guilt or despair.[21] Sex and motherhood were preliminary tastes of the fuller abundance to come, not contrary to it. Likewise, she saw her obedience to the church as taking Jesus' words with radical seriousness; her anger against the church was because it did *not* take them seriously enough.

Put most simply, her radicalism was a vision of the good life through communal sharing. The radicalism of this vision means limitation for some so that others may be invited to the table. "There is always room for one more; *each of us will have a little less*"(italics added).[22] The first part of the statement—the inclusive invitation to the abundant life—is only possible if the second part is observed: some must take less. Day discovered this hard reality for middle-class Americans like herself through the nitty-gritty of her own long journey as a successful journalist who gradually, through voluntary imprisonments for women's suffrage and against prostitution, through periods of spiritual discouragement and despair, through accepting the unlovely aspects of poverty (bad food, noise, little privacy) came to realize that she was happy. This is not a realization that comes at the front end of life or through thinking. Day's insights are hard-won, embodied ones, hammered out through the events, decisions, and consequences in her own life.

What she saw in her personal journey was a microcosm of the larger story of God's kingdom as a present reality. The banquet of life was not just for her, but for everyone, and it was available now if Christ's disciples would help it become so. At the heart of this kingdom was a new way of seeing and being: seeing oneself as one with the poor and living in that reality. The urgency and concreteness of her alternative vision meant that Father Zossima's words in

The Brothers Karamazov became her lifelong watchword: "Love in practice is a harsh and dreadful thing compared to love in dreams." And yet her life of voluntary poverty was not miserable: it was *abundant*.

For both Day and Woolman, however, voluntary poverty meant cutting out hindrances that would keep them from seeing clearly and acting obediently. This is a crucial lesson that we middle-class North American Christians might learn from them. Economic limitations were self-imposed by both of them so that their vision was unencumbered and action—whatever they saw as necessary to be done—would be possible. By living with few possessions, each of them realized the gross injustices of conventional economic arrangements that fostered greed, rationalization, and indifference by the well-off. Jesus' revolutionary views on poverty seemed to them not radical but self-evident. Having acknowledged the common sense of an alternative economic vision, one in which all had a place at the table by each taking less, the issue was *how* to implement it in their own time.

Neither Woolman nor Day was very successful. In fact, as we have noted, they were often seen as fools tilting at windmills. Eventually, of course, the slaves were freed and Woolman is remembered as one of the earliest abolitionists. Perhaps eventually, the Jubilee Year initiative for third-world debt forgiveness will be realized and the widening gap between the richest and the poorest human beings will shrink, and Day will be eulogized as one who saw the possibility for an abundant life other than the consumer one. But success is not the main criterion for judging these folks. They are, I believe, most valuable to us as cautionary tales and as models. As cautionary tales, they remind us middle-class North American Christians how deeply we are embedded in the consumer view of the good life: it is the ocean in which we live—most of the time unconsciously. But, say Woolman and Day, there is another possibility, the possibility that Jesus tells about in his parables, lives in his eating practices and healings, dies for on the cross, and appears to his disciples to work for: this possibility is an abundant life, a life of love and joy and delight, but only reached if some take less so all might partake. Woolman and Day were models of this possibility: in their own ambivalent and marred lives they tried to live the cruciform abundant life. As middle-class North Americans they knew that this abundant life must be a cruciform one for them—as it must be for us.

The implications for our personal and work lives are obvious, if painful. What the implications are, however, for each of us individually we must discover. To discover this we must do with less so that we can even see other possibilities, especially the particular ways and paths where we can be most effective and are willing to be persistent. The value of attending to the "lives of the saints" is not to mimic them but to pass back to one's own life and read it from a new and different perspective—the perspective of God's abundant life for all—and then to implement that new reading in concrete, mundane, practical ways. John Cobb and Herman Daly voice a poignant hope in their book, calling for an ecological economic worldview:

> Love of earth is not altogether dead within the human heart. . . . There is still a willingness to live a frugal and disciplined life if that can be seen as truly meaningful in relation to the massiveness of the problem. Capacity for sacrifice is not altogether gone. In short there is a religious depth in myriads of people that can find expression in lives lived appropriately to reality. That depth must be touched and tapped, and it must be directed by an honest and encompassing view of reality. If that is done, there is hope.[23]

We have looked briefly, with the help of Woolman and Day, at what it might mean for individuals to live their lives appropriately to reality—reality as understood within the ecological economic paradigm, especially as that is made concrete and radicalized by the story of Jesus. We must now turn to another equally difficult question concerning "life in the Spirit": whether a frugal, disciplined life can be "truly meaningful in relation to the massiveness of the problem." Does it *matter* how we live? As we turn to the church and political life, two sources of systemic good and evil in society, the answer is not assured.

Life in the Church

It is hard to deny what one recent critic says about mainline Protestantism: "Having made more accommodations to modernity than any other religious tradition, liberal Protestantism shows many signs of tired blood. . . ."[24] Roman Catholicism may seem somewhat healthier, with its long history of encyclicals on economics and as the fertile ground for many liberation theologies. And while right-wing and charismatic Christian groups do not suffer from tired blood, they offer scant support for the ecological economic paradigm. Overall, the churches' record is not an outstanding one. *Does* it matter to Christendom how we live? Walter Brueggemann thinks so, as we see in this stirring call to the churches.

> Consumerism is not simply a market strategy. It has become a demonic spiritual force among us and the theological question facing us is whether the gospel has the power to help us withstand it. . . . As we walk into the next millennium, we must decide where our trust is placed. The great question facing the church is whether our faith allows us to live a new way.[25]

It would be difficult to put the issue more sharply; for Brueggemann, the church must choose between "life" and "death," between "God" and "mammon."[26] Is the question of which abundant life we choose—the consumer one or the ecological one—*the* theological question of our day? Is it in any way similar to the question that Christians in Germany faced with Nazism?[27] Is the devastation and impoverishment that our middle-class North American lifestyle is causing the planet and other people an issue of such radical seriousness that our answer to it defines the state of our faith? If so, no one would not know it from polls on concerns and issues troubling North Americans: world poverty and environmental degradation scarcely make it to the bottom of lists, if they appear at all. But we need to remember that the biggest issues seldom do. Nazism was able to cloak itself as a "good" for many, and our booming economy is certainly able to do so as well. Staying hidden is the best policy for any "demonic spiritual force."

The foregoing chapters have tried to make the case that whether we choose one or the other of two economic models *is* a matter of life and death, a matter of the health and happiness of the world's human population and the well-being of everything else. If it is of such importance, can the churches be of any help? Again, we are helped by Brueggemann as he sketches the two economic models:

> The market ideology wants us to believe that the world is profane—life consists of buying and selling, weighing, mea-

suring and trading, and then finally sinking into death and nothingness. But Jesus presents an entirely different kind of economy, one infused with the mystery of abundance and a cruciform kind of generosity.[28]

From the parables and healing stories of Jesus, from his ministry of siding with the oppressed and his death as a consequence of such identification, we have seen what this "different kind of economy" entails: an abundance that demands a cruciform life. We were created from the overflow of divine love—the universe is a manifestation of God's super-abundant love—and we are fulfilled by God's desire to be reunited with each and every one of us. But this fulfillment does not occur magically or apart from the deepest intricacies, dilemmas, and despairs of fleshly existence. The way is slow because it goes through the thick of things, through the particular needs and desires of each creature, through the forces for well-being of each system and sub-system of the planet. This means a give-and-take among all the creatures and entities on our planet, involving sacrifices by some so that others may survive. A "cruciform kind of generosity," then, is the way back to God, the way to the fulfillment of *this* abundant life because it is a vision of abundance that will include each and every creature, especially the most vulnerable and oppressed.

What, then, is the task of Christian churches at the beginning of the millennium, faced as they are with a global society characterized by a notion of abundance that is in direct opposition to divine abundance—a notion of abundance that is impoverishing and devastating "God's body"? That task, I believe, is to say "no with thunder" as Karl Barth and his colleagues did in the Barmen Declaration of 1934. This will mean, as it meant for those Christians, a cruciform life, perhaps most clearly seen in Dietrich Bonhoeffer's imprisonment and eventual death for his involvement in an attempted assassination plot on Hitler's life. But others—Barth himself, Ruldolf Bultmann, Paul Tillich—paid different prices, some losing university posts, some accepting exile. All had to take a position on *the* theological question of their day and pay the price of their refusal to accept "a demonic spiritual force." We should not exaggerate: Nazi ideology and market capitalism are not the same kind of evil; the former is patently much more evil and much more clearly evil. But market capitalism and the uncontrolled consumerism that accompanies it is dangerously evil in two ways: it is not easy to identify as evil, and it has the potential for enormous destruction, for it is responsible for undermining the life support systems of the planet as well as for contributing to an unknown number of "silent deaths" from poverty and starvation.

Thus, whether or not the churches can reverse the direction toward disaster that rampant consumerism's kind of abundance supports, they must preach and teach a different view of abundance. They must say No to the abundant life of our culture. Since Constantine, churches in the West have been, to one degree or another, "established," considered to be an advantageous part of society's public life. The churches have responded with various degrees of accommodation to their various cultures. We are now at a time, I believe, when the churches should recall their origins prior to the Constantinian establishment; they were then fringe groups, sects, counter-cultural voices. They need to remember the radical message of Jesus that lies at their foundation, the message of the social revolutionary, who upended the conventions of his day, helping people to see a different kind of abundant life. As the North American mainline churches, both Protestant and Catholic, lose their established powers (including buildings, capital, clergy benefits, etc.) they have the opportunity to regain influence; that is, the power to envision and advocate a different way of life, one that is aligned with the ecological economic model. They have the opportunity to preach justice for the planet and its peoples.[29] Freed from having to please the establishment, they can do the work that the church as counter-cultural voice should do: demand, as Leonardo Boff insists, "the minimum social justice required to ensure that life has its basic dignity."[30]

This is the counter-cultural mission of the Christian churches: the promulgation of a different view of the abundant life. For middle-class North American Christians it will mean that the churches must call us to a sacrificial, cruciform lifestyle. We must begin to *live* differently. Having seen another possibility, another paradigm of abundance from the neo-classical economic one, we must individually and collectively devise alternative ways of working, eating, cultivating land, transporting ourselves, educating our children, entertaining ourselves, even of worshiping God. Of course, the voice of the churches can be but one of many others in society attempting to live differently. The religions of the world, including Christianity, are the source of basic worldviews that implicitly govern much of our economic and cultural behavior. They are, as well, about the business of helping people to see differently. Hence, one of their most important contributions to a global alternative economic paradigm is re-envisionment. They should see themselves as advocates for such an alternative paradigm within the public discourse. The Christian churches (and all other religions as well) should be part of the conversation for the public good—not as cogs in the wheels of the establishment but as counter-cultural voices for an alternative kind of abundant life for all members of the global family.

Life in Society

> In the final analysis, it is the power of individuals, channeled through civil society, that will drive governments, international institutions, and businesses toward sustainability.[31]

"The power of individuals, channeled through civil society": one would wish for an easier, quicker solution. But democracies do not work that way. The reason that the religions of the world must play a key part in achieving an alternative abundant lifestyle is that minds, hearts, and wills must be changed in order for laws to be. "Loving nature," which many people claim to do, or even simplifying one's lifestyle at the individual level will not bring about the systemic, institutional changes necessary for planetary justice and sustainability. Loving nature and living frugally are excellent ways to prepare ourselves for *the* change that our society needs and that the religions can help bring about: a paradigm change. This must be a change in our most basic sense of the good life. Malcolm Young claims that the problem is not that Americans do not love nature, but that they are enmeshed in a success story—the consumer one—that is ruining the planet.

> The value of autonomy, broad access to industrial products, individualism, efficiency, consumer choice, affluence and privacy which we regard too highly in North America has been etched into the landscape of our efforts to create a modern utopia. We defile our environment not through the failure of our dominant values but through their success.[32]

It is precisely from within this success story that American citizens presently vote. These historically formed values of who we are and what we value need to be changed in order for us to vote for the legislators and the laws that will help reorient society in a just, sustainable direction. This task is mainly a practical, not a theoretical one; it is thinking differently for the purpose of acting differently. How we think and feel about ourselves and our place in the scheme of things, especially at the level of basic assumptions, is critical to how we act.

But *do* basic assumptions change? An illustration of one such change that has occurred over the past several decades is the status of women: who women are and where they fit into the scheme of things. On this matter, in almost every country in the world and in every religious, civil, business, and family setting, a paradigm shift is occurring. These shifts vary enormously in style, depth, and breadth, but they are occurring: support for the human rights of women is now assumed to be "the way things should be" even in cultures where these rights are not recognized. There has been a basic shift to a new paradigm on one of the most important assumptions in all societies—the status of women. Since the dawn of human history women have been considered inferior in most if not all cultures; in the future, it seems this may not be so. That such deep change can occur on this critical issue is hopeful; perhaps our notions of the good life are also not set in stone.

And *how* do basic assumptions change? By many ways and means, but one of those factors is religion. The particular task of the religions in this enterprise is helping people to see differently, especially to see ourselves differently. The religions are—or should be—an essential partner in bringing this about. I am not claiming that a change in our assumptions will bring about the needed political and economic policies, but in a democracy such policies are not instituted unless the electorate demands them. Changing minds, hearts, and wills is certainly one task in the planetary agenda; it will also need the particular insights, skills, and powers of governments, businesses, non-profit organizations, as well as of every citizen. Whether or not we have the time to change is a very serious question, but playing ostrich or fiddling while Rome burns is not the solution. To be able to face ourselves in the mirror each morning, not to mention facing our grandchildren, we need to do what we can. I am suggesting that one essential task for the Christian churches (and other religions) is to enter the public discourse on justice and sustainability at the level of worldview, of who we are and how we fit with other human beings and other life-forms on our planet.

As we draw to a close, I would like to turn our attention once again to the issue of evil. I believe it belongs here under "Life in Society," although earlier we addressed it under the doctrine of God. When considered as a "God question," people often ask: "How could a good God permit evil?" or "Why do bad things happen to good people?" or "How can God be just if such horrendous evil exists?" The common supposition is that God is somehow responsible for both natural and moral evil: whether the event is a hurricane or the Holocaust, God caused or at least permitted it to happen. *Great* evil, evil in which people lose their limbs, lives, and loved ones, whether in a plane crash, war, or a massive flood involves God, directly or indirectly. I believe it is time we shifted our glance on the matter of evil from God to ourselves. The great issue before us should be *our* involvement in almost every kind of evil presently occurring on our planet. Whether we consider poverty and starvation, genocide, ethnic hatred and warfare, racial and sexual discrimination, greed and hoarding, species decline, deforestation, air and water pollution, land degradation, global warming, and even floods, droughts, and tornadoes, human beings now are responsible, directly or indirectly, to a lesser or greater degree—and some more than others—for all of the above. We should stop fretting about "theodicy"—how and why God is responsible for evil—and consider the increasing and appalling extent to which we are. This would be a salutary task for the religions, and especially Christianity, to take on: to help us see ourselves clearly as the oppressors that we are. Rather than Christianity focusing its concern with evil on God, let us place the blame where, in our time, it primarily belongs: on the privileged middle and upper classes of the world whose greedy lifestyle is causing greater evil to millions of impoverished people and to millions of dying species, as well as to the very health of our planet, than any so-called "act of God" ever has. We are bringing about this evil continuously, silently, and insidiously simply by living the way we do.

So how can we not despair? What possible prospects are there for any significant changes occurring? I began this book with two quotations: one from Irenaeus, "The glory of God is every creature fully alive" and the other from Bishop Serapin of the fourth century, "We beg you, God, make us fully alive." The first statement is the prophetic one, the description of life as it should be and as we, God's helpers, should make it be. But the second statement is the sacramental one, the trust that God is able to bring this about, through our willingness and work. In other words, *we are not alone.* The prophetic witness of God in Christ tells us what we must do; the sacramental embodiment of God in Christ surrounds us with God's empowering presence as we attempt to do it. The first and last words—the words of creation and resurrection—are Yes, not No. The No is enclosed within the Yes: we only discover what sin and evil are as we realize the joy of God's love, the love of others, and the love that is the world. That is the reality that I have gradually come to realize over the last fifty years; it is not what we must do or can do, but what God can and does do through us. We are instruments of divine love and reflections of divine glory. We were created in God's image, in the image of love, and our goal is to grow more fully into that image by loving each other and the world in concrete, practical, daily ways; in other words, in just and sustainable ways. But we are not left on our own to do this: God is with us, all of us, every second of every day. Our task is to become aware of God's presence. As we do so we will both see the world differently and be empowered to act differently in and toward it. We are called to see differently—and then to live differently, as differently as we can, with God's help.

 **Epilogue**

As I write these closing comments, the United Methodist Church, with a vote of two to one, has reaffirmed its negative position on homosexuality. The upcoming Presbyterian and Episcopal conventions have also once again slated this issue for consideration. The Southern Baptist Convention, the largest Protestant body in the United States, is poised to condemn once more the ordination of women. The Roman Catholic Church, under the leadership of John Paul II, has increasingly focused on issues of homosexuality, abortion, priestly celibacy, and the ordination of women. In all cases, personal, sexual issues surface as the church's interpretation of sin and evil; public, economic issues seem to be of less concern.

It is very discouraging. Not only do the establishment churches spend their time and energy on these lesser matters, but they do so to the exclusion of the more important ones. By so doing, they proclaim to the world that what the church really cares about is sex, not economics—personal morality, not public good. Perhaps it is intentional. The sexual issues provide a distraction, allowing the churches to avoid naming the real sin: consumerism and market capitalism as forces opposed to the abundant life for all people and the planet.

The churches appear to be in a state of cultural captivity; this is certainly nothing new—it has happened many times over the centuries. But what to do? The usual strategy, and a fairly effective one, has been for small, marginal groups to form in protest: the monastic movements, the Reformation sects including the Quakers, the Catholic Worker movement, and Latin American base communities were all counter-church movements from within the church. Like the NGOs, which have arisen out of despair over governmental inaction to deal with the negative consequences of free trade on poor people and the environment, so it may be time for Christians to once again work against the church in order to be truly for it.

Let us recall John Dominic Crossan's comment that the open table and radical egalitarianism of Jesus' Kingdom of God "is more terrifying than anything we have ever imagined," and even if we cannot accept it, *we should not explain it away.* This is what the John Woolmans and Dorothy Days insist that the church acknowledge: if it cannot accept the radical abundance of God's open table for all, it should not call it something more acceptable. For us well-off Christians, sin is not principally personal or sexual; rather, it is our refusal to acknowledge our terror at the prospect of the systemic economic changes needed for the just and sustainable distribution of the world's goods to all people and other creatures. *That* is truly terrifying for us. But if it is at the heart of Christian faith, then it should be acknowledged, even if it means we will not be righteous—or even comfortable.

Is there hope for us—we middle-class North American Christians? Can we at least be honest, if not good? It might help if we could keep our "wild space" intact. Being a Christian, even a middle-class North American one—as I envision it—involves having a wild space. That wild space is the shocking suggestion—even if only a suspicion—that *all* really are invited to the banquet, that every creature deserves a place at the table. This is not the hegemonic view of our society *or* the church: it is counter-cultural and counter-church. It is a different vision of the good life, but wild as it may seem, it is not necessarily wrong or impossible. Its two key principles are very mundane ones: justice and sustainability. Could the wild space become the whole space—the household of planet earth where each of us takes only our share, cleans up after ourselves, and keeps the house in good repair for future dwellers? I do not know, but perhaps we Christians could at least admit what life abundant truly should be, terrifying as it may be.

Appendix: A Manifesto to North American Middle-Class Christians

Preamble

IT IS TIME FOR AN ECOLOGICAL REFORMATION. The Protestant Reformation and Vatican II brought the importance of the human individual to the attention of Christians. It was a powerful revolution with many impressive religious and political results. But our current version of this model—the individualistic market model, in which each of us has the right to all we can get—is devastating the planet and making other people poor. This model is bankrupt and dangerous. We now need a new model of who we are in the scheme of things and therefore how we should act in the world.

The Individualistic Model

The model of human being as individual, which comes from the Protestant Reformation and the Enlightenment, is deeply engrained in American culture. It is the assumption of our Declaration of Independence, symbolized by the phrase "life, liberty, and pursuit of happiness." These goals are oriented to *individuals*—to their rights and desires. Likewise, American Christianity has been focused on individual well-being, either as salvation of believers or comfort to the distressed. This model of human life supports the growth of deep-seated assumptions about who we are and what we can do: we are a collection of individuals who have the right to improve our own lives in whatever ways we can. We see ourselves as basically separate from other people, while acknowledging the right of others also to improve themselves to the best of their abilities. This picture of ourselves is so deeply embedded in our culture that for most people it is simply "the way things are." It is seen as a description of the way human beings should respond to other people and to nature. But it is not a description; it is a model, a *way* of seeing ourselves and nature. It is, moreover, a way that increasingly is proving to be harmful to most of the world's people and to nature.

This individualistic model of human life, which is now joined by twenty-first-century market forces, has resulted in rampant consumerism by North Americans. We feel we have the *right* to whatever level of material goods and comfort we can amass for ourselves. The top 15 percent of the world's people now account for 86 percent of private consumption.[1] We middle-class North Americans are a large part of that 15 percent. What began centuries ago as a reformation to free the human individual religiously and politically has resulted in our present model of human life, which is on course to ruin the planet.

Destruction and Denial

However, this ruinous course is not common knowledge because the market forces benefiting from the individualistic model do not want people to slow down consumption or to question what over-consumption is doing to our planet and to poor people. There is very little public discussion of the key consequences of this model: climate change (global warming), the increasing gap between the rich and the poor, the extinction of other species, and the rapid decline in natural resources. We are being kept in denial about the seriousness of these major global issues by powerful business lobbies and timid politicians, but also by our own reluctance to disrupt the most comfortable lifestyle that any people on earth have ever enjoyed.

Global Warming: An Example

And yet, once the curtain is drawn aside and we take a peek at the deeply disturbing consequences of even one issue driven by our voracious consumerism, most of us may begin to question our model of human life. For example, global warming is becoming up-close-and-personal. Nine of the earth's recorded eleven warmest years have occurred since 1986, and 1999 was the warmest year yet, with 2000 shaping up to be warmer still. Floods, droughts, hurricanes, tornadoes, and other weather events are becoming more frequent and more extreme. Increasingly, the world's best weather experts agree that we are changing the weather with major and disastrous consequences.[2] The weather is the largest, most complex, and most important of all earth systems. Even minor changes have implications for food production, disease, water scarcity, air quality, desertification, biodiversity—as well as justice between peoples. Since global warming is the result of energy use, especially the burning of fossil fuels, the 15 percent of the world's people who use five times the energy of the rest of the world's population should pay special attention to this issue. We are creating a worldwide problem that heavily impacts others, specifically poor people and nature. Our cars and airplanes especially, but also the multitude of other ways energy makes our lives comfortable and privileged, must come under scrutiny. *Should* we live this way if it is achieved at the expense of nature's well-being and that of other people? *Can* we continue to live this way?

A cold, hard look at the individualistic market model of human life says no—we should not and we cannot. We *should* not as Christians because this model is contrary to our clearest and deepest traditions: that the Redeemer is also the Creator, that God is on the side of the oppressed, that God loves the world and dwells in it. We *cannot* continue to live this way because our planet is no longer able to support such a model of human life. If all people on earth were to live as North Americans do, we would need four more Earths to produce sufficient energy.

The Ecological Model: Who We Are

The individualistic market model has failed us: it has limited religious viability, and it is proving to be dangerous to our planet. We need another model of human life: we need an Ecological Reformation. An Ecological Reformation would base its model of human life on how reality is understood in *our* time. The individualistic model arose several hundred years ago and is no longer supported by the science of our day. The picture of reality emerging from cosmology, evolutionary biology, and ecology focuses on relations and community, not on individuals and objects. According to this picture, everything in the universe has emerged from a Big Bang fifteen billion years ago when a tiny bit of matter exploded and over billions of years became the galaxies and stars and, about four billion years ago on our planet, life itself. All life grew from one cell into millions of species, into the rich, diverse, and infinitely interesting forms we know—from mushrooms and mice to wheat and giant cedars, from fungi and frogs to chimpanzees and human beings. We are all related: we all came from the same beginning. There never has been a grander, more awe-inspiring creation story, and it is available to Christianity and to other religious traditions as a way to reimagine God the creator in twenty-first-century terms.

This story also provides us with a new model of human life, one that is based on the best science of our day—in other words, on reality as presently understood. In this story, human beings are not individuals with the power to use nature in whatever ways they wish. Rather, we are *dependent* on nature and *responsible* for it. In a sharp reversal, we do not control nature, but rely utterly on it. In this picture, human beings are products of nature and depend for our every breath and bite of food on it. We cannot live for more than a few minutes without air, a few days without water, a few weeks without food. The rest of nature does not, however, depend on us; in fact, if human beings were to disappear from the earth tomorrow, all plants and animals would be better off. We are among the neediest, the most vulnerable of all earth's creatures, dependent on nature's gifts every moment of our lives.

New House Rules: What We Should Do

Our radical dependence on nature means that we are also responsible for it. As the species currently laying waste the planet—and aware that we are doing so—we must accept responsibility for our actions. The ecological model of human life not only tells us who we are but also what we must do: it gives us guidelines on how we should act. In other words, it is a functional creation story, one that has practical implications for how we live at personal and public levels.

We could call these implications our new "house rules." The common creation story tells us that the earth is our home—it is where we evolved and where we belong. It also tells us what we must do for all of us to live decently and happily here. House rules are what one pins on the refrigerator as guidelines for sharing the space, the food, the resources of the home. The basic rules are: Take only your share, clean up after yourself, and keep the house in good repair for future occupants. The ecological model comes with some definite house rules, clearly seen in the fact that "ecology" and "economics" come from the same word root having to do with laws for living in a household. The basic rule is that if everyone is to have a place at the table, the limits of planetary energy must be acknowledged. Energy that is consumed is not recycled, but goes into the atmosphere as carbon dioxide. The house rules of our home set limits to growth—both of our consumer desires and the size of the human population. We need, then, to become "ecologically literate," to learn what we can and cannot do if our home is to continue to exist in a sustainable way. We must fit our little economy into the Big Economy, earth's economy, if our economy is to survive.

Christianity and the Ecological Model

As Christians we need to do all this and more. The Protestant Reformation and Vatican II supported the model focused on the well-being of the human individual. Protestants and Catholics should also support the ecological model. It *is* the picture of reality in our time, and Christianity has always been most effective when it has reconstructed its doctrines in light of reality as currently understood. The new model is also religiously rich and suggestive; it has enormous worship and liturgical potential. But of greatest importance, it is in profound agreement with the two deepest traditions in Christianity—the sacramental and the prophetic. This new model, which could be summarized by a version of Irenaeus's watchword—the glory of God is every creature fully alive—provides Christians with new ways to say that God is *with* us on the earth and that God is *for* us, especially the oppressed. This new model suggests to Christians that the way to picture God's presence with us is the eschatological banquet to which all are invited, all people and all other creatures.

The Abundant Life

The ecological model, then, suggests a new vision of the "abundant," the good, life. It is not and cannot be the consumer model of individual gain; it must be a shared life where "the rich must live more simply, so that the poor may simply live."[3] We must envision models of the abundant life based not on material goods, but on those things that really make people happy: the basic necessities of food, clothing, and shelter for themselves and their children; medical care and educational opportunities; loving relationships; meaningful work; an enriching imaginative and spiritual life; and time spent with friends and in the natural world. In order to move toward this good life, we will need to make changes at every level: personal, professional, and public—how we live in our houses, how we conduct our work lives, and how we structure economic and political institutions. It is a life that for us North Americans may well involve limitation and significant change in our level of comfort. Christians might see it as form of discipleship, a cruciform life of sacrifice and sharing burdens.

A Call to Action

The Ecological Reformation is the great work before us. The urgency of this task is difficult to overstate. We do not have centuries to turn ourselves around and begin to treat our planet and our poorer brothers and sisters differently. We may not even have the next century. But the scales are falling from our eyes and we see what we must do. We must change how we think about ourselves and we must act on that new knowledge. We must see ourselves as both radically dependent on nature and as supremely responsible for it. And most of all, we North American privileged people who are consuming many times our share at the table must find ways to restructure our society, our nation, and the world toward great equitability. Christians should be at the forefront of this great work—and it is a *great* work. Never before have people had to think about the well-being of the entire planet—we did not ask for this task, but it is the one being demanded of us. We Christians must participate in the agenda the planet has set before us—in public and prophetic ways—as our God "who so loved the world" would have us do.

 **Notes**

Preface

1. *The Confessions of St. Augustine,* books 1–10, trans. F. J. Sheed (New York: Sheed and Ward, 1942) 1.5.

2. Dorothy Day, *The Long Loneliness: The Autobiography of Dorothy Day* (New York: Harper and Row, 1952) 44.

Part I: The Practice of Planetary Theology
Chapter 1: A Brief Credo

1. Annie Dillard, *Pilgrim at Tinker Creek: A Mystical Excursion into the Natural World* (New York: Bantam, 1975) 269; Alice Walker, *The Color Purple* (New York: Washington Square, 1978) 178.

2. Gordon Kaufman, *Theology for a Nuclear Age* (Philadelphia: Westminster, 1985).

3. Eberhard Bethge, "Turning Points in Bonhoeffer's Life and Thought," in Peter Vorkink, ed., *Bonhoeffer in a World Come of Age* (Philadelphia: Fortress, 1968) 79.

4. Teresa of Avila, *The Interior Castle,* trans. Kieran Kavanaugh and Otilio Rodriguez (New York: Paulist, 1979) 100.

5. Pierre Teilhard de Chardin, *Writings in Time of War,* trans. René Hague (London: Collins, 1968) 14.

6. Charles Birch, Nairobi World Council of Churches Assembly, 1975.

7. John B. Cobb Jr., *Becoming a Thinking Christian* (Nashville: Abingdon, 1993) 39ff.

8. John Woolman, *The Journal* and *A Plea for the Poor* (John Greenleaf Whittier Edition Text; New York: Corinth, 1961) 51.

9. "A Collect for Peace," *The Book of Common Prayer* (New York: Seabury, 1979) 99.

Chapter 2: Theology Matters

1. Dorothee Soelle, *Theology for Skeptics: Reflections on God,* trans. Joyce L. Irwin (Minneapolis: Fortress, 1995) 103.

2. As quoted by Robert McAfee Brown, *Gustavo Gutiérrez: An Introduction to Liberation Theology* (Maryknoll, N.Y.: Orbis, 1990) 99.

3. For two helpful books on this subject, see John B. Cobb Jr., *Becoming a Thinking Christian* (Nashville: Abingdon, 1993) and Howard W. Stone and James O. Duke, *How to Think Theologically* (Minneapolis: Fortress, 1996). Cobb states his purpose as follows: "I have written this book in the hope of renewing a unifying Christian vision that can function as the real basis of life in the world" (60); Stone and Duke claim that most Christians do not know how to state their faith except to echo familiar phrases: "Sound bytes about the body of Christ, people of God, Christ-event, kerygma, and group process are not yet a deliberative theology of the church" (23).

4. Johann Baptist Metz, "The Last Universalists" in Miroslav Volf et al., eds., *The Future of Theology: Essays in Honor of Jürgen Moltmann* (Grand Rapids, Mich.: Eerdmans, 1996) 48.

5. David Tracy, "Theology and the Many Faces of Modernity," *Theology Today* 51 (1994) 104.

6. For an interesting analysis of postmodernism and its relationship to theology, see Paul Lakeland, *Postmodernity: Christian Identity in a Fragmented Age* (Minneapolis: Fortress, 1997).

7. For expansion on the following points, see my other books, especially *Metaphorical Theology: Models of God in Religious Language* (Minneapolis: Fortress, 1982) chaps. 1, 4; *Models of God: Theology for an Ecological, Nuclear Age* (Minneapolis: Fortress, 1987) chaps. 1, 2; *The Body of God: An Ecological Theology* (Minneapolis: Fortress, 1993) chaps. 2, 3.

8. H. Richard Niebuhr defines radical monotheism in an interesting and important fashion, linking being and value, thus setting a framework for the affirmation of all of creation: "Radical monotheism dethrones all absolutes short of the principle of being itself. At the same time it reverences every relative existent. Its two great mottoes are: 'I am the Lord thy God; thou shalt have no other gods before me' and 'Whatever is, is good'" (*Radical Monotheism and Western Culture* [New York: Harper and Bros., 1943] 37). In this single quotation, Niebuhr has combined the typically Protestant defense of the transcendence of God with the characteristically Catholic insistence on the value of the natural order.

9. One only has to recall Augustine's comment that all theology is but the babble of babies or Thomas Aquinas's statement at the end of his highly productive life that everything he had written was straw to see the sensibility at work.

10. Thomas Aquinas's treatment of religious language makes the same point. All language about God, he says, is analogical, using familiar terms, such as *love,* for God, although we do not know *how* they apply to God. Because God is the cause of love (as of everything else), we can assume that there is a relationship between what we know of love and God's love (the analogy of intrinsic attribution). As a qualifier, however, Thomas added that all we know is that just as our loves are in proportion to our being, so God's love is in proportion to the divine being (the analogy of proper proportionality)—and what that equation is, we do not know! Hence, Thomas was very modest about our statements about God, while he was certain about God being Love-Itself. See the *Summa,* ques. 13.

11. The term is Langdon Gilkey's, who defines it, however, more narrowly than I do. He sees it as the contemporary move in light of massive injustice and ecological deterioration to wager on a vision of Christian faith in order to take political stands to ameliorate these conditions. "All liberating political theologies rest on a centered vision, a *relative absolute.* This was clear in the Barmen challenge to Hitler; it is clear in the current liberation theologies" ("Events, Meanings, and the Current Tasks of Theology" *JAAR* [December 1985] 723). While fundamentalist theology of all ages absolutizes its own insights, good theology never does; thus, I think the term "relative absolute" can be used for the basic insight of all appropriate theologies.

12. For further and extensive treatments of this matter, see my other books, especially *Metaphorical Theology* and *Models of God.*

13. Elizabeth Sewell, *The Human Metaphor* (South Bend, Ind.: University of Notre Dame Press, 1964) 80.

14. See George S. Hendry, *Theology of Nature* (Philadelphia: Westminster, 1980) chap. 1.

15. For extensive treatment of this subject, see my book *Super, Natural Christians* (Minneapolis: Fortress, 1997).

16. Rebecca Chopp puts it well: "Theology is not primarily a debate about ontological or epistemological categories, but rather fashions discourse and practices for living justly" ("Feminist and Womanist Theologies," in David F. Ford, ed., *The Modern Theologians: An Introduction to Christian Theology in the Twentieth Century* [2d ed.; Cambridge, Mass.: Blackwells, 1997] 398).

17. Juan Luis Segundo, *Liberation of Theology,* trans. John Drury (Maryknoll, N.Y.: Orbis, 1975) 26.

18. Douglas John Hall, speaking of the North American context as the one we should embrace, writes: "They are called to this cruciform vocation, not out of any fascination with the negative, but because the rhetorical positive lauded by the image makers of the First World is sustained at an inestimable cost to millions of God's beloved creatures, human and extrahuman, and threatens the future of the planet itself" (*Thinking the Faith: Christian Theology in a North American Context* [Minneapolis: Fortress, 1991] 19).

19. As quoted by Brown, *Gustavo Gutiérrez*, 75.

20. Julio Lois, "Christology in the Theology of Liberation," in Ignacio Ellacuría and Jon Sobrino, eds., *Mysterium Liberationis: Fundamental Concepts of Liberation Theology* (Maryknoll, N.Y.: Orbis, 1993) 172. Another quotation is apt as well: "When all is said and done, the dissident God revealed to us in Jesus' practice cannot be truthfully professed in a society such as ours without our adopting this dissidence in practice. Access to the God of Jesus by the route selected by liberation christology evinces that to profess God is to 'practice God' (Gutiérrez)," 182.

21. As quoted by Aruna Gnanadason, "Women and Spirituality in Asia," in Ursula King, ed., *Feminist Theology from the Third World: A Reader* (Maryknoll, N.Y.: Orbis, 1994) 354.

22. This is a very complex issue, and my generalization does not begin to suggest its intricacies and nuances. Nonetheless, in many studies, this retreat has been followed, culminating in the earlier part of our century with Karl Barth's claim that creation was principally the backdrop for redemption and Rudolf Bultmann's focus on human trust in God as the central theological issue. Neither Neoorthodoxy nor Existentialism paid much attention to the natural world, a legacy that dies hard in present-day local congregations.

23. No case need be made for this in the Hebrew Scriptures, from Genesis, including the Noah material, to the psalms, and the large Wisdom tradition (which has been so well studied lately in Christianity by Elisabeth Schüssler Fiorenza, Jürgen Moltmann, and Elizabeth A. Johnson). But in Christianity, a strong case can be made as well, beginning with the Gospel of John and coming up through Irenaeus's wonderful theology, Augustine, Thomas Aquinas, the medieval mystics, to contemporary Roman Catholic theologians Teilhard de Chardin and Karl Rahner. Feminist the-

ologians have made especially strong contributions in this area and, increasingly, third-world liberation theologians are doing so as well, such as the work of Leonardo Boff.

24. This is the thesis of Paul F. Knitter's book, *One Earth Many Religions: Multifaith Dialogue and Global Responsibility* (Maryknoll, N.Y.: Orbis, 1995). The "common ground" of the various religions is, he claims, eco-human well-being.

25. Juliet Schor, author of *The Overspent American,* comments that the "new consumerism," a consumerism that is pressing people not just to keep up with the Joneses down the street but with the television jet set, brings little satisfaction. She notes that it is having "broader effects on our ability to construct a good society. As the pressures on private spending have escalated, support for public goods, and for paying taxes, has eroded. Public education, social services, public safety, recreation, and culture are being squeezed. This then ups the ante to spend privately, as people respond by buying security systems, enrolling their children in private schools, and spending time at Discovery Zone rather than the local playgrounds. In the end, we find ourselves impoverished socially, culturally, and spiritually, despite being surrounded by a mountain of stuff" (*The Boston Globe,* 17 May 1998, sec. E).

26. M. Douglas Meeks says it well: "The table manners at the Lord's Table become our manners for the whole of our lives. Our manners at this Table are meant to be our manners at all tables. If the question of the Lord's Table is the question whether all of God's creatures will have daily bread, then the church must become a trustee of public responsibility" ("The Future of Theology in a Commodity Society," in Volf et al., eds., *The Future of Theology,* 265).

Chapter 3: The Matter of Theology

1. Erich Heller, *The Disinherited Mind: Essays in Modern German Literature and Thought* (Cleveland, Ohio: World, 1961) 211.

2. John Cobb says that Christian identity should be applied to all issues, not just religious ones: "To be a theologian is to desire that all the beliefs by which we live be Christian"; "I have written this book in the hope of renewing a unifying Christian vision that can function as the real basis of life in the world" (*Becoming a Thinking Christian* [Nashville: Abingdon, 1993] 59–60).

3. Heller, *The Disinherited Mind*, 211.

4. Peter Hodgson's definition of theology is similar: "Theology, as the practice of the Christian community, is a constructive activity that requires critical interpretations and practical applications of faith's language about God in the context of contemporary cultural challenges and their theological implications" (*Winds of the Spirit: A Constructive Christian Theology* [Louisville, Ky.: Westminster John Knox, 1994] 10).

5. Ernest Gombrich as quoted in Nelson Goodman, *Languages of Art: An Approach to a Theory of Symbols* (Indianapolis: Bobbs-Merrill, 1968) 7–8.

6. Frederick Ferré, "Organizing Images and Scientific Ideals: Dual Sources for Contemporary Religious World Models," in J. P. van Noppen, ed., *Metaphor and Religion* (Brussels, Belg.: Free University of Brussels, 1983) 71–90.

7. See my book *The Body of God: An Ecological Theology* (Minneapolis: Fortress, 1993) for a theology built on this model.

8. See Jacquelyn Grant, *White Women's Christ and Black Women's Jesus: Feminist Christology and Womanist Response* (Atlanta: Scholars, 1989).

9. With acknowledgment to Antonio Gramsci, whose list of characteristics varies somewhat from the one I am giving.

10. I cannot find the reference. I believe "wild space" is the creation of two anthropologists. If any reader knows the reference, please send it to me care of Fortress Press.

11. Dorothee Soelle, *Theology for Skeptics: Reflections on God*, trans. Joyce L. Irwin (Minneapolis: Fortress, 1995) 111–12.

12. Miroslav Volf, "Theology, Meaning, and Power," in Miroslav Volf et al., eds. *The Future of Theology: Essays in Honor of Jürgen Moltmann* (Grand Rapids, Mich.: Eerdmans, 1996) 112.

13. Revelatory insights of this sort lie at the heart of theology. Paul Tillich expresses it this way: "One could say that in each system an experienced fragment of life and vision is drawn out constructively even to cover areas where life and vision are missing. And conversely, one could say that in each fragment a system is implied which is not yet explicated. . . . A fragment is an implicit system; a system is an explicit fragment" (*Systematic Theology*, vol. 1 [Chicago: University of Chicago Press, 1967] 58).

14. The feminist literature on this issue is now immense. Early on, feminist theologians spoke of "woman's experience" to differenti-

ate it from what modern theology called human experience, which the feminists saw as a mask for male experience. It soon became evident, however, that there was no such thing as woman's experience: it too seemed to be a mask, this time for Western, white, affluent women's experience. Women experience differently depending on their differing social, cultural, historical contexts. The realization that people experience differently does not detract from the importance of the category in theology; it simply means that we must be open to a variety of interpretations of Christian faith.

15. Peter Hodgson claims that revelation is not truths about God but events in the world that have "the shape of freedom": "God is revealed as liberating power by the way in which God's word works in the world" (*Winds of the Spirit*, 128). To Hodgson, revelation is not verbal, but the power of God acting in the world, shaping it in ways that are liberating and healing to human and natural life.

16. *Black Elk Speaks: Being the Life Story of a Holy Man of the Oglala Sioux*, as told through John G. Neihardt (Lincoln: University of Nebraska Press, 1961) 43.

17. Hans Küng, *Theology for the Third Millennium: An Ecumenical View*, trans. Peter Heinegg (New York: Doubleday, 1988) 51.

18. There is nothing novel about this assertion. Martin Luther would agree with it and so would Elisabeth Schüssler Fiorenza: Luther found in Paul's description of justification by grace through faith the transformative revelation that was salvation for him, and Schüssler Fiorenza claims that Scriptural revelation for women is what liberates them from oppression. In both cases, what matters is the experience of liberating love, not truths about God and the world.

19. Hans-Georg Gadamer, *Truth and Method* (New York: Seabury, 1975) 264.

20. As Edward Schillebeeckx puts it, "What was experience for others yesterday is tradition for us today; and what is experience for us today will in turn be tradition for others tomorrow" (*Interim Report on the Books Jesus and Christ* [New York: Crossroads, 1981] 50).

Part II: The Context of Planetary Theology
Introduction

1. David A. Crocker and Toby Linden, introduction in David A. Crocker and Toby Linden, eds., *Ethics of Consumption: The Good Life, Justice, and Global Stewardship* (Lanham, Md.: Rowman & Littlefield, 1998) 1.

2. Steven C. Hackett, *Environmental and Natural Resources Economics: Theory, Policy and the Sustainable Society* (Armonk, N.Y.: M. C. Sharpe, 1998) 4.

3. Max Oelschlaeger, *Caring for Creation: An Ecumenical Approach to the Environmental Crisis* (New Haven, Conn.: Yale University Press, 1994) 3.

4. Twenty million people die annually not from plane crashes, natural disasters, or even droughts but just because they are poor. See Thomas Pogge, "A Global Resources Divided," in Crocker and Linden, eds., *Ethics of Consumption,* 501–36.

5. Larry L. Rasmussen, *Earth Community, Earth Ethics* (Maryknoll, N.Y.: Orbis, 1996) 87.

6. The United Nations *Human Development Report* for 1998 states that "for more than one billion of the world's poor people increased consumption is a vital necessity and a basic right" (New York: Oxford University Press, 1998) iii.

7. David Malin Roodman, "Building a Sustainable Society," in Lester Brown et al., eds., *State of the World 1999* (millennial ed.; New York: W. W. Norton, 1999) 170.

Chapter 4: The Contemporary Economic Model and Worldview

1. Max Oelschlaeger, *Caring for Creation: An Ecumenical Approach to the Environmental Crisis* (New Haven, Conn.: Yale University Press, 1994) 96.

2. See Steven C. Hackett, *Environmental and Natural Resources Economics: Theory, Policy and the Sustainable Society* (Armonk, N.Y.: M. E. Sharpe, 1998) 4–5.

3. Herman E. Daly and John B. Cobb Jr., *For the Common Good: Redirecting the Economy toward Community, the Environment, and a Sustainable Future* (2d ed.; Boston: Beacon, 1994) 113.

4. Milton Friedman, *Essays in Positive Economics* (Chicago: University of Chicago Press, 1953) 4.

5. Hackett, *Environmental and Natural Resources,* 33.

6. Nathan Keyfitz, "Consumption and Population," in David A. Crocker and Toby Linden, eds., *Ethics of Consumption: The Good Life, Justice and Global Stewardship* (Lanham, Md.: Rowman and Littlefield, 1998) 485.

7. Adam Smith, *The Wealth of Nations* (New York: Modern Library, 1937) 14.

8. Revered as a paradox, the "invisible hand" claims that "individuals acting according to their human nature ('red in tooth and claw' as Hobbs reminds us) as infinitely acquisitive and selfish, will ultimately (and unintentionally) work out the best means of organizing production and consumption within a society" (Malcolm C. Young, "The Invisible Hand in the Wilderness: Economics, Ecology and God" [M.A. thesis, Harvard University, 1998] 67).

9. See Herman E. Daly, *Beyond Growth: The Economics of Sustainable Development* (Boston: Beacon, 1996) 50ff.

10. "Protestantism displayed a large measure of consonance with the capitalist spirit of private judgement and self-control. It was not a difficult step from the right of people to possess and develop their own souls unfettered by the church to the right of people to possess the means of production and enjoy their fruits unfettered by civil institutions" (Norman K. Gottwald, "Values and Economic Structures," in Michael Zweig, ed., *Religion and Economic Justice* [Philadelphia: Temple University Press, 1991] 58–59).

11. Behind this view also is Kantian idealism and Cartesian dualism, with humanity alone as subject and everything else arranged as its object. "In short, the typical modern dualism reappears in economic theory from Adam Smith to the present. On the one side there are human beings, the satisfaction of whose wants is the single end of economic activity. On the other side there is everything else, all of which comes into consideration only as means to the end of satisfying human wants" (Daly and Cobb, *For the Common Good,* 107).

12. Lester R. Brown and Christopher Flavin, "A New Economy for a New Century," in Lester R. Brown et al., eds., *State of the World 1999* (millennial ed.; New York: W.W. Norton, 1999) 4.

13. Ibid., 15.

14. "In calculating GDP, pollution is not only counted as a positive, but it may be done so three times: when an economic activity produces it, when it is cleaned up, and when associated health costs occur" (Barry Marquardson, "GDP Fails as a Measurement," *Globe and Mail* [July 16, 1998]).

15. Oelschlaeger, *Caring for Creation,* 96.

16. "Just when we are moving to an ever greater validation of the sacredness of the individual person, our capacity to imagine a social fabric that would hold individuals together is vanishing. This is in

part because of the fact that religious individualism . . . is linked to economic individualism which, ironically, knows nothing of the sacredness of the individual. . . . What economic individualism destroys, and what our kind of religious individualism cannot restore, is solidarity, a sense of being members of the same body" (Robert N. Bellah, "Is There a Common American Culture?" *JAAR* 66, no. 3 [1998] 622).

17. Ibid., 616.

18. Communism is not more community oriented than capitalism, as a "collective" does not rest on a model of the intrinsic relationality of all beings. Moreover, communism, as practiced to date, has proven as destructive of nature as capitalism, if not more so. Nonetheless, as long as it was around, it not only provided a strong critique of capitalism's form of individualism, but also, simply by its existence, undercut market capitalism's claim to be the only possible model of economics.

19. John Cobb calls it the religion of "Economism": its god is endless growth; its priests are the economists; its evangelists are the advertisers; its laity are the consumers; its cathedral is the shopping mall ("Economism or Planetism: The Coming Choice," *Earth Ethics* 3 [fall 1991]). Max Oelschlaeger claims that ". . . economic policy is a secular religion, and the GNP and the rate of economic growth are our holiest of holiest. Almost every American has been socialized to believe in them as absolutes" (*Caring for Creation,* 68). Malcolm Young adds: "Economic thinking represents the most compelling system of meaning in our time. Its universality and the energy which we devote toward achieving its ends make it far more important than almost any other means of making sense of the world. . . . Profit and possession, personal and national income, growth and development, production and consumption have become ends in themselves" ("The Invisible Hand in the Wilderness," 180, 181).

20. Joerg Rieger, "Developing a Common Interest Theology from the Underside," in Joerg Rieger, ed., *Liberating the Future: God, Mammon, and Theology* (Minneapolis: Fortress, 1998) 7.

21. Keyfitz, "Consumption and Population," 498.

22. Neva R. Goodwin, introduction in Neva R. Goodwin, Frank Ackerman, and David Kirion, eds., *The Consumer Society* (Washington, D.C.: Island, 1997) xxx.

23. Young, "The Invisible Hand in the Wilderness," 52.

24. Ibid., 181.

25. Unpublished paper by Stephanie Kaza, "Overcoming the Grip of Consumerism," delivered at the 1998 International Buddhist-Christian Theological Encounter, Indianapolis, Ind., 13–16.

26. Goodwin, "Volume Introduction," xxxi.

27. United Nations, *Human Development Report 1998* (New York: Oxford University Press, 1998) 2.

28. "It is now widely accepted among researchers that, as Michael Argyle, an Oxford University experimental psychologist put it in a recent article, 'money has little effect (on happiness), except at the lower end of the income scale'" (John Cassidy, "No Satisfaction: The Trials of a Shopping Nation," *The New Yorker* [January 25, 1999] 89).

29. Ibid.

30. Juliet Schor, "We Want What We Cannot Afford," *The Boston Globe* (May 17, 1998) sec. E, p. 3. See also her book, *The Overspent American: Upscaling, Downshifting, and the New Consumer* (New York: Basic, 1998).

31. Ibid.

32. See Judith Lichtenberg, "Consuming Because Others Consume," in Crocker and Linden, eds., *Ethics of Consumption,* 155–75.

33. Ibid., 170.

34. United Nations, *Human Development Report 1998,* iii.

35. Kevin Gallagher, "Overview Essay: Globalization and Consumer Culture," in Goodwin et al., eds., *The Consumer Society,* 301–8.

36. Brown and Flavin, "A New Economy for a New Century," 4.

37. Or, in more technical terms, "scale refers to the physical volume of the through-put, the flow of matter-energy from the environment as low-entropy raw materials and back to the environment as high-entropy wastes" or it is "the product of population times per capita resource use" (Robert Costanza et al., *An Introduction to Ecological Economics* [Boca Raton, Fla.: St. Lucie, 1997] 80).

38. United Nations, *Human Development Report 1998,* 4.

39. Ibid., 2. See also Alan Durning: "People living in the nineties are on average four-and-a-half times richer than their great-grandparents were at the turn of the century . . ." (*How Much Is Enough? The Consumer Society and the Future of the Earth* [New York:

W.W. Norton, 1992] 23), and the report in *Forbes* magazine that the 225 richest people in the world have a combined income of more than $1 trillion, which approaches the combined annual incomes of the poorest one half of humanity (Brown and Flavin, "A New Economy for a New Century," 20).

40. United Nations, *Human Development Report 1998*, 2.

41. "At the foundation of human development is the principle of the universalism of life claims, acknowledging the life claims of everyone—women, men and children—without discrimination. It demands a world where consumption is such that all have enough to eat, no child goes without education, no human being is denied health care, and all people can develop their potential capabilities to the full extent. The human development perspective values human life for itself. . . . Nor does it value one person's life more than another's" (Ibid., 39).

42. "Most Consuming More, and the Rich Much More," *New York Times* (September 13, 1998).

43. John Kenneth Galbraith notes in *The Affluent Society* that when private goods and services increase, there is a decreasing trend in public services. "The problem is not economics; it goes back to a far deeper part of human nature. As people become fortunate in their personal well-being, and as countries become similarly fortunate, there is a common tendency to ignore the poor" (as quoted in United Nations, *Human Development Report 1998*, 42). Galbraith wrote those words in 1958; the growing gap between the rich and the poor over the last 40 years has proven him right.

44. Janet N. Abramowitz, "Valuing Nature's Services," in Lester R. Brown et al., eds., *State of the World 1997* (New York: W.W. Norton, 1997).

45. Ibid., 109.

46. Lester R. Brown, "The Legacy of Rio," in Brown et al., eds., *State of the World 1997*.

47. Bangladesh, a country that may well be flooded through global warming, produces 183 kg of carbon dioxide per capita versus an average of 11,389 kg per capita in the industrialized countries (United Nations, *Human Development Report 1998*, 57).

48. "The poor are both agents and victims of environmental degradation. They suffer most directly the consequences of degra-

dation, whether caused by their own actions or by the consumption of others. Moreover, the poor often have no alternative when the environmental resources they depend on are degraded—the environment is an integral and irreplaceable aspect of their life support system" (Allen L. Hammond, "Natural Resource Consumption: North and South," in Crocker and Linden, eds., *The Ethics of Consumption*, 466).

49. *Intergovernmental Panel on Climate Change: Second Assessment—Climate Change 1995*, published by the World Meteorological Organization and the United Nations Environmental Programme. It should be noted that this report was the consensus of 2,500 weather scientists and it was published without a dissenting minority statement.

50. During a single month in the spring of 1999, I clipped seven articles from Canadian newspapers that mentioned the effects of global warming: two submerged islands in the South Pacific that are the first victims of global warming; the movement of butterflies north, noted as the first evidence of a large-scale biological response to global warming; feeble West Coast salmon and skinny polar bears as evidence of global warming threatening the ocean food chain; a report by the Red Cross that human-caused "natural disasters" displaced more people than war and conflict together in 1998, with this trend of "environmental refugees" projected to increase; the global transition of dryland, the source of much of the world's foods, into barren land as the result of climate change; a review of Alan Durning's book *Green Collar Jobs*, in which he says that many jobs are getting "greener" but people's lifestyle and leisure time are getting "browner," as illustrated by the increase in SUVs, which burn twice the fossil fuel of conventional cars and are slated to outsell them by 2005; the increase in rainfall in Vancouver over the last several years, which was attributed to global warming. There was one piece of good news that month: British Columbia has received $30 million for fuel-cell research, the research that lies behind emissions-free cars.

51. The Hadley Centre for Climate Change in Britain claims that such a prospect is likely, with temperatures shooting up to six degrees Celsius over the next century, which would put them at the top of the range from the 1995 IPCC report. Such conditions would turn parts of the Amazon rainforest into a desert, over 200

million people would be flooded out of their homes, millions would die from hunger as the American continental breadbasket dries up, epidemics would be rampant, etc. See Stephen Hume, "No Longer Any Doubt: It's Getting Warmer," *Vancouver Sun* (December 30, 1998) sec. A, p. 10.

52. Martin Luther King Jr., *A Testament of Hope: The Essential Writings of Martin Luther King, Jr.*, ed. James Washington (New York: Harper and Row, 1986) 250.

53. "Globalization does not serve world community—it is just individualism writ large" (Daly, *Beyond Growth*, 148). Moreover, the backbone to classical economics, the notion of "comparative advantage," by which each nation presumably had an "advantage" in terms of producing particular crops for export, has been undercut by globalization, since investment can now go wherever the costs are lowest. Thus, rich nations can move capital around to benefit their stockholders, making poor nations unequal partners. See Amata Miller, "Global Economic Structures: Their Human Implications," in Michael Zweig, ed., *Religion and Economic Justice* (Philadelphia: Temple University Press, 1991).

54. Young, "The Invisible Hand in the Wilderness," 66.

55. The standard economic theory "assumes that consumers come to the market with well-defined, insatiable desires for private goods and services; these desires are not affected by social interactions, economic institutions, or the consumption choices or well-being of others" (Frank Ackerman, "Overview Essay on the History of Consumer Society," in Goodwin et al., eds., *The Consumer Society*, 149).

56. As Juliet Schor puts it, "In the neo-classical scheme, workers get what they want. In the 'work and spend' world, they want what they get" ("A New Economic Critique of Consumer Society," *Ethics of Consumption*, ed. Crocker and Linden, 134).

Chapter 5: The Ecological Economic Model and Worldview

1. Robert Costanza et al., *An Introduction to Ecological Economics* (Boca Raton, Fla.: St. Lucie, 1997) 179.

2. Max Wyman, "The Story as Communion" (an interview with Barry Lopez), *Vancouver Sun* (July 4, 1998) sec. G, p. 9.

3. Herman E. Daly and John B. Cobb Jr., *For the Common Good: Redirecting the Economy toward Community, the Environment, and a Sustainable Future* (2d ed.; Boston: Beacon, 1994) 138.

4. M. Douglas Meeks defines economy as *oikonomia* even more broadly: ".... the relations of human beings for producing and distributing the conditions of life against death" ("Economy and the Future of Liberation Theology," *Liberating the Future: God, Mammon, and Theology*, ed. Joerg Rieger [Minneapolis: Fortress, 1998] 45).

5. David Abram, *The Spell of the Sensuous: Perception and Language in a More-Than-Human-World* (New York: Vintage Books, 1996) 46–47.

6. Commenting on global warming and air pollution, Abram notes it as an example of our refusal to acknowledge our dependence on the earth: "Yet our disregard for the very air we breathe is in some sense the most profound expression of this oblivion.... Only as we begin to notice and to experience, once again, our immersion in the invisible air do we start to recall what it is to be fully a part of the world" (ibid., 260).

7. Ibid., 257.

8. As quoted in ibid., 271.

9. Ibid., 264.

10. A new environmental ethic could emerge by re-visioning ourselves with and in the land: ".... through a rejuvenation of our carnal, sensorial empathy with the living land that sustains us" (ibid., 69).

11. These views are epitomized by Locke and Rousseau: Neo-Lockeans believe self-interest and private property are inherent (hence nature should also be owned), while Rousseauvians highlight social cooperation and interdependence (hence alienation from others and nature leads to war). For further discussion, see Stephen C. Hackett, *Environmental and Natural Resources Economics: Theory, Policy and the Sustainable Society* (Armonk, N.Y.: M. E. Sharpe, 1998) 20ff.

12. Costanza et al, *An Introduction to Ecological Economics*, 24.

13. Stephen C. Hackett puts the matter succinctly: "Private property regimes and market systems of allocation rest on an ethical foundation of individualism, which states that all values, rights, and duties originate with individuals and not in society as a whole. In contrast, the sustainability ethic holds the interdependent health and well-being of human communities and earth's ecology over time as the basis of value" (*Environmental and Natural Resources Economics*, 209).

14. S.Viederman,"Sustainability's Five Capitals and Three Pillars," in Dennis C. Pirages, ed., *Building Sustainable Societies: A Blueprint for a Post-Industrial World* (Armonk, N.Y.: M. E. Sharpe, 1996) 46.

15. Robert Costanza insists that a critical element of ecological economics' view of the good society begins with "the vision of the earth as a thermodynamically closed and nonmaterially growing system, with the human economy as a subsystem of the global ecosystem. This implies that there are limits to biophysical through-put of resources from the ecosystem, through the economic subsystem and back to the system as wastes ..."(*An Introduction to Ecological Economics,* 79).

16. As Herman Daly notes,"Economic logic remains the same—economize on the limiting factor," but now the limiting factor is natural, not human–made, capital (*Beyond Growth: The Economics of Sustainable Development* [Boston: Beacon, 1996] 8).

17. Ibid., chap. 14.

18. United Nations, *Human Development Report 1999,* as quoted in the *Vancouver Sun* (July 12, 1999) sec. A, p. 6.

19. Ibid.

20. Economists vary on their estimates of what limited inequality must be for sustainability, but the figure of a ten to twenty times differential is common. For instance, the CEO of a company would be paid ten to twenty times more than the lowest-paid worker; thus, if the worker received $25,000 a year, the CEO would have a salary between $250,000 and $500,000 (certainly a handsome income). At the present time the differential in most large companies is several times that figure, often (counting stock options and other benefits) in the multi-millions.

21. For suggestions on specific strategies, laws, alternative taxes, subsidies, etc. to encourage the goals of sustainability and distributive justice, see Costanza, *An Introduction to Ecological Economics;* Daly and Cobb, *For the Common Good;* Daly, *Beyond Growth;* and Hackett, *Environmental and Natural Resources Economics.*

22. "Libertarian economists look at *Homo economicus* as a self-contained individual who is infinitely mobile and equally at home anywhere. But real people live in communities, and in communities of communities. Their very individual identities are constituted by their relations in community" (Daly, *Beyond Growth,* 163).

23. Daly and Cobb, *For the Common Good,* 188.

24. As quoted in the *Vancouver Sun,* (July 12, 1999) sec. A, p. 6.

25. United Nations, *Human Development Report 1998* (New York: Oxford University Press, 1998) 38.

26. United Nations, *Human Development Report 1999,* as quoted in the *Vancouver Sun* (July 12, 1999) sec. A, p. 6.

27. It is difficult to point to any specific country as an example without laying oneself open to all sorts of qualifications and caveats: yes, Canada is a consumer culture, and probably most Canadians have accepted the neo-classical anthropology and so on, but there is a difference between the top ten countries in the HDI list and the bottom ten. The *quality of life for ordinary people* varies enormously between the top and bottom ten, and that is the key point.

28. Herman E. Daly, "Consumption:Value Added, Physical Transformation, and Welfare," in David A. Crocker and Toby Linden, eds., *Ethics of Consumption: The Good Life, Justice and Global Stewardship* (Lanham, Md.: Rowman and Littlefield, 1998) 20–21.

29. Larry L. Rasmussen, *Earth Community, Earth Ethics* (Maryknoll, N.Y.: Orbis, 1996) 127.

30. Robert Costanza et al. touch on this basic change in anthropology in the following statement: "In ecological economics we consider maintenance of the capacity of the earth to support life as an objective, shared value that is constitutive of our identity as persons in community" (*An Introduction to Ecological Economics,* 159).

31. James A. Nash, "On the Subversive Virtue: Frugality," in Crocker and Linden, eds., *Ethics of Consumption,* 416–36.

32. "Frugality in classical Christian ethical interpretations is an expression of love—seeking the good or well-being of others in response to their needs and to the God who is love. The source of the sacrificial dimension in frugality is love of neighbor, for love always entails giving up at least some of our self-interests and benefits for the sake of the welfare of others in communal relationships" (ibid., 429).

33. Ibid., 433.

34. Ibid., 421.

35. Alan Durning, *How Much Is Enough? The Consumer Society and the Future of the Earth* (New York: W.W. Norton, 1992) 169.

36. Nash, "On the Subversive Virtue: Frugality," 427.

37. Janet N. Abramovitz, "Valuing Nature's Services," in Brown et al., eds., *State of the World 1997* (New York: W.W. Norton, 1997) 109.

38. Rasmussen, Introduction, *Earth Community, Earth Ethics,* 8.

39. Abramovitz, "Valuing Nature's Services," in Brown et al, eds., *State of the World 1997*, 110.

40. Costanza et al., *An Introduction to Ecological Economics*, 95.

41. Abramovitz, "Valuing Nature's Services," in Brown et al., eds., *State of the World 1997*, 96.

42. Daly and Cobb, *For the Common Good*, 107.

43. "Since an isolated system of abstract exchange value flowing in a circle has no dependence on an environment, there can be no problem of natural resource depletion, nor environmental pollution, nor any dependence of the macroeconomy on natural services, or indeed on anything at all outside itself" (Daly, *Beyond Growth*, 47). But the ecological model sees it differently: "The macroeconomy is an open sub-system of the ecosystem and is totally dependent upon it, both as a source for inputs of low-entropy matter/energy and as a sink for outputs of high-entropy matter/energy" (ibid., 48).

44. Robert Bellah as quoted in Durning, *How Much Is Enough?* 147.

45. *The Globe and Mail* (July 26, 1999) sec. A, p. 13.

46. Costanza et al., *An Introduction to Ecological Economics*, 179.

Part III: The Content of Planetary Theology
Introduction

1. For a helpful sketch of similarities and differences among orthodox, liberal, and liberation theologies, see Dorothee Soelle, *Thinking about God: An Introduction to Theology* (Philadelphia: Trinity, 1990) chaps. 1–4.

2. Susan Thistlethwaite, "On Becoming a Traitor: The Academic Liberation Theologian and the Future," in Joerg Rieger, ed., *Liberating the Future: God, Mammon, and Theology* (Minneapolis: Fortress, 1998) 23.

3. Joerg Rieger, "Developing a Common Interest Theology from the Underside," in Rieger, ed., *Liberating the Future*, 129.

4. Ibid., 129.

5. Ibid., 128–29.

6. Frederick Herzog, *God-Walk: Liberation Shaping Dogmatics* (Maryknoll, N.Y.: Orbis, 1988) 46.

7. Rieger, "Developing a Common Interest Theology from the Underside," in Rieger, ed., *Liberating the Future*, 132.

8. Dietrich Bonhoeffer, *Letters and Papers from Prison* (New York: HarperCollins, 1959). See esp. letters of April 30, 1944, and July 18 and 21, 1944.

Chapter 6: God and the World

1. Julian of Norwich, *Revelation of Love*, trans. and ed. John Skinner (New York: Doubleday, 1996) 62.

2. Augustine, *On the Trinity*, book 9, 4.4.

3. H. Richard Niebuhr expresses it as confidence in being: "When the confidence is so put into words the resultant assertion is not that there is a God but that Being is God, or, better, that the principle of being, the source of all things and the power by which they exist, is good, as good for them and good to them. It is relied upon to give and conserve worth to all that issues from it. What otherwise in distrust and suspicion, is regarded as fate or destiny or blind will or chance is now trusted. It is God" (*Radical Monotheism and Western Culture* [New York: Harper and Bros., 1943] 38).

4. Langdon Gilkey, "God," in Peter C. Hodgson and Robert L. King, eds., *Christian Theology* (Minneapolis: Fortress, 1982) 89-90.

5. David Tracy, "The Paradox of the Many Faces of God in Monotheism," in Hermann Haring and Johann Baptist Metz, eds., *The Many Faces of the Divine* (Maryknoll, N.Y.: Orbis, 1995) 32.

6. This line of thinking is ancient and honorable, beginning in Christian theology with Paul and John and including Irenaeus, Augustine, Thomas, Luther and Calvin as well as contemporary theologians as divergent as Karl Barth and Karl Rahner. There are many varieties of it—a Barthian one where human knowledge follows God's initiative and action ("the analogy of faith") and a Rahnerian one where human beings know God "naturally" because they were created by God to do so ("the supernatural existential"). While Thomas and Luther, for example, disagree on how much human beings can know of God apart from revelation, they are in surprising agreement that we do not know anything as purely natural beings (because for both theologians, there is no such thing— God created us and hence creation will always be like the creator, whether as in cause and effect in Thomas or as a mask of God in Luther).

7. Dorothee Soelle, *Theology for Skeptics: Reflections on God*, trans. Joyce L. Irwin (Minneapolis: Fortress, 1995) 12.

8. One of the basic insights of liberation theology is an epistemological breach with modern theology: what matters is not primarily what we know about God but how we practice God's love
(orthodoxy vs. orthodoxy). They insist it is not the existence of
God but the presence of God that matters; not whether we can
intellectually affirm that God exists, but rather whether we identify with God's presence in the world. It is not whether God is but
where God is—and they find God in the world, especially in those
who are oppressed and suffering. While both kinds of theology
affirm issues of knowledge and action, the emphasis is different: for
liberation theologies knowledge follows action whereas for modern theologies ethics is the outcome of theology.

9. The positive and negative as ways to God is as old as the
medieval distinction between cataphatic and apophatic theology
and as contemporary as Paul Tillich's notion of the "sacred void," a
negative route through despair to the affirmation that even the
negative owes its existence to God and is connected to the positive.
Protest theology is a form of negative theology: it claims that our
expressions of horror and disgust at such events as the Holocaust
and nature's destruction are ways of making a light affirmation—
"reality ought not to be this way"—through confrontation with
the dire negativities of existence. See, for instance, Erik Borgman,
"Negative Theology as Postmodern Talk of God," in Haring and
Metz, eds., *The Many Faces of the Divine*.

10. See my book, *The Body of God: An Ecological Theology* (Minneapolis: Fortress, 1993) 136–41.

11. The literature here is immense, stretching back well into the
nineteenth century. For one critique of it, see my book, *Models of
God: Theology for an Ecological, Nuclear Age* (Minneapolis: Fortress,
1987) chap. 3.

12. See *The Body of God*, esp. chaps. 5, 6.

13. H. Richard Niebuhr, *Radical Monotheism*, 32.

14. John Macquarrie traces the history and forms of panentheism, including his own version called "dialectical theism," claiming
that it goes back to Dionysius the Areopagate's notion of divine
transcendence overflowing into immanence; Johannes Scotus Eri-
gena's concept of human beings as "theophanies," manifestations of
God on the finite level; Nicholas of Cusa's doctrine of internal
relations in which "God is in all things and all things in God, or, to

put it another way, all things are an unfolding (explicato) of God, while he in turn is an enfolding (complicatio) of all things" (109); G. F. Hegel's view that the true God is not the transcendent, self-subsistent God but the One who needs nature to be complete and hence goes out (as creator) and returns; process theologies of many kinds, all of which insist that God is becoming as well as being, responsive and changing as well as infinite and eternal. See his *In Search of Deity: An Essay in Dialectical Theism* (London: SCM, 1984). What Macquarrie overlooks is the many feminist relational theologies that in one way or another affirm divine immanence as the neglected aspect of God. See, for instance, the work of Rita Nakashima Brock, Chung Hyun Kyung, Mary Daly, Carter Heyward, Elizabeth A. Johnson, Catherine Keller, Rosemary Radford Ruether, Letty Russell, Dorothee Soelle, Marjorie Suchocki, Sharon Welch, Delores Williams.

15. See my book *Super, Natural Christians: How We Should Love Nature* (Minneapolis: Fortress, 1997) chaps. 4, 5.

16. I am not using the traditional terms—Father, Son, and Holy Spirit—for many reasons, the chief one being that these terms have become God's "names," the only proper names, and thus they pretend to be descriptions of God (which, I believe, no terms can be). God is not really father, son, or holy spirit. Nor is God really creator, liberator, or sustainer. We must begin with our own experiences of God's love in conversation with the church's tradition: I believe that the three terms I have used express both my own experience better and are consonant with the tradition (though not identical with it). Moreover, as active, dynamic terms they focus attention not on God as a being (like a father or son), but on divine activity in regard to the world. Finally, they avoid the androcentric bias of the father/son language. Some will, however, claim that my view of the trinity is focused on the external functions rather than the internal "persons" of the trinity (on the "economic" rather than the "immanent" trinity). This is only the case if one separates action and being. For an excellent discussion of this and other related points, see Catherine Mowry LaCugna, *God for Us: The Trinity and Christian Life* (San Francisco: HarperSanFrancisco, 1991).

17. Behind this simple statement lies a nest of problems. Some claim that the trinity is really about God in God's self (thus, the

"immanent" trinity is what matters and it secures God's relationality within divinity—the three "persons" have their sociality among themselves, not with the world). Others insist that the trinity is an inference from God's action in the world (especially in Jesus Christ, but also in creation and in God's spirit with the world). This latter position suggests that the "economic" trinity is most important, for it tells us about God's transcendence toward the world and immanence in the world, rather than being primarily a statement about the divine being. The position put forth in these pages borrows from both positions, but more from the latter than the former; that is, the trinity, as I see it, is principally a statement about God and the world, but it is also, I believe, about God—but only with the slight ontological claim that models have.

18. Martin Buber, *I and Thou* (New York: Scribner's, 1970) 18.

19. Understood this way, the trinity is not strictly speaking a Christian doctrine; Martin Buber's "In the beginning is relationship" suggests that belief in radical transcendence and radical immanence is a Jewish as well as a Christian understanding of God (see, for instance, the various personifications of God in the Hebrew Scriptures as Wisdom, Logos, and Spirit—through these means, God is Emmanuel, God with us).

20. Catherine Mowry LaCugna, "The Trinitarian Mystery of God," in Francis Schüssler Fiorenza and John P. Galvin, eds., *Systematic Theology: Roman Catholic Perspectives*, vol. 1 (Minneapolis: Fortress, 1991) 177.

21. LaCugna, *God for Us*, 16.

22. See *The Body of God*, chaps. 2, 3.

23. The major models of creation are based on common human activities—giving birth, making a work of art, and speaking. Since all expressions of God's activities are necessarily metaphorical and no one model can be adequate, it is appropriate to use all three models, since they complement and enrich one another. Any one of them alone presents difficulties: giving birth (pantheism), art (distance), speaking (disembodiment). The advantage of the three together is that one can speak of creation in bodily, appreciative, and humanly significant ways.

24. For further elaboration of this point, see *Super, Natural Christians*, chap. 3.

25. This movement out of the world and into the self is a long one, beginning with Luther and crystallized in the theology of

Schleiermacher, with its apotheosis reached in twentieth-century existentialism. Religion's "place" was no longer the entire cosmos as the Middle Ages believed, but had been reduced to the human self. This reduction is still with us in most popular Christianity, both Catholic and Protestant, with the exception being the process and liberation theologies that are insisting on the political and cosmological contexts as the appropriate ones for doing theology.

26. This is, I believe, the basic incarnational affirmation; not that "God became man in Jesus Christ" but that God is present in mediated form in everything and everyone. This understanding of incarnation is prevalent in many religious traditions, including the Jewish as well as forms of Hinduism and Native religions. The distinctive aspect of Christianity is its belief in the paradigmatic incarnation in Jesus of Nazareth; that is, Christians are those who look Godward through Jesus, seeing him as telling us of God in a distinctive, though not the only, way.

27. See *Super, Natural Christians,* 164ff., and *The Body of God,* chaps. 2, 6.

28. As Langdon Gilkey points out in an essay on contemporary views of God, no theologian these days wants to be accused of having a "Greek" view of God—that is, God understood in static, unchanging terms; all views of God, from Karl Barth to process theology and including feminist and liberation understandings, are of God as dynamic, active, and involved in the world ("God," in Hodgson and King, eds., *Christian Theology*). These positions vary greatly, however; some important contributions are by Teilhard de Chardin, John Cobb, David Griffith, Schubert Ogden, Maurice Wiles, Edward Farley, Marjorie Suchocki, Elizabeth A. Johnson, Gordon Kaufman, Gustav Gutiérrez, and John Macquarrie.

29. There is, however, a lively literature that does want to claim that to one degree or another, the world process is guided by, illumined by, or caused by God. See, for instance, the works by John Templeton as well as the many books supported by his Foundation.

30. H. Richard Niebuhr, *Faith on Earth: An Inquiry into the Structure of Human Faith* (New Haven, Conn.: Yale University Press, 1989) 67.

31. *Random House Webster's College Dictionary* (New York: Random House, 1997) 1334.

32. See John Hick, *Evil and the God of Love* (New York: Harper and Row, 1966).

33. One example, among myriad others, is the Turkish earthquake that occurred in August, 1999. As reported in the *Globe and Mail*, "Shoddy construction and municipal corruption were major reasons for the soaring death toll from Turkey's disastrous earthquake" ([August 19, 1999] sec. A, p. 10). The earthquake was not caused by human beings, but its extreme impact on human life was.

34. United Nations, *Human Development Report 1998* (New York: Oxford University Press, 1998).

35. Julian of Norwich, *Revelation of Love*, 62–63.

Chapter 7: Christ and Salvation

1. Even though millions appear still to accept this story as literal truth, the work of Rudolf Bultmann is definitive for the academic and theological communities in regard to this issue. While all, including myself, may not agree with Bultmann's existentialist rewriting of the mythic story, his criticism of it in light of the contemporary scientific worldview is persuasive. Rather than a reduction of the story to existentialist philosophy, I would suggest a remythologization in the context of the contemporary worldview, as revisionist theologians as disparate as Pierre Teilhard de Chardin, John Cobb Jr., Marjorie Suchocki, and the liberation theologians have done. These thinkers have used scientific, economic, and sociological materials to retell the story in terms that are not only credible to contemporary people but speak also to the critical, painful, and pressing issues of our time.

2. Again, as with the mythological issue, the religion and science issue poses the question of Jesus wrongly. A case in point is the current debate over creationism and evolution; here the doctrine of creation—the affirmation that one's being is totally dependent on God—is confused with a scientific account of how human beings and everything else came to be. One can—and I do—embrace evolution theory enthusiastically *and at the same time* affirm the doctrine of creation. In fact, evolution provides an excellent way to remythologize the Genesis creation story in terms appropriate to our time. The difficulty with traditional Christology is not mythology (or images, metaphors, etc.) but the particular mythology used. It is from a different era; we need to find ways to speak of Jesus imagistically and metaphorically in terms relevant to our own time.

3. For a helpful typology of meanings of "incarnation," see Sarah Coakley, *Christ without Absolutes: A Study of the Christology of Ernst Troeltsch* (Oxford, Eng.: Clarendon, 1988) 104ff.

4. Curiously, this common understanding of orthodox Christology is heretical—it is Docetic in implying that Jesus is not fully human. As a "miracle" (supported by the virgin birth and the immaculate conception of Mary), Jesus was not conceived and born like the rest of us, but descends from heaven, comes to earth from the outside, in a manner impossible for human beings. In this sense, even within orthodox terms (the Chalcedonian formula), it is "bad" theology.

5. Even though there are several classical views of the atonement, the Anselmic substitutionary sacrificial one, or variations of it in the ransom theory, the Christus Victor theory, etc., are widespread, whether one looks at Roman Catholic, Reformed, Anglican, or Evangelical traditions. While these Christian bodies disagree on many things, there is surprising unanimity on Christ's work: the stress is on Jesus "doing it all."

6. For further discussion of this see my book, *The Body of God: An Ecological Theology* (Minneapolis: Fortress, 1993) esp. chaps. 1, 2, 6.

7. Lynn White Jr., "The Historical Roots of Our Ecological Crisis," *Science* 155 (March 10, 1967) 1203-7.

8. For a brief treatment of these categories see George S. Hendry, *Theology of Nature* (Philadelphia: Westminster, 1980) chap. 1.

9. Christologies with prophetic motifs include those of Rosemary Radford Ruether, H. Paul Santmire, James A. Nash, Larry L. Rasmussen.

10. Outstanding work on wisdom Christologies has been done by Elisabeth Schüssler Fiorenza and Elizabeth A. Johnson.

11. Elizabeth A. Johnson, "Wisdom Was Made Flesh and Pitched Her Tent among Us," in Mary Anne Stevens, ed., *Reconstructing the Christ Symbol* (New York: Paulist, 1993) 113.

12. Ibid., 97.

13. The wide range of sacramental Christologies include the disparate ones of Pierre Teilhard de Chardin, Karl Rahner, Matthew Fox, Carter Heyward, Brian Swimme, Thomas Berry, and Eastern Orthodoxy.

14. John Hick, ed., *A Gerard Manley Hopkins Reader* (New York: Oxford University Press, 1953) 13.

15. Augustine, *The Confessions of St. Augustine,* books 1–10, trans. F. J. Sheed (New York: Sheed and Ward, 1942) 10.6.

16. Jürgen Moltmann, *The Way of Jesus Christ: Christology in Messianic Dimensions* (San Francisco: Harpers, 1989) 275. Elsewhere he writes: "Christology can only arrive at its completion at all in a cosmic christology" (278).

17. Among others, see the christologies of John Cobb Jr., Rita Nakashima Brock, Jay McDaniel, and Charles Birch.

18. Even a partial listing of ecologically significant liberation Christologies is not possible. I will simply mention a few theologians whose work in this regard I have found helpful: Leonardo Boff, Dorothee Soelle, Chung Hyun Kyung, Delores Williams, Gustavo Gutiérrez, Ada-María Isasi-Díaz, Mercy Amba Oduyoye.

19. Leonardo Boff, *Ecology and Liberation: A New Paradigm,* trans. John Cumming (Maryknoll, N.Y.: Orbis, 1995) 26.

20. Chung Hyun Kyung, "Welcome the Spirit; Hear Her Cries: The Holy Spirit, Creation, and the Culture of Life," *Christianity and Crisis* 51 (July 15, 1991) 223.

21. See, for instance, *Sustainable Growth—A Contradiction in Terms?* (Geneva: Visser 't Hooft Endowment Fund, 1993).

22. Sarah Coakley gives six definitions of incarnation; her first two definitions suggest incarnation as I am using the term. The first definition says that it is characteristic of God to reveal the divine self to humanity; the second definition, that in Jesus God takes a special initiative for the sake of humankind (*Christ without Absolutes,* 104). I would, however, modify Coakley's object of divine incarnation from humanity to include as well the natural world.

23. "But creatures cannot attain to any perfect likeness of God so long as they are confined to one species of creatures; because, since the cause exceeds the effect in a composite and manifold way. . . . Multiplicity, therefore, and variety, was needful in the creation, to the end that the perfect likeness of God might be found in things according to their measure" (as quoted in Arthur O. Lovejoy's *The Great Chain of Being: A Study of the History of an Idea* [Cambridge, Mass.: Harvard University Press, 1933] 76).

24. As Moltmann says, "Logos christology is originally Wisdom christology and is as such cosmic christology" (*The Way of Jesus,* 282). For Spirit, see chapter 5 of my book *The Body of God: An Ecological Theology* (Minneapolis: Fortress, 1993).

25. The prophetic and the sacramental as critical to environmental ethics are mentioned in different ways by both Rosemary Radford Ruether and Elizabeth A. Johnson. Ruether's treatment occurs as "The Covenantal Tradition" and "The Sacramental Tradition" in *Gaia and God: An Ecofeminist Theology of Earth Healing* (San Francisco: Harper, 1992). Johnson compares covenantal and sacramental ecological ethics to orthodox Christologies: the ascending, historical, salvation history, from below (covenantal) and the descending, metaphysical, incarnational, from above (sacramental) in *Consider Jesus*, 70.

26. We are not suggesting that a Christian's faith is based on the state of historical Jesus research at any particular time; nonetheless, Christianity has always claimed some continuity between "the Christ of faith" and "the Jesus of history." Recent research, which has moved out of narrow church contexts of interpretation to sociological, cultural, and political ones of first-century Mediterranean society, has reached a remarkable consensus on some broad outlines of Jesus' life; most notably, that he was a social revolutionary opposed to the structures of domination and domestication of his day. This consensus is expressed in different ways by New Testament scholars such as E. P. Sanders, Burton Mack, Elisabeth Schüssler Fiorenza, Marcus Borg, John Dominic Crossan, and Richard Horsley. See, for instance, Marcus J. Borg, *Jesus in Contemporary Scholarship* (Valley Forge, Pa.: Trinity, 1994). Nicholas Lash states the Christian's dilemma succinctly: "If I were to become convinced that Jesus did not exist, or that the story told in the New Testament of his life, teaching and death was a fictional construction ungrounded in the facts, or a radical *mis*interpretation of his character, history and significance, then I should cease to be a Christian" (*Theology on Dover Beach* [New York: Paulist, 1979] 84).

27. Borg, *Jesus in Contemporary Scholarship*, 194.

28. Ibid., 172.

29. "Consistently, Jesus undermined the world of conventional wisdom with its safe and prudent ethos, its notion of reality organized on the basis of rewards and punishments, its oppressive hierarchies, its categories of righteous and sinners" (ibid., 1).

30. Over the last few decades, with the rise of liberation theologies and the current quest for the historical Jesus, this continuity is widely acknowledged among many different kinds of Christology.

As Roger Haight expresses it: "A sense of historicity is leading theologians and Christians generally to put more stock in the saving power of Jesus' public career and ministry, in contrast to the almost exclusive dogmatic Pauline concentration of the dynamic and power of salvation in Jesus' death" (*Jesus: Symbol of God* [Maryknoll, N.Y.: Orbis, 1999] 58).

31. John Dominic Crossan, *Jesus: A Revolutionary Biography* (San Francisco: HarperSanFrancisco, 1994) 73–74.

32. Ibid., 68.

33. Ibid., 113–14.

34. See ibid., 179–81.

35. See Marcus Borg's treatment of the linkage between eschatology and social world. He argues that the shift in recent scholarship from seeing Jesus as an eschatological figure to a teacher of subversive wisdom changes also the view of Jesus' work from atonement/cross theology to the call to a new way of living in the world—from an individualistic, forgiveness of sins paradigm to a radical social transformation of perception and of life (*Jesus in Contemporary Scholarship*, 10ff.).

36. Ibid., 13.

37. Ibid., 152.

38. Borg underlines this by saying that Jesus was a "spirit person," whose experiential relationship with God was the source of everything he was and did (ibid., 152).

39. This is the heart of a Christology claiming that Jesus was "fully God and fully human" but in non-substantialist terms; Charlene Burns has written a doctoral dissertation, "The Incarnation as Affective *Metoché*," about this Christology (Vanderbilt University, 2000). Among other sources in this fine study, Burns mentions the work of Kristen Renwick Monroe, *The Heart of Altruism: Perceptions of a Common Humanity* (Princeton, N.J.: Princeton University Press, 1996). Summarizing Monroe's study, Burns (183) writes:

> The one predominant theme found to occur in the thinking of all the individuals classified as altruists in Monroe's study had to do with world view: "Altruists see the world as one in which connections exist and extend through nature, beyond the death of any one particular individual" (Monroe, 123). . . . The core of the altruists' identity is that they are linked to humankind as a

whole: "All life concerns them. All death diminishes them.
Because they are part of mankind" (Monroe, 216).
This is not a particular empathetic responding to the needs of one
individual, although the capacity for empathy is an integral part of
it. Altruism seems to be a global participatory relation to humankind as a whole.

40. From Annie Dillard, *For the Time Being* (New York: Knopf,
1999) 172.

41. "Deification" is one of the oldest theories of Christ's work,
very prominent in the Eastern church, less so in the Western
church, where Anselm's sacrificial substitutionary atonement
became standard—and still is in most churches. Deification, then,
has as good credentials in the tradition as does the reigning theory;
it is also widely embraced today, in different ways, by liberation,
feminist, and ecological theologians.

42. Crossan, *Jesus: A Revolutionary Biography*, 55.

43. This perspective is widespread among contemporary theologians. Hans Küng denies sacrificial atonement theories, claiming that
the test for being a Christian is not supporting that theory (or any
other); rather, "the test is the faith in the one and only God, the actual following of Jesus Christ, in trust and in the power of the Holy
Spirit" ("Christian Self-Criticism in the Light of Judaism," trans.
Kenneth Brewer and Steffen Losel, in Robert F. Berkey and Sarah A.
Edwards, eds., *Christology in Dialogue* [Cleveland: Pilgrim, 1993] 246).
Latin American theologian Julio Lois says that while the cross is central in Christianity, it is not as a substitutionary atonement but as solidarity with the crucified of the earth—we follow the Crucified One
by "embracing the cause of those crucified by the sin of the world"
("Christology in the Theology of Liberation," in Ignacio Ellacuría
and Jon Sobrino, eds., *Mysterium Liberationis: Fundamental Concepts of
Liberation Theology* [Maryknoll, N.Y.: Orbis, 1993] 183). John Macquarrie sees Christ as representative, not substitute: "The representative also steps in for us, but he holds the place open for us so that we
can step in ourselves. The Christian must consciously appropriate the
work of Christ on his or her behalf, and take up the cross" (*Jesus
Christ in Modern Thought* [Philadelphia: Trinity, 1990] 402).

44. Dillard, *For the Time Being*, 168.

45. Crossan, *Jesus: A Revolutionary Biography*, 55.

46. Dillard, *For the Time Being*, 168.

Chapter 8: Life in the Spirit

1. Walter Brueggemann, "The Liturgy of Abundance, the Myth of Scarcity," *Christian Century* (March 24-31, 1999) 346 (italics added).

2. Hans Küng, *Credo: The Apostles' Creed Explained for Today* (New York: Doubleday, 1993) 162 (italics added).

3. Marcus J. Borg, *Jesus in Contemporary Scholarship* (Valley Forge, Pa.: Trinity, 1994) 172.

4. Brueggemann, "The Liturgy of Abundance, the Myth of Scarcity," 346.

5. Küng, *Credo,* 162.

6. This radical-sounding statement is in the tradition of Irenaeus, Spinoza, Hegel, Rahner, Tillich, and many others. It does not deny the incarnation of God in Jesus Christ, but sees that incarnation as the epitome or paradigm of what is evident elsewhere—that God is with us here and now in the world, in the flesh, in matter.

7. Julian of Norwich, *Revelation of Love,* ed. and trans. John Skinner (New York: Doubleday, 1997) 177–78.

8. Arthur Michael Ramsey as quoted by Alister E. McGrath, *Christian Theology: An Introduction* (2d ed.; Oxford, Eng.: Blackwell, 1994) 323.

9. Julio Lois, "Christology in the Theology of Liberation," in Ignacio Ellacuría and Jon Sobrino, eds., *Mysterium Liberationis: Fundamental Concepts of Liberation Theology* (Maryknoll, N.Y.: Orbis, 1993) 173.

10. Pablo Richard, "Theology in the Theology of Liberation" in Ellacuría and Sobrino, eds., 164.

11. John Woolman, *The Journal* and *A Plea for the Poor* (New York: Corinth, 1961).

12. Robert Coles, "In This Pagan Land," *America* (Nov. 11, 1972) 380.

13. Woolman, *Journal,* 8–9.

14. Ibid., 43.

15. Ibid., 157.

16. Ibid., 222.

17. Dorothy Day, *The Long Loneliness: The Autobiography of Dorothy Day* (New York: Harper and Row, 1952) 44.

18. Ibid., 317.

19. Ibid.

20. Wes Michaelson, "Encountering Dorothy Day," *Sojourners* (December 1976) 17.

21. Day, *The Long Loneliness*, 159.

22. Ibid., 263.

23. Herman E. Daly and John B. Cobb Jr., *For the Common Good: Redirecting the Economy toward Community, the Environment, and a Sustainable Future* (2d ed.; Boston: Beacon, 1994) 380.

24. Wade Clark Roof and William McKinney, *American Mainline Religion: Its Changing Shape and Future* (New Brunswick, N.J.: Rutgers University Press, 1987) 20–21.

25. Brueggemann, "The Liturgy of Abundance," 342, 345.

26. Ibid., 345.

27. For an excellent treatment of this period and the way Christians in Germany responded, see H. Jackson Forstman, *Christian Faith in Dark Times: Theological Conflicts in the Shadow of Hitler* (Louisville, Ky.: Westminster John Knox, 1992).

28. Brueggemann, "The Liturgy of Abundance," 346. Brueggemann spells out the churches' narrative of abundance in more detail: "The gospel story of abundance asserts that we originated in the magnificent, inexplicable love of a God who loved the world into generous being. The baptismal service declares that each of us has been miraculously loved into existence by God. And the story of abundance says that our lives will end in God, and that this well-being cannot be taken from us. In the words of St. Paul, neither life nor death nor angels nor principalities nor things—nothing can separate us from God" (343).

29. Schubert Ogden defines justice as "giving everyone her or his own," which he expounds from a creation perspective in the following way: "Even as God's work as Creator is in the deeper interest of every creature in a cosmic order that frees it to realize its own interests as fully as possible in solidarity with all its fellow creatures, so acting rightly toward others and, even more so, creating right structures of social and cultural order are by way of realizing the same deeper interest, thereby carrying forward God's own work of creation" (*Doing Theology Today* [Valley Forge, Pa.: Trinity, 1996] 119).

30. Leonard Boff and Virgil Elizondo, eds., *Ecology and Poverty: Cry of the Earth, Cry of the Poor* (Maryknoll, N.Y.: Orbis, 1995) 74. Also

note: "The challenge is to make people see one another as members of a great earthly family together with other species and find their way back to the community of other living beings, the planetary and cosmic community" (75).

31. David Malin Roodman, "Building a Sustainable Society," in Lester R. Brown et al., eds., *State of the World 1999* (New York: W. W. Norton, 1999) 182.

32. Malcolm C. Young, "The Invisible Hand in the Wilderness: Economics, Ecology and God" (M.A. thesis, Harvard University, 1998) 10.

Appendix: A Manifesto to North American Middle-Class Christians

1. United Nations Development Programme, *New York Times* (September 13, 1998).

2. *Intergovernmental Panel on Climate Change: Second Assessment— Climate Change 1995,* published by the World Meteorological Organization and the United Nations Environmental Programme.

3. Charles Birch, Nairobi World Council of Churches Assembly, 1975.

Index

CPSIA information can be obtained at www.ICGtesting.com
Printed in the USA
LVOW07s1246130116

469733LV00011BA/23/P